JOHANNINE CHRISTIANITY IN CONFLICT

SOCIETY
OF BIBLICAL
LITERATURE

DISSERTATION SERIES

William Baird, Editor

Number 60
JOHANNINE CHRISTIANITY IN CONFLICT:
Authority, Rank, and Succession in
the First Farewell Discourse

by D. Bruce Woll

D. Bruce Woll

JOHANNINE CHRISTIANITY IN CONFLICT:

AUTHORITY, RANK, AND SUCCESSION IN THE FIRST FAREWELL DISCOURSE

Scholars Press

Distributed by
Scholars Press
101 Salem Street
P.O. Box 2268
Chico, California 95927

JOHANNINE CHRISTIANITY IN CONFLICT:
Authority, Rank, and Succession
in the First Farewell Discourse

D. Bruce Woll

Library of Congress Cataloging in Publication Data

Woll, D. Bruce
    Johannine Christianity in conflict.

    (Dissertation series / Society of Biblical
Literature ; no. 60)
    Bibliography: p.
    1. Bible. N.T. John XIII, 31-XIV–Criticism,
interpretation, etc. I. Title. II. Series:
Dissertation series (Society of Biblical litera-
ture) ; no. 60.
BS2615.2. W64   226'.506   81-1795
ISBN 0-89130-471-1 (pbk.)   AACR2

Printed in the United States of America
1 2 3 4 5
Edwards Brothers, Inc.
Ann Arbor, Michigan 48104

ACKNOWLEDGMENTS

This dissertation has been nourished, above all, in the classes taught by my adviser, Professor Jonathon Z. Smith. I wish to thank him for his unfailing support and encouragement. I wish to thank my readers, Professor Robert Grant and Professor Jay Wilcoxen, for their comments. I am grateful also to my fellow students, Gene Gallagher, Jim Tabor, and Pat Cox, for their criticisms, comments, and insights. Finally, I am grateful to my wife, Ruth, for her loyalty in the face of what has appeared to her, at times, to be a quixotic enterprise.

TABLE OF CONTENTS

INTRODUCTION: "ANOTHER PARACLETE,"
A SUCCESSOR TO JESUS?

The "crisis of categories" in New Testament scholarship is by now widely recognized, in part as a result of James M. Robinson's explicit naming of the crisis in 1871 in the introductory essay to *Trajectories Through Early Christianity*.[1] Robert Kysar concludes his recent book-length review of contemporary Johannine research by underscoring the need for attention to the categories being used in interpretation. According to Kysar, "the quest for new categories must be the pressing item on the agenda for any who would profess to work at the task of penetrating the mystery of the evangelist's thought."[2] In the study which follows I propose to engage in this quest by arguing that the category of authority, together with related terms such as power, legitimation, rank, succession, and hierarchy, are basic to an understanding to the Gospel in that they point to one of the predominant and controlling aspects of the situation addressed by the Gospel.[3]

I shall not attempt a comprehensive review of the theme of authority and related themes. Instead, I shall analyze in detail one text, the first farewell discourse (13:31-14:31), which, I will argue, is pivotal for an understanding of the processes of social interaction of which the Gospel was a part.

I wish to begin by calling attention to the theme of succession, which is addressed in a central way in the first farewell discourse.[4] In what is, upon reflection, one of the most remarkable expressions in the Fourth Gospel, Jesus promises his disciples, after announcing his imminent departure, that "another Paraclete" will be sent from the Father (John 14:16, 17). In other words, Jesus tells the disciples that another figure will take his place when he leaves. He will have a successor.

Can the Johannine Jesus have a successor? It is impossible to avoid the inference that Jesus himself is the prior Paraclete.[5] But if this is the case, how can there be "another Paraclete?" Can anyone take the place of Jesus, the "only-begotten Son?"

Jesus and the Paraclete are implicitly accorded the same title
by the promise in 14:16. According to Hans Windisch, the
Paraclete promised in the farewell discourses is the "double"
(*Doppelgänger*) of Jesus.[6] But how can the Johannine Jesus have
a "double"? The Gospel makes it clear that the Son can have no
equal, that he stands in a unique relation to the Father (1:18;
14:6). The Gospel makes it clear that unlimited authority is
invested in the Son (3:35; 13:3), that he is "the way, the truth,
the life," "the light of the world," "the bread of life." Can he
be replaced, at his departure, by someone else?

Clearly the promise of the Spirit as another Paraclete
raises fundamental questions about our understanding of the
authority, power, and status of the Johannine Jesus.
Clearly, too, the Paraclete passages constitute one of
the most striking and significant anomalies in a Gospel otherwise
marked by its massive christocentricity.[7] The promise of the
Paraclete raises questions about the limits of the Son's
authority. Is it an authority which is limited temporally by
the departure? It raises questions about the rank and status of
Jesus, questions which are an explicit concern of the author.
The centrality and exclusivity of the Son are called in question
by the promise of the Paraclete. Does the departure mean removal
from his position as the central object of seeing, hearing,
believing and knowing on the part of the disciples? It raises
questions about the uniqueness of the Son. If there is to be a
Paraclete after the Son, how many Paracletes are there? Was
Jesus *preceded* by a Paraclete? Hans Windisch calls attention to
this possibility by noting Oswald Spengler's reference to the
"astounding doctrine," contained in the Paraclete promise, that
Jesus is not the bringer of the final and total revelation but
is only "the second envoy, who is to be followed by a third."[8]

The issue of rank is not a consideration that is extraneous
to the text of the Paraclete sayings. Some commentators have, in
fact, called attention to evidence in these sayings which seems
to suggest that the Paraclete is a superior figure to Jesus!
In 16:12,13, for example, Jesus tells the disciples that the
Spirit of Truth will guide them into "all the truth," in
contrast to Jesus, who, because of the limitations of the
disciples, cannot reveal everything. According to Hans Windisch,

there is here "a sudden glimpse of a thought which ascribes
a certain superiority" to the Paraclete, though it is
immediately qualified. More astonishing is the view, advanced
by Günther Bornkamm, that underlying the relationship of Jesus
to the Paraclete is the eschatological pattern of forerunner to
fulfiller (*Vorläufer-Vollender*).[9] In other words, he holds
that according to the Paraclete tradition appropriated by the
author Jesus is the forerunner to the Paraclete! Though, as
we shall argue below, there are serious problems with Bornkamm's
view, it cannot be claimed that his position has no foothold
whatsoever in the text. Not only can one cite 16:12,13, referred
to by Windisch, but 16:7 also may be interpreted in this way.
According to this text Jesus departs so that the Paraclete can
come, suggesting that Jesus makes way for the Paraclete.
Furthermore, closely related to the promise of the Paraclete in
14:16,17 is the promise to the disciples that they, together
with the Paraclete will be successor figures to Jesus, and that,
as such, they will do "greater" works than those done by Jesus
himself (14:12).[10]

The discussion of the issues surrounding the promise of
the Paraclete as a successor figure to Jesus has been disappointing in several respects.[11] In the first place, scholars have,
for the most part, not addressed the central issue of rank, i.e.,
why it is that in the Fourth Gospel of all places the Spirit is
depicted so explicitly as a successor figure to Jesus, with the
implicit threat to the exclusive position of Jesus contained
therein.[12] For example, a great deal of the discussion devoted
to the Paraclete sayings has focused on the question of the
origin of the title, *parakletos*. What is not generally noted is
that one of the main reasons *this* title seems to call for
explanation is that the way it is used makes the implicit threat
to the exclusive christology of the Gospel unavoidable. Likewise,
the related issue of whether the Paraclete is, or was originally,
the title of a concrete personal figure is above all important
for the bearing such an understanding would have on the exclusive
claims made by the Johannine Jesus on his own behalf.

In the second place, scholars have, for the most part,
overlooked the situation of authority conflict, suggested by the

succession idea, as a possible context for interpreting the Paraclete promise.[13] In the third place, there has been a tendency to treat the Paraclete passages in isolation from their immediate context in the farewell discourses.[14] Where the attempt has been made to incorporate the Paraclete promises into the sequence of thought in the discourses, the succession relationship has generally received short shrift, or been ignored altogether.[15] Related to these three factors is the unsatisfactory treatment of the farewell discourses in Johannine scholarship generally.

Focusing our attention, for the moment, on the last point, it must be said that Johannine scholarship has scarcely begun to define the important role played by the farewell discourses in the Gospel as a whole. The fact of their importance is evident from the amount of space they occupy, approximately one-fifth of the Gospel. Their importance has been noted, of course. According to Siegfried Schulz, for example, the farewell discourses constitute the "theological highpoint of the Gospel," the "heart" of its theology.[16] But Schulz does not define wherein this importance lies.

A variety of factors have combined to produce the disappointing results of contemporary Johannine scholarship with respect to the farewell material. In the first place, the large amount of attention which has been paid to the hypothesis of a Signs Source in recent years has diverted attention away from the farewell discourses.[17] In the second place, most treatments of the discourse material have tended to disregard the formal differences between the farewell material and the obviously similar discourse and dialogue material occurring in the first twelve chapters of the Gospel. That is to say, there has been a tendency to lump together, from a formal point of view, all of the discourse and dialogue material in the Gospel as "revelation discourse" and thus to minimize the formal distinctiveness of the farewell material.[18] In the third place, a large number of studies of speech material in the Gospel have remained at the level of thematic analysis, with little attention to formal or compositional questions, and therefore with little attention to the coherence and structure of the larger literary units clearly marked in the Gospel.[19] In the fourth place, undoubtedly the most important obstacle to a satisfactory statement of the function of the farewell discourses within the Gospel has been the controversy over their organization, which has monopolized attention. It has long been recognized that there is more than one farewell discourse in the Gospel, but there is little agreement on the number, scope, and sequence of the literary units contained in chapters 13:31 through chapter 16.[20]

Because of the preoccupation with the questions of organization and rearrangement of the farewell material comparatively little attention has been paid to the question of the *function* of the farewell discourses within the Gospel. In the present study I shall focus primary attention on the question of the role played by the farewell speech material in the Gospel. I wish to inquire into the reasons why so much of the Gospel is cast in a form which underscores the *separation* of Jesus from the disciples.

I shall not attempt to treat the farewell speech material as a whole, but, as noted above, will focus on the first farewell discourse. According to Wilhelm Heitmüller, writing more than fifty years ago, this text "can, in a certain sense, be called the heart of the Gospel."[21] Whether, and if so, in what sense, this is an accurate statement of the importance of this discourse, is a central question of this study. In answering this question, we shall be attempting to discover, at the same time, the reasons for the prominence of the Paraclete tradition within this Gospel.

PART I

ANALYSIS OF THE FIRST FAREWELL DISCOURSE

CHAPTER I

THE FIRST FAREWELL DISCOURSE AND
JOHANNINE SCHOLARSHIP

The Farewell Discourses and the First
Farewell Discourse

One of the most glaring disjunctions in a Gospel noted
for its *aporiae* is found in John 14:30-31. Here, in the middle
of the farewell discourses, Jesus says to his disciples, "Arise,
let us depart from here." This summons follows what is clearly
intended as a conclusion to the final words of Jesus. In 14:27
Jesus pronounces the benediction of peace, summarizes the main
themes of the preceding discourse (14:28), announces the coming
of "the prince of this world" in the person of Judas (vs. 30,
cf. 13:27), and then signals the departure with the words quoted.
As has frequently been pointed out, these words form a natural
transition to the passion narrative beginning in 18:1, which,
in fact, opens with the arrival of the traitor, Judas, as Jesus
had announced.[1] One does not expect three more chapters of
discourse, dialogue, and a farewell prayer to intervene before
the party does, in fact, depart. The conclusion in 14:27-31
leaves chapters 15-17 "in mid-air."[2]

How is one to account for this disjunction? A traditional
explanation of conservative scholars has been that the discourse,
dialogue, and prayer recorded in chapters 15-17 occurred,
historically, on the way to the garden.[3] But, as Raymond Brown
points out, this overlooks the fact that the exit from the room
does not occur until 18:1, which reads, "After saying these
things, Jesus went out (*exelthen*) with his disciples. . . ."[4]
A second explanation is P. Corssen's suggestion that Jesus'
words in 14:31 are a secondary insertion.[5] Corssen's explanation
rests on the premise that a reader would have been reminded of
Mark's account of the coming of the traitor (Mark 14:41), and
would have been tempted to add words from the Marcan account in
order to harmonize the two narratives!

A third type of explanation is represented by attempts to treat Jesus' summons as metaphorical language. H. Zimmermann, for example, suggests that the words, "Arise, let us depart from here," belong to the well-known ambivalent expressions typical of the Gospel. The real meaning of the words, he suggests, is a summons to resurrection. Chapters 15-16 reflect the situation of the church after the departure of Jesus; chapter 14, on the other hand, still reflects the situation prior to the departure. So 14:31 is a summons to the disciples to move from the one condition to the other.[6]

These three explanations fail to do justice to the fact that 14:27-31 as a *whole* forms the conclusion of Jesus' farewell, and that the only appropriate sequel is the account of the betrayal in 18:1ff. They do nothing to dispel the impression that chapters 15-17 have been inserted into the Gospel in such a way as to break apart an originally smooth transition.

The one explanation which deserves serious consideration as an alternative to the view that chapters 15-17 are secondary is the view that they have been misplaced. Those holding this view have proposed various ways to rearrange the order of the farewell material. Confidence in such explanations has waned as their number has waxed.[7] Chapters 15 and 16 have been inserted, sometimes with, sometimes without the farewell prayer of chapter 17, after 13:20; 13:24; 13:30; 13:31a; 13:32; 13:35 and 13:38.[8] The place of chapter 17 has been particularly troublesome in such attempts. Some rearrangement theories retain it after chapter 14, thus failing to solve the original difficulty posed by 14:31.[9] In other proposals, the prayer ends up in the middle of the discourse and dialogue, which is equally unsatisfactory.[10] Rudolf Bultmann proposed to resolve these difficulties by placing chapter 17 *before* the discourses, so that in his rearrangement the order of the material is as follows: 1) Announcement of betrayal (13:21-30), 2) The Prayer (ch. 17), 3) Introduction to the farewell discourses (13:31-35), 4) Chapters 15-16, 5) Chapters 13:36-14:31.[11] But Bultmann's proposal has not proved any more convincing than other rearrangements. All such proposals, Bultmann's included, which originate in the attempt to do away with a compositional disjunction, have introduced new compositional problems, and, furthermore, do not take into account the implications of the fact that 13:31-14:31 and 15:1-16:33 contain large sections of parallel material, which suggests more than one original farewell composition and thus lends added weight to the view that one or the other is secondary.[12]

Julius Wellhausen was apparently the first to take the position that chapters 15-17 are a secondary addition.[13] He appealed not only to the natural connection between 14:31 and 18:1, but also to theological differences which, he claimed, marked the secondary version of the farewell off from the original in chapter 14. This neat solution was set forth in a more complicated form by Wellhausen a year after he first proposed it, and it, or versions of it, have been adopted recently by a number of scholars. G. Richter, for example, has argued that there are two theological tendencies behind the two explanations of the foot-washing in chapter 13, and that the same tendencies distinguish the two versions of the farewell discourses.[14] A radical version of this approach is represented by Jürgen Becker's recent argument that there are four distinct compositions in 13:31-16:32, representing four distinguishable theological tendencies.[15] The first (13:31-14:31) and the last (16:16-33) have, he argued, clear affinities, as do the second (15:1-17), and the third (15:18-16:15). Only the first, however, was composed by the "evangelist." The rest all show a shift in focus from christology to ecclesiology. Other scholars have accepted the view that there are two or more originally independent farewell compositions, but argue that the differences between them do not warrant assigning them to different authors.[16]

It is not our purpose here to follow out the details of this discussion. It seems clear that the farewell material in the Gospel is composed of several originally distinct compositions, including two which parallel each other at several points.[17] Our interest in the rest of this study is in the first of these compositions, the farewell discourse in 13:31-14:31. We shall argue that this discourse, with dialogue elements in it, is a coherent literary unit with a single theme and purpose, and that it fulfills a fundamental role in relation to the Gospel as a whole. Our analysis supports the view that this discourse could have stood alone in the original version of the Gospel.[18] Whether or not chapters 15-17 were written by the author and added to the Gospel later by a redactor, or were written by the redactor, or someone else, is a question we shall leave aside.

The Structure of the First Farewell Discourse

Attempts to Outline the Discourse

"The internal organization of ch. xiv," says Raymond Brown, "is not easy to discern."[19] Though many commentators have treated 13:31-14:31 (or at least ch. 14) as a unit, there have been few attempts to discuss the structural principles by which the discourse is organized. Many scholars divide up the discourse into units for purposes of discussion without explaining the basis for their subdivisions.[20] They appear to treat the discourse as a collection of little units strung together rather loosely around the general theme of the departure of Jesus. Adolf von Harnack did, in fact, characterize the farewell situation as a *Sammelbecken* where the author brought together a variety of diverse speech traditions.[21] Judging from the many different outlines of the discourse which have been proposed it would seem, indeed, as if there is little overall organization or structure to the chapter.[22] It is significant that in none of the rearrangement theories has there been an attempt to insert additional material between 14:1-14:31. Chapter 14 has been put in different places in different theories--as the last unit in the farewell material (Spitta, Bultmann), or just before the prayer (Moffatt, Bernard, Lewis, Wendt, Macgregor). In all such theories, however, chapter 14 has been treated as a single unit. Though this is negative evidence for the unity of at least 14:1-31, it is nonetheless impressive.[23]

The beginning of the discourse remains to be considered. It has been held by a number of scholars that 13:31-38 forms the introduction to the farewell material. However, it has also been the case that many of the rearrangement theories have found it convenient to insert chapters 15-16 (and sometimes ch. 17) into 13:31-38 at one point or another.[24] If one rejects theories of displacement, there is little reason to question the view that 13:31-38 functions as the introduction to the discourse. As Raymond Brown points out, though 13:31-38 is obviously a composite in which vss. 31-32, 33, and 34-35 are "more juxtaposed than connected," nevertheless, "one can trace the logic that led to the union of these disparate elements."[25] We shall trace this "logic" in the following chapter in detail.

A further question is whether 13:31-38 whould be considered as the introduction to the farewell discourses as a whole, or only the introduction to the first discourse in chapter 14. In the present form of the Gospel 13:31-38 clearly does function as the introduction to the farewell material in chapters 14-17. We would suggest, however, that this is a secondary function acquired with the addition of chapters 15-17.[26] We intend to show that the first farewell discourse is organized systematically in order to express a single message, and that 13:31-38 fits into the structure of the discourse in such a way as to indicate that it was composed originally as part of the first farewell discourse alone.

Turning to the central part of the discourse, 14:1-26, we find that some scholars have divided up the chapter by motif. Rudolf Bultmann, for example, divides the discourse into two units, 14:1-14, dominated by the key-word, *pisteuein*, and 14:15-24, held together by the word *agapan*, with 14:25-31 forming the conclusion.[27] But Raymond Brown, who adopts this same outline, concedes that these units are not major subdivisions, and, in fact, states that his decision to treat them separately in his commentary "is really a question of practicality."[28] Brown is just as tentative when it comes to his analysis of the first "unit," vss. 1-14. "With hesitancy," he proposes a division into vss. 1-4, 6-11, and 12-14, with vs. 5 as a transitional question.[29] Brown, at least, acknowledges the difficulties with this sort of analysis.

Some scholars have called attention to the elements of dialogue, that is, the questions of the disciples which occur at 13:36; 14:4, 8, and 22, as evidence of conscious composition. Many scholars follow this principle in taking 14:1-4 as a unit, with Thomas's question in vs. 5 introducing a second unit (14:5-7),[30] and Philip's question introducing a third unit (14:8ff).[31]

Uncertainty over whether to divide by motif or by dialogue explains the lack of consensus on whether to make a break between vss. 20 and 21,[32] taking vss. 21-24 as dealing with the love motif, or between vss. 21 and 22,[33] Judas's question in vs. 22 being taken as introducing this unit.[34]

A glance at the three questions makes clear the fallacy of viewing them as a principle of subdivision. In all three cases, the question of the disciple is prompted by the previous statement of Jesus which, in fact, introduces the particular motif in question. In vs. 4 Jesus introduces the theme of "the way," which Thomas's question then picks up. In vss. 6,7 Jesus introduces the theme of knowing the Father, which Philip's question picks up in vs. 8. In vs. 21, Jesus introduces the motif of the manifestation of Jesus to his own, which Judas's question picks up in vs. 22. The same applies to Peter's question in 13:16, which harks back to Jesus' words in vs. 33. In other words, the questions are not used to *introduce* the theme but to *advance* it.[35]

The consistency in the way the questions of the disciples are used suggests possible compositional intention. C. H. Dodd and others have pointed to another piece of evidence of the same, in the use of the expression, *me tarassestho humon he kardia*, in 14:1 and again in 14:27.[36] Chapter 14, says Dodd, "is clamped together by the repeated use" of this expression.[37] More important, after noting the closeness of 14:1-3 to the traditional language of the church's eschatology, Dodd goes on to suggest that from vss. 4 on we have "Johannine reinterpretation" of this traditional eschatology. "It would seem that the evangelist was conscious of putting forward a bold reinterpretation of what was believed to be the teaching of Jesus."[38] But Dodd does not show how this works out in a detailed analysis of the whole.

Becker's Analysis: An Expository Structure

Dodd's suggestions have received more sustained application to the details of the discourse in the recent analysis of Jürgen Becker.[39] As with Dodd, Becker starts with the observation that the repetition of the exhortation in 14:1 and 14:27 is evidence of conscious composition. The discourse is divided into

three parts. The introduction, 13:31-38, is marked off from
the central part of the discourse (14:1-16) by the first
exhortation in 14:1. The conclusion (14:27-31) is marked off
by the second exhortation in 14:27.

What is important is Becker's treatment of the central
part of the composition, 14:1-26. The first verses of this
part, 14:1-3, contain a "word of revelation," taken from the
tradition, which answers Peter's question, raised in the introduction, as to where Jesus is going (13:36).[40] But this saying,
which expresses the traditional Parousia expectation of the
early church,[41] serves merely as a "text" which the author
reinterprets in the verses which follow. Becker's analysis
here coincides with Dodd's view, noted above, that from vss. 4
on we have "Johannine reinterpretation" of a traditional word.
Becker, however, goes a step further in working out the formal
structure of the reinterpretation found in vss. 4-26. The
basis of the reinterpretation, he suggests, is the "I am" saying
in vs. 6, which functions in exactly the same way as the "I am"
saying in 11.24f. "Just as by the I-am word of the resurrection
(11:25ff.) the evangelist in John 11 interpreted anew and thereby
corrected the church's faith--represented by Martha in 11:24--so
the statements in 14:4ff. serve him now to exegete in his own
sense the apparently widespread view of his church represented
in 14:2ff."[42] Two expressions from the "text" are selected by
the author for commentary, dividing up the exegesis into two
parts. The first part, vss. 4-17, takes up the expression
poreuomai (vs. 2) and treats the theme of Jesus' departure
(cf. *hupagein* in vss. 4, 5, and *poreuomai* in vs. 13). The
second part, vss. 18-26, takes up the expression *palin erchomai*
(vs. 3) and treats the theme of Jesus' return (cf. vs. 18).
"Thus," concludes Becker, "14:4-26 is an exegesis of the word
of revelation in 14:2ff. which has come down to the evangelist
from the church, organized around two main themes."[43] Becker
does not use the word "text" to refer to the word of revelation
in 14:2-3, but it is, we would suggest, an accurate description
of the way he views its function in the discourse. Confirmation
of this analysis is to be found in the speaker's summary of the
discourse in 14:28, which picks up the same two themes, departure
and return: "You heard what I said to you, 'I am going away and

I am coming (back) to you."[44]

It is striking to observe that Becker's analysis coincides with the homiletical midrash form which Peder Borgen has demonstrated in the case of the bread discourse in John 6.[45] In the homily form described by Borgen the exposition of the text proceeds by paraphrasing and interpreting one portion of the text after another, so that the parts of the text serve as the basis for the subdivisions of the homily. The terms of the text are paraphrased in the exposition (cf. *hupagein* in vs. 4 as a "paraphrase" of *poreuomai* in vs. 3), the opening and closing statements of the homily have central terms in common (14:28 repeats the themes of 14:3), and subordinate quotations are used in the exposition (with which we may compare the way the "I am" saying in vs. 6 functions in Becker's analysis).[46] The major difference between the farewell discourse and Borgen's homily form is obviously the fact that the former uses sayings of Jesus as its "text" whereas in Borgen's examples the text is taken from the Old Testament Scriptures. But Wayne Meeks has pointed out that in the bread discourse the composition begins not with the O.T. text in vs. 31, but with the saying of Jesus in vs. 27, and Meeks concludes from this that "the form of explication" observed by Borgen "may have had a wider application in rhetoric than only the exposition of sacred texts."[47] It should also be pointed out that the oldest strata of rabbinic materials does not, in fact, exegete scripture but rabbinic utterances.[48]

The possibility that the homiletic form described by Borgen is applicable to sayings of Jesus has been noted by David Aune, who recalls B. W. Bacon's suggestion to the same effect.[49] Aune points out that the words of Jesus are, in another respect, treated as scripture. The typical Johannine fulfillment formula is applied to them in John 18:9 (quoting 17:12) and John 18:32 (quoting 12:32f.). But Aune's conclusion that the words of Jesus are "regarded as equal in value to the words of the Old Testament" does not do justice to the fact that the Gospel subordinates the "writings" of Moses to the words of Jesus (5:46, 47).[50]

The Critique of Becker's Analysis: Discontinuity

Becker's analysis of the expository form of the discourse appears convincing, especially in light of the comparison with Borgen. There are problems, however, with his interpretation. According to Becker, the purpose of the discourse is to correct the false eschatology which holds that the departure of Jesus has created a distance, a discontinuity, between Jesus and the believer which will exist until the future return of Jesus at the Parousia. "Discontinuity" means, in this instance, the absence of Jesus.[51] The central message of the discourse is "continuity," understood as the presence of Jesus now in the church.[52]

In this interpretation Becker represents a type of analysis of the first farewell discourse which characteristically focuses attention on Jesus' promise to come back to the disciples (14:18ff.), along with the related promises that the disciples will see him soon (14:19,20), that they will "live" (14:19), and that they will be united with Father and Son in reciprocal union (14:20,23).

This text, 14:18-24, is clearly a crux in the interpretation of the discourse.[53] A number of scholars have taken the promise of the coming of Father and Son to be the climax of the discourse, calling attention to the movement from the *monai* in heaven in 14:3 to the *mone* with the believer in 14:23. But there have been a variety of interpretations of the meaning of this promise. Discussion has turned on the question of the mode of realization or actualization of the "coming" of Jesus and the Father, the "seeing" of Jesus by the disciples, and the indwelling of vs. 20. Older scholars spoke of "mysticism," as in Hans Windisch's reference to the "mystically reinterpreted parousia of Jesus."[54] In recent years scholars have rejected the term "mysticism" but the alternative attempts to characterize the relationship between Father, Son and believer set forth in these verses have not been much more illuminating. Barnabas Lindars' reference to a "faith-union maintained by the imagination and the will" is not untypical of the language of those who reject "mysticism." The coming of Father and Son to the believer, spoken of in 14:23, must, Lindars says,

> be an interior apprehension of Jesus and the Father
> in the hearts of those who love Jesus. This can
> hardly be a mystical experience of an esoteric
> kind, which would not be accessible to all. It is
> more likely to be something akin to the Pauline
> concept of being "in Christ," a faith-union
> maintained by the imagination and the will.[55]

Other scholars have stressed the conditions of love and obedience
imposed by Jesus (14:21,23,23) and have talked in terms of
ethical realization of salvation.[56] According to Bultmann, the
language of Easter (14:19), Pentecost (14:16,17), and Parousia
(14:18) has been demythologized, that is to say, reinterpreted
existentially by the author to refer to "stages through which
the life of the believer has to pass."[57] David Aune sees in
this language a reference to a "cultic" coming of Jesus "in
the form of a pneumatic or prophetic *visio Christi* within the
setting of worship 'in the Spirit' as celebrated by the
Johannine community."[58] Kundsin understands the passage to
be referring to the coming of Jesus to Christian martyrs in
the hour of death.[59]

Most of these interpretations have in common the assumption that the departure of Jesus is viewed by the author as
having created a problem of distance and discontinuity in the
relationship of the believer to Jesus. It is assumed that the
central message of the discourse is to resolve this problem
by disclosing the fact of a present unity with Jesus, the fact
of his presence in the church, the continuation of his
salvation despite the delay of the Parousia or the loss of
eyewitness contact with Jesus. As a result, scholars have
labored to answer the question of *how* Jesus continues to be
present as the question which is presumably answered in the
text.

There are, however, tensions and anomalies in the discourse which are not accounted for on such an understanding.
Focusing on Becker, we find that, in his view, 14:1-3, which
implies a period of separation from Jesus until the Parousia,
reflects a view which the author does not share. However, the
implication of a period of separation is to be found already in
13:33 and 36. If 14:1-3 implies a "salvation-empty present"
for the church, the same is true of 13:33 and 36. In this

regard 13:33 is a remarkable statement. Jesus explicitly places his followers in the same position as "the Jews," or outsiders, non-followers. None of them will be able to follow Jesus when he goes away. Following directly upon Jesus' triumphal announcement of his own and the Father's reciprocal glorification, the relegation of the disciples, on this occasion, to the same rank as "the Jews" is all the more shocking. Why such an offensive way of disclosing the disappointing truth that the disciples will not accompany him to heaven? 13:33 cannot be attributed to a "tradition" which the author is going to correct, since it explicitly picks up a theme which the author has developed and stressed on two previous occasions (7:33 and 8:21). But if the author himself clearly emphasizes the separation and absence occasioned by the departure, this creates a problem for the view that the theme of the discourse is the *presence* of Christ.

A second problem has to do with Becker's treatment of the succession theme in 14:12-17. These verses presuppose the *absence* of Jesus ("because I go to the Father," vs. 12) and make provision, in his absence, for the disciples (vs. 12), indwelt by "another Paraclete" (vss. 16, 17), to take his place. The idea of Jesus' absence, in other words, is *not* corrected, as Becker's interpretation demands. It is presupposed in these verses (vss. 12-17).

We encounter here what is perhaps the fundamental difficulty in the way of an interpretation of the first farewell discourse as a coherent whole. On the one hand, we have in vss. 18ff., the verses to which Becker appeals, the promise that Jesus will, in effect, be his own successor, a notion implied already in vss. 4-11 in the insistence on the exclusivity of Jesus' mediatorship. On the other hand, we have in vss. 12-17 the promise that Jesus will be succeeded by *others*--the disciples, the other Paraclete. We have, in other words, two logically incompatible sequels to Jesus' departure placed side by side in the discourse.[60]

Many scholars, Becker among them, have resolved the problem by assuming that Jesus and the other Paraclete must, in one way or another, be identified.[61] But even if we make this

assumption we must still ask why the author has placed these
two promises together in this fashion. We must account, in
this instance, not only for *what* the author has presumably
intended to say, but also for *how* he has said it.

It is worth pointing out, in this connection, that in the
discourse as a whole there is a marked pattern in the way in
which it sets forth Jesus' absence and presence. From 13:31-
14:3 it is emphasized that Jesus will go away and that the
disciples will be left behind. In 14:4-11 it is emphasized
that Jesus continues to be the only way for the disciples to
know and see the Father, implying that he remains, in some
sense, present. In 14:12-17 it is explicitly stated that Jesus
goes away and that the disciples remain behind to do his works.
In 14:18-24 it is explicitly stated that Jesus will be present,
indwelling the disciples. Both sides of this alternating
sequence of absence, presence, absence, presence must be
accounted for in any interpretation of the discourse.

A third weakness in Becker's analysis occurs in his
treatment of the teaching and remembering role assigned to the
Paraclete in the promise of 14:25,26. In these two verses
Jesus tells the disciples that the promised Spirit-Paraclete
will "teach you all things and will *remind you of all that I
have said to you*." According to Becker this means nothing
more than the "confirmation" of the presence of Father and Son
in the church, "denn wer der Gegenwart Christi gewiss ist, hat
'alles.'"[62] But this comment ignores completely the specific
temporal horizon of the promise, the relation in which the author
stands to the words spoken by Jesus as words spoken *in the past*.
It also trivializes what is one of the most important pieces of
evidence to the fact that the author himself is aware of Jesus
as a figure of past time.[63] According to the author, the Paraclete will direct the attention of the believer backwards in
time to the tradition of Jesus' words.

To sum up, Becker has assigned the distance and discontinuity to someone other than the author, namely, to a "tradition"
to be corrected. But there is evidence in the farewell discourse
that the author himself affirms, even emphasizes the temporal
discontinuity. To fully understand the issue, it is necessary

to place it in the context of the interpretation of the Gospel
as a whole.

The Function of the First Farewell Discourse: Continuity or Discontinuity, Presence or Hierarchy?

Continuity in the Gospel: Christocentrism and the Problem of Interpretation

Becker's position, which, in effect, relegates the departure of Jesus to the status of external occasion for the
farewell discourses, reflects Ernst Käsemann's interpretation
of the Gospel. Becker's formulation of the theme of the farewell discourse as the *praesentia Christi* is taken from Käsemann's
summary formulation of what he, Käsemann, considers to be the
"center" of the Gospel.[64] It is not surprising, therefore, that
Becker pays so little attention to the emphasis on discontinuity
in the discourse and in the Gospel, since few have stated the
other side of the matter, the evidence for the continuity of
the Son across the boundaries of time and space in the Gospel
of John more forcefully than Ernst Käsemann.

According to Käsemann, the temporal transcendence of the
Son relativizes the importance of human history to the point
where history, in John, "can be regarded as a process only in
the most external and superficial sense."[65]

> The dimension of the past is retained only in so far
> as it points forward to his presence; all of the future
> is nothing but the glorified extension and repetition
> of this presence. History remains the history of the
> Logos, since it is the sphere of his past, present and
> future epiphany. The sole theme of history is the
> *praesentia Christi*. What else may happen on earth is
> only scenery and props for this theme. These earthly
> events are in part only intimated or roughly sketched
> so that some narratives recede into twilight. Dogmatic
> reflection determines the structure and the subdivision
> within this Gospel.[66]

Rightly pointing to the dominant role played by the glory and
pre-existence of the Son, or "protology," in John, Käsemann
draws the conclusion "that the incorporation and position of the
passion narrative of necessity becomes problematical. Apart
from a few remarks that point ahead to it, the passion comes

into view in John only at the very end. One is tempted to regard it as being a mere postscript."[67]

Käsemann's argument is directed against those who have interpreted the passion in terms of a "christology of humiliation," a journey from lowliness to glory.[68] But this is not the only way in which the author's emphasis on the "passion" can be interpreted. While accepting Käsemann's case against such an interpretation of the passion, we cannot follow him in downplaying the importance of the departure of Jesus in the Gospel, and must, instead, pose all the more sharply the question of the reason for the author's emphasis on the final hour of Jesus' sojourn on the earth.[69]

It will be useful to follow Käsemann's argument a bit further. Käsemann has pressed the fact of the christocentrism in John to the point where the eschatological categories within which much of twentieth-century Johannine scholarship has attempted to encompass the Gospel have broken down. The emphasis on pre-existence, Käsemann argues, expresses a fundamental shift in outlook in comparison with the earlier Christian tradition, a shift from eschatology to protology as the center of the Christian message.[70] John's "eschatology," he says, "no longer emphasizes the end and the future, but the beginning and the abiding."[71] But this shift from eschatology to protology is an aspect of a more fundamental shift, the reversal in order of priority of eschatology and christology. Primitive eschatology was from the beginning christologically oriented. In John's Gospel, however,

> eschatology is no longer the force that determines christology; the opposite is the case. Christology determines eschatology and eschatology becomes an aspect of christology. In Christ, the end of the world has not merely come near, but is present and remains present continually.[72]

I have quoted Gerhard Krodel's translation, but a more literal translation points to the fact that what is in view is the defining or determining *boundaries* of the Johannine world view. According to Käsemann, "eschatology is no longer the *horizon* of christology, but rather the reverse. Christology is the horizon of eschatology."[73]

What kind of category is it that has become determinative in the Johannine world view? To talk about "christology" is to make use of a confessional category for analytical purposes. What is in view is a divine *person*. By "person" I mean the central speaker in the Gospel, who in his self-testimony speaks of himself as one whose self-consciousness is continuous from "before the creation" (17:5). But the word "person" has misleading connotations involving distinctions, for example, between "person" and "nature" deriving from later christological and trinitarian controversies. Käsemann points out, correctly we would argue, that the way in which the Gospel of John talks about the Son "can no longer be explained on the basis of a purely soteriological interest. The internal divine relationship of the revealer as the Son is just as strongly emphasized as his relation to the world."[74] But Käsemann can only describe what is involved here by making reference to the subsequent dogmatic controversies. "With the christological mystery is connected what later times called the mystery within the Trinity."[75] Similarly he describes Johannine christology in the language of subsequent debate as "naive docetism."[76] What is obscured by such categories is the question of the specific problems which characterized the *author's* time and place and which he has chosen to address.[77] To call the author's christology "naive" docetism is to admit that this position was taken without conscious choice, which is to say that the issue of the "real" nature of Christ in the sense of the later debates *had not yet been raised*. What then *is* the context of interpretation in which we are to place the christocentricity? What issues *was* the author addressing which led him to take the positions he did? If Käsemann is correct in insisting that the determinative context is not apocalyptic eschatology, even though eschatological language is used, and if, on the other hand, it is not christological and trinitarian dogmatics of a subsequent era, how are we to characterize it? What categories are appropriate to the situation of the Gospel?

It is worth emphasizing the way in which the christocentricity of John has posed for other scholars the issue of appropriate interpretative categories. Theo Preiss, for example, speaks of the simplicity of Johannine thought as rising from "a strict convergence of all the themes towards the Person of him whose speeches, delivered in a mysterious monotone, culminate in those sovereign formulae: 'I am the light of the world . . . the resurrection, and the life. . . .'" But he also points out that the convergence, or "christo-centric character" makes the "thought" of the Gospel "so resistant to any systematic analysis."[78] George MacRae argues that while in the "I am" pronouncements Jesus is claiming to be the fulfillment of all of the expectations symbolized, there is also "the further assertion that no such symbolization reaches the reality of Jesus as Son of God."[79] W. D. Davies has argued recently that in the Fourth Gospel "geographic dimensions have been transcended and that 'holy places' as such, can be dispensed with in the 'holy Person.'"[80] F. Hahn speaks of a "blurring of horizons" in the Gospel.[81] Rudolf Bultmann holds that the central riddle of the Gospel is the fact that Jesus claims to be the Revealer, but reveals nothing other than the fact that he is the Revealer, the point being the destruction of all dogma, the repudiation of "revelation" understood as objectifiable content which can be coded and controlled within human categories.[82] Hoskyns refers to the "self-contained allusiveness" of the Gospel, whose author is determined that the reader shall be "overwhelmed by the singleness of the theme."[83] Meeks, following Hoskyns, talks about the "self-referring quality" of the whole gospel, which gives the reader the impression that Jesus is "playing some kind of language-game" whose rules neither Jesus' hearers nor the gospel's readers could possibly know."[84] At the heart of the self-referring quality of the Gospel is, I suggest, a formal characteristic of Jesus' speech, namely, that almost all that Jesus says about all other figures in the Gospel--Father, Paraclete, disciples, the world--takes the form of testimony by Jesus about *himself-in-relation* to the other figures. As Meeks says, we find in the gospel a

> closed system of metaphors, which confronts the
> reader in a fashion somewhat like the way a Semitist
> once explained to me how to learn Aramaic: "Once you
> know *all* the Semitic languages," he said, "learning
> any one of them is easy." The reader cannot under-
> stand any part of the Fourth Gospel until he under-
> stands the whole. Thus the reader has an experience
> rather like that of the dialogue partners of Jesus:

either he will find the whole business so
convoluted, obscure, and maddeningly arrogant
that he will reject it in anger, or he will
find it so fascinating that he will stick with
it until the progressive reiteration of themes
brings, on some level of consciousness at least,
a degree of clarity.[85]

Discontinuity in the Gospel: the
Stress on the Departure

In light of the relativizing, blurring effect of the
Gospel's christocentrism, the emphasis which the author places
on the departure of Jesus takes on fundamental significance.

Temporally, the departure is viewed throughout the
Gospel as marking an important boundary line. The first words
of the farewell discourse, in 13:31, mark off the time of
departure and glorification from the preceding time: "Now is
the Son of Man glorified . . ." The "now" of this announcement
stands in contrast to the "not yet" of the earlier statement
in 7:39 where, in an editorial remark, the author observes that
"the Spirit was not yet (*oupo*) present because Jesus was not
yet (*oudepo*) glorified." The importance of the announcement in
13:31, 32 is underscored by the fact that this announcement to
the disciples alone repeats the announcement made at the end of
the public ministry (12:23ff.), and echoes the author's solemn
remarks at the opening of the foot-washing scene in 13:1ff.

The division in time marked by the glorification of Jesus
is also marked by a shift from misunderstanding to understanding
on the part of the disciples. Referring to the fulfillment of
Old Testament prophecy in the triumphal entry into Jerusalem,
the author points out that the disciples did not comprehend
these things "at first" (*to proton*), "but when Jesus was
glorified, then they remembered that these things were written
concerning him and that they had done these things to him"
(12:16). In this editorial comment, as in 13:1ff. and 7:39,
the voice of the author is heard directly. The remembering
motif, which we find here, in 12:16, and which we noted in the
farewell discourse at 14:26, occurs also in 2:17 and 22.[86]

These references belong to a pattern of anticipation and
arrival which is pervasive in the Gospel. From the beginning
of the ministry of Jesus the reader's eye is drawn forward to
the coming event. Jesus' words to Nathaniel at his call set
the tone: "Because I said to you, I saw you under the fig tree,
do you believe? You shall see greater things than these. And
he said to him, 'Truly, truly, I say to you, you will see
heaven opened, and the angels of God ascending and descending
upon the Son of Man'" (1:50, 51). At the wedding at Cana
Jesus' rebuke to his mother is explained with the words, "my
hour is not yet come" (2:4), just as later Jesus escapes
death because, the narrator informs the reader, "his hour was
not yet come" (7:30; 8:20). As early as 6:70 Jesus hints at
the coming betrayal: "Did I not choose you, the twelve, and one
of you is a devil?" To Judas Jesus makes the pointed remark at
the beginning of the final Passover, "The poor you always have
with you, but you do not always have me" (12"4f.). In the
dialogue with Nicodemus Jesus points forward to the departure
and glorification in the enigmatic words concerning the "lifting
up" of the Son of Man (3:14), a motif repeated at 8:28 and 12:32.
In 6:62 Jesus refers to his "ascent" to the place from whence
he came.

Just as the remembering motif in the farewell discourse
picks up a motif repeated earlier, so the motif of departure
as separation in 13:33 occurs earlier. In 7:33 Jesus tells his
hearers that he is "going away" and that they will not be able
to follow him. His statement is met with misunderstanding:
"Where does this fellow intend to go that we won't find him?
Surely he isn't going off to the Diaspora among the Greeks to
teach the Greeks? What is this he is talking about: 'You will
look for me and not find me,' and 'Where I am, you cannot
come?'" (7:33-36).[87] In 8:21f. the author repeats this scene,
with variations. This time the hearers make the sarcastic
suggestion that perhaps Jesus means to commit suicide when he
speaks of going away to a place where his hearers will not be
able to follow, thus misunderstanding him again.

If the whole of the public ministry anticipates the
coming hour, the point of view taken at the close of the public
ministry and in the farewell supper and discourses is that the

hour anticipated has now arrived. The announcement of the
arrival of "the hour" of glorification is made for the first
time in an address given by Jesus in 12:23-33. Its importance
is indicated by the fact that it is punctuated by the dramatic
sound of a voice from heaven in which the Father himself
announces the coming glorification. The speech of Jesus is
followed by a short exchange with "the crowd" which recalls the
two earlier dialogues concerning the departure and separation.
In the latter two cases, as we have seen, the hearers misunderstand what Jesus means when he talks about "going away." Now
they raise an objection. The Messiah, they say, will, according
to the law, "remain for ever. How can you say that the Son of
Man must be lifted up? Who is this Son of Man?" Jesus' reply
is a warning which once more contains a veiled reference to his
departure (12:34-36).

The farewell discourses assume the arrival of the hour.
"From now on" the disciples "know" and "have seen" the Father
(14:7). "No longer do I call you servants," Jesus tells his
disciples, they are now "friends" (15:15). The point of view
becomes retrospective when Jesus speaks of the guilt which the
world has incurred by its rejection of Jesus: "If I had not
come . . . but now they have no excuse. . . . If I had not
done among them the works . . . but now . . ." (15:23,23). The
disciples have become "witnesses" because they have been with
Jesus "from the beginning" (15:27, cf. 16:4). The retrospective
point of view becomes even more marked in the farewell prayer.
Jesus' prayer is based upon what he has accomplished. He has
glorified the Father (17:4), accomplished his work (vs. 4),
manifested his name (17:6,26), given the disciples his words
(17:8, 14), kept them (17:12), guarded them (17:12), sent them
(17:18), given them the glory given to him (17:22). They in
turn have kept the word (17:6), received the words (17:8),
believed that Jesus is from the Father (17:8), and have
therefore been hated by the world (17:14).

The division is also a spatial one. Spatial terms abound
in the Gospel to describe the "death" of Jesus. It is a
departure, a change of location, a return to heaven, an ascent.
The terms used include the following: *hupagein* (7:33; 8:14,21f.;

13:33, 36; 14:4f.,28; 16:5,10,17), *poreuesthai* (14:2f.; 12:28; 16:7, 2, 8), *erchesthai* (to the Father, 17:11, 13), *aperchesthai* (16:7); *aphienai* (16:28), *anabainein* (3:13; 6:62; 20:17), and *hupsothenai* (3:14; 8:28; 12:32). The verb *doxasthenai*, as we shall argue, likewise has a primary spatial aspect.

The division in time and space is, in fact, incorporated into the compositional structure of the Gospel by the author's choice of the farewell discourse form, which, in contrast to the apocalyptic discourse form in Mark and Matthew, often pointed to as parallel, highlights the fact of departure. According to Günter Bornkamm, we find in John "as never before" that the farewell of Jesus from the earth and the situation of the disciples who are left behind has become "das eigentlich beherrschende Thema."[88] "Jesus' farewell," says Bornkamm, "is not merely the external occasion, but precisely the theme itself in these (farewell) discourses."[89]

It is evident that the emphasis placed by the author on the departure of Jesus cannot simply be erased by pointing to the continuous presence of the Son across the boundaries of time and space. What then is its status, function, and meaning?

The issue may be posed in sharper terms by looking at some of the ways scholars who have recognized the emphasis on the departure have interpreted it. Louis Martyn, for example, points out that "more than once Jesus announces the termination of his sojourn," and affirms his view "that the problem posed by Jesus' departure to the Father is a real one."[90] He finds in the Gospel "two levels" of narrative which are distinguished in terms of their time reference. The Gospel is, on one level, a witness to events in Jesus' earthly lifetime, the level of the *Einmalig*. It is, at the same time, "a witness to Jesus' powerful presence in actual events experienced by the Johannine church."[91] By *Einmalig*, Martyn says, "I mean something like 'back there' as opposed to 'now and here.' . . . I wish only to distinguish two levels in John's way of presenting certain parts of his Gospel. The reader will not go far wrong if he renders my use of *einmalig* by the expression "once upon a time.'"[92] The Gospel is a "two level drama" in which the author is actually writing about his own present time in the form of a narrative about the past sojourn of Jesus on earth.

There is, however, a tension in Martyn's study between his insistence on the *distinction* between the two levels in the narrative, on the one hand, and his insistence on the unity or "integrity" of the two levels, a tension which leaves the status of the distinction unclear. Is it a distinction drawn by the author of the Gospel, one he is conscious of making? In his analysis of chapter 5 Martyn raises this question directly. "Does John present this drama on the two levels with which we are now familiar?" he asks. In answer, he cites 5:18, with the observation that in this "editorial comment," "the *two* levels of the drama are clearly and distinctly indicated":

> For this reason the Jews sought all the more to kill him, because he *not only* broke the sabbath, *but also* called God his Father, making himself equal with God.[93]

Later, however, when he brings up the question again, he concludes, "I doubt that he was himself *analytically conscious* of what I have termed the two-level drama, for his major concern in this regard was to bear witness to the essential *integrity* of the *einmalig* drama of Jesus' earthly life and the contemporary drama in which the Risen Lord acts through his servants."[94] He even concludes, in still another reference, that John does not "in any overt way" indicate to the reader a distinction between the two "stages"![95]

How are we to understand these statements? How could the author have concerned himself with the *integrity* of the two levels or stages unless he was himself conscious of the distinction between them? Martyn suggests that the author was not "analytically" conscious of the two-level drama, which implies that he was conscious of it in some *other* way. How would this other way be described? What Martyn presumably means by "analytically conscious" is the consciousness of the two levels of the drama which the historical critic discerns. This is suggested by Martyn's observation that "only the reflective scholar intent on *analyzing* the Gospel will discover the seams which the Evangelist sewed together so deftly."[96] It goes without saying that the author was hardly conscious of the distinction *in this way*. This does not, however, mean that he was not conscious *in other ways* of the distinction between his own time and the past time of which he wrote. In his final chapter,

Martyn draws upon the farewell discourse in chapter 14 in order
to show how the "integrity" between the two levels is secured
by the figure of the Paraclete. He fails to recognize, however,
that the discourse offers crucial evidence of the way in which
the author was conscious of the *distinction*.

Martyn's failure to address this feature of the Gospel,
a feature which is so critical to his postulate of a two-level
drama is due to his failure to distinguish in precise terms
between the *author's* approach to the relationship between the
time of Jesus and the time of the church, on the one hand, and
the insights of the *historical critic*. This affects not only
the distinction between the two stages but also the understanding
of the "integrity" or continuity. One must draw a sharp
distinction between the unity of the two times as understood by
the author and the anachronistic blurring together of the two
historical periods perceived by the historical critic. We are
driven back again to the question of the *author's* situation,
the issues *he* was addressing.

Wilhelm Thüsing in his study of exaltation and glorification in John, speaks of "two stages" in the saving work of
Jesus.[97] He has, in fact, attempted to work out in meticulous
detail the relationship of the two stages. Stage one, he argues,
covers the earthly life of Jesus including his death, which is
understood as "exaltation" (*hupsothenai*).[98] Stage two refers
to the "working out" of the exaltation which takes place in
the work of the Paraclete in the church.[99] Stage one constitutes
the "setting up" of the saving sign of the cross; stage two, the
working out of the saving effects. Stage one is the enthrone-
ment on "the throne of the cross"; stage two is the rule from
the "throne next to the Father." Stage one exhibits the glory
of obedience; stage two the glory of rule. Stage one is the
seed; stage two the unfolding or growth.[100]

Thüsing insists on the unity of the two stages as parts
of a single "work."[101] There is a relationship of analogy
between them,[102] and even a projection of one stage into the
other in the way the evangelist presents them.[103] Furthermore,
the first stage *contains* the second in seed form. The first
stage is more than just a beginning or a cause (*Ursache*) of the
second. "It is a 'beginning' of a special kind, a beginning

which contains everything within itself."[104]

Thüsing's study is marred, as Käsemann has pointed out, by his adoption of the obedience/reward pattern to interpret the descent and ascent of the Son.[105] The effect is to obscure the real point of the author's emphasis on the division enacted by the departure. The issue at stake is, as Thüsing holds, a matter of authority and rank. Contrary to Thüsing, however, it is a matter of the authority and rank of Jesus *in relation to the authority and rank of the disciples*. The central issue is *not* the authority and glory of the earthly Jesus in relation to the authority and glory of the exalted Son.

We can clarify our thesis further by a comparison with Rudolf Bultmann's interpretation of the departure. Bultmann has recognized more clearly than most that the distance opened up between Jesus and the believer by the departure is, for the author of the Gospel, something necessary and *positive*. The theme of the farewell discourses, according to Bultmann, is "the indirectness of revelation."[106] Bultmann understands this "indirectness" in terms of his demythologizing "idea of revelation." Indirectness means, for Bultmann, anti-mythological, anti-dogmatic, anti-mystical revelation. Against Bultmann, however, we would hold that John's opposition to dogma and myth must be understood as opposition to *someone else's* dogma and myth, not to dogma and myth per se. John's critique of miracle, myth, and dogma takes place on the basis of his own miracle, myth, and dogma.

There is in the farewell discourses an insistence by Jesus upon mediation or "indirectness." Bultmann is in fact correct in holding that this is the dominant theme. However, the indirectness or mediation which Jesus insists upon has to do with the status of the disciples as agents in relation to Jesus. His access to the Father is direct, unmediated; theirs is mediated. They are dependent upon him, and therefore *subordinate* to him. The issue, in the first farewell discourse at least, is rank, hierarchy, place, not "revelation."

*Summary: Theme and Outline of the
First Farewell Discourse*

We may summarize. The large amount of farewell material
in the Gospel of John poses the following question: Why is there
such an emphasis on the departure of Jesus in a Gospel in which
the transcendence of the Son across space and time boundaries
is so radically conceived? In a community with a christology
of this sort it is highly improbable that the absence of Jesus
would have been experienced as a problem. The departure of
Jesus is not treated as a problem in the Gospel, or as a symbol
of a problem to be overcome, be it the loss of eyewitness
contact with Jesus or the delay of the Parousia.[107] On the
contrary, it is one of the prominent motifs in the Gospel. We
are led to ask: In what sort of situation would an emphasis on
the *departure* of the Son have made sense?

In seeking to answer this question, a fundamental premise
in what follows is that the Johannine christology reflects a
Christian community which was still charismatically active, a
community in which direct access to the Spirit was a dominant
fact of experience.[108] In such a community the problem of a
"salvation-empty present" would have been highly unlikely. The
praesentia Christi would have been so pervasive and fundamental
that the connection with the Son could hardly have been threatened
by the delay of the Parousia or the loss of eyewitness contact
with Jesus. On the contrary, it would have been far more
likely for such a community to face exactly the opposite kind
of problem, namely, *too much* "salvation," that is to say, too
many claimants to saving powers, too many successor figures,
resulting in rivalry and "charismatic competition." In such a
situation, we suggest, it was altogether possible for some to
perceive a threat to the rank and authority of Jesus in the way
in which others understood their authority.[109]

Here is a clue to the *Sitz im Leben* of the Gospel's
teaching concerning the departure of Jesus. The issue addressed
is one of rank; specifically, the rank and authority of Jesus
in relation to subsequent authority figures. In relation to this
issue the departure of Jesus occupied an ambivalent place. On
the one hand, it could be understood to mean that Jesus was a
figure of the past, a figure whose place could be taken by

succeeding authorities. On the other hand, as we shall see
when we turn to our analysis of the first farewell discourse,
the departure of Jesus could also be interpreted as the manifestation of his supreme glory, his unique relationship with the
Father, and, as such, as a dividing line, marking off Jesus
from all successors.

We shall argue, in what follows, that the first farewell
discourse addresses a threat to the supremacy of the Son, and
that the theme of the discourse is not the presence of the Son,
but his *preeminence*, demonstrated in his triumphant return to
the Father, alone. The problem addressed is not eschatological,
historical, or hermeneutical distance from the Son to be overcome, but the opposite, an illegitimate collapsing of hierarchical distance between Son and followers.

The theme of the preeminence of the Son does justice to
the whole of the first farewell discourse, not just certain
parts of it. Before turning, in the next four chapters, to a
detailed demonstration of this thesis, it will be useful to
indicate in summary fashion how the discourse is organized
around this theme.

The preeminence of the Son is set forth in the discourse
in relation to the disciples. It is essential to a proper
interpretation of the discourse to recognize that there are two
sides to the portrait of the disciples in the discourse. On the
one hand they are viewed in terms of their *access to heaven*. On
the other hand, they are viewed in terms of their *agency on
earth*. Roughly speaking, the first half of the discourse (13:31-
14:11) focuses primarily on the question of the disciples' access
to heaven, whereas the second half (14:12-26) focuses primarily
on the disciples' role as agents. The former aspect has been
generally emphasized, to the neglect of the latter.

The *subordinate* status of the disciples is revealed in the
conditions and circumstances of their access to the divine
source of power and authority, represented by the Father, in
contrast to the conditions and circumstances of Jesus' access.
Two possible ways for the disciples to gain access to the
Father are in view in the discourse. One way is for the disciples to ascend to heaven (14:3). The other way is for Father,
Son, or Spirit to descend to the disciples (14:23). What is

made clear in the discourse is that the basis for the
disciples' work is not *their* ascent to heaven, but *Jesus'* work,
his ascent, *his* return.

The introductory section of the discourse, 13:31-14:3,
announces the return of Jesus to the Father, and makes it clear
that the disciples do not go with him. Several main themes of
the discourse are anticipated here; the contrast between Jesus
and the disciples in their relation to heaven, the departure and
return of Jesus as the basis for the disciples' access to
heaven, and the opening up of an interim period during which
the disciples are separated from Jesus. Chapter II of the dissertation analyzes this introductory section.

In the rest of the discourse (14:4-26), attention focuses
on the interim period between Jesus' return to heaven and the
disciples' reunion with him in heaven, during which time the
disciples take the place of Jesus as his visible agents on
earth. It is made clear in this part of the discourse that
just as the disciples are dependent upon the departure and
return of Jesus for their ultimate ascent to heaven, so during
the interim period they are dependent upon the departure and
return of Jesus for their authority as his successor-agents.
In this way, we may note, Becker's expository pattern, which
turns on the two motifs, departure and return, is retained as
the basic structural feature of the discourse in my analysis.
The departure and return of Jesus, which are announced in
13:31-14:3 as events which define the beginning and end of the
interim period, are expounded in 14:4-26 with reference to the
agency of the disciples during this interim period. The basis
for their agency will be their access to the Father (14:23).
However, it is made clear that Jesus continues, in the period
after his departure, to be the only one to have *direct* access
to the Father (14:4-11). The disciples' access is *mediated*.
As such, their agency is subordinate to and dependent upon the
agency of Jesus. Chapter III of the dissertation focuses upon
the agency of Jesus as set forth in 14:4-11. Chapter IV deals
with the agency of the disciples as set forth in 14:12-24.

One further point is taken up in Chapter V. The subordination of the disciples to Jesus has a horizontal, or
temporal dimension, as is made unavoidably clear in 14:25, 26,

where the promise is made that the Spirit will recall to the
disciples all that Jesus has said. The implication is that the
disciples do not say anything new, but repeat what Jesus has
said. Regardless of what this is interpreted to mean in actual
practice, it implies that the teaching of the disciples is subordinate to the prior teaching of Jesus. We take this to mean,
further, that the *time* of the disciples is dependent upon and
therefore subordinate to the prior, paradigmatic time of Jesus'
visible agency.

After we have analyzed the discourse in Part I, we turn
in Part II to a discussion of its function in relation to the
Gospel as a whole and in relation to the situation in the
Johannine community which appears to be reflected in the discourse.

CHAPTER II

THE HIERARCHY: THE PRIOR ASCENT
OF THE SON (13:31-14:3)

In this chapter we shall limit our attention to the
introductory section of the first farewell discourse. It should
be noted that I include 14:1-3 within the introduction. The
break between 13:38 and 14:1 is not as sharp as some have maintained.[1] The fact that Jesus shifts from addressing Peter alone
to addressing the disciples as a group is no more determinative
of the basic structure of thought than are the subsequent
occasions when Jesus addresses individual disciples in the
singular (Thomas, in 14:4-6; Philip, in 14:9; Judas, in 14:34).[2]
The use of the formula *me tarassestho humon he kardia* in 14:1
and 14:27 does not function as a neat demaracation of the parts
of the discourse. In 14:27 this is particularly clear since,
on any reading, the concluding section begins at least with
the blessing of peace at the beginning of vs. 27.[3]

Taking 13:31-14:3 as the introduction to the discourse,
we have, in these verses, three succeeding announcements of
Jesus' imminent departure.[4] The first announcement (13:31-32)
interprets it in terms of Jesus' relationship to the Father.
The second (13:33-38) interprets it in terms of Jesus' relationship to the disciples. A sharply drawn contrast opens up
between what the departure means for Jesus, namely, glorification with the Father, and what it means for the disciples,
namely, separation from Jesus. The third announcement (14:1-3)
makes it clear that the separation will be temporary.[5] After a
certain period of time, during which Jesus will prepare "a
place" for the disciples in his Father's house, he will return
and "take" (*paralempsomai*) the disciples to himself.

This threefold announcement of the departure of Jesus
sets the stage for the rest of the discourse by drawing a sharp
line of distinction between Jesus and the disciples. It is a
distinction in the relationship of Jesus and the disciples
respectively to the Father, or the Father's house. There is,

first of all, a distinction in the sequence or order of ascent
to heaven. Jesus goes first. The disciples cannot follow until
"afterwards" (13:36). There is, secondly, a distinction of
"place." The temporal discontinuity is based upon and gives
expression to a discontinuity or hierarchy in rank, status, or
position in "the Father's house." Jesus goes first to heaven
because he is *from* there. He goes first because he belongs
there originally. The ascent of the disciples depends upon
Jesus' prior return and preparation of a place for them. (14:2).
His place is original; theirs is secondary, derived, and
dependent upon him. Jesus goes first, in other words, because
he *is* first.[6]

The hierarchical aspect is not an extraneous consideration.
On the contrary, it is present in the opening lines of the
discourse, which describe the departure of Jesus as an event
of glorification of Son and Father. Our first task, in the
discussion that follows, will be to show that the glorification
motif interprets the departure of Jesus as an exhibition of the
true position and power of the Son. We shall then focus our
attention on the temporal aspect of the hierarchy. In the third
part we shall concentrate on the primacy of "place" attributed
to the Son in these introductory verses.

The Doxasthenai *Motif*

The first farewell discourse opens with a "hymn of
triumph."[7] The first five lines form a pronouncement of victory:

Now has the Son of Man been glorified
And God has manifested his glory in him.
Because God manifested his glory in him,[8]
God will glorify him in himself,
And will glorify him immediately.

The motif of glorification is one of the richest and most important in the Gospel.[9] It is unnecessary here to attempt a
comprehensive analysis of the theme. I want to focus attention
on only one aspect, the legitimating significance of the glorification of Jesus.

The noun, *doxa* is used frequently in the Gospel in the
context of legitimation controversy. In 5:41-44 Jesus denies
accepting "glory" from men, but accuses the Jews of doing so.

They receive glory "from one another" and do not seek the
glory "which is from the one God" (5:44). The verb, *doxazo*,
is used twice in 8:54 in a similar context. In this, one of
the most violently polemical encounters between Jesus and "the
Jews," Jesus argues that the claims he is making, even though
they place him above Abraham (8:53), are legitimate because
God is the source of his glory: "If I glorify myself (*ego
doxazo emauton*), my glory amounts to nothing. The one who
glorifies me is the Father whom you claim as 'our God,' even
though you do not know him" (8:54). Here the issue is the
source of one's "glory," or honor, esteem, recognition. In
7:18 Jesus lays down a test by which to judge between legitimate
and illegitimate prophets: "The one who speaks from himself
seeks his own glory; but he who seeks the glory of him who sent
him, this one is true and there is no deceit in him." Here the
issue is, Whose glory is being sought, the prophet's own glory,
or the glory of God? To seek one's own glory is to be a false
prophet. As is clear from 8:54 there is a reciprocal relationship between seeking God's glory and being glorified by God.
The true prophet seeks God's glory, and is glorified by God.

A legitimating act may be understood as demonstrating
the correctness of whatever claims one has made or have been
made for one. What is at stake in the controversies in John is
control over the channels of access to truth from God. The
criterion by which rival claims are measured is relationship to
the "one God," to whom both parties appeal. Jesus' claim
throughout the Gospel is to be from God, to be speaking the
words of God, to be one with God. The return of Jesus to the
Father's house is the demonstration of the truth of his claims
to be *from* God. His return to heaven is the demonstration of
his heavenly rank.[10]

The use of the term, *doxasthenai*, to describe the return
of Jesus to heaven links the return to the legitimation controversies. The term, *doxasthenai*, is only one of a number of
words used in the Gospel of John to characterize the death of
Jesus. Most of the other terms used are, strikingly, words
denoting spatial movement as was noted above.[11] The death of
Jesus is interpreted in the Gospel of John above all as a change
of place.

The verb, *doxasthenai*, as used of Jesus in 13:31, has a twofold reference to place. First, in the sense of "geograph-ical" location, it refers to his return to heaven from earth. Second, in the sense of "social" position or place, Jesus' return to heaven is a demonstration of his rightful, original, rank. The two senses are explicitly conjoined in the Gospel itself in referring to Jesus' descent: "He who is from above is above all" (3:31). Both are present in his ascent. As a return to his place "above all," Jesus' "glorification" is the vindication of his claims to be *from* above. The glorification is an act of legitimation.

Thus the opening lines of the farewell discourse signal the fact that the discourse is related to the earlier public disputes over the claims made by Jesus on his own behalf. These lines also suggest the real measure of Jesus' claims. He claims to share glory with God. The Father and the Son of Man are glorified in one another. The reciprocal glorification must be understood in light of the reciprocal indwelling of Father and Son, which Jesus claims later on in the discourse (14:10, 11). Jesus claims to be one with God. This is the true measure of his status. He places himself so close to an equal rank with the Father that he is obliged to point out explicitly, also in the farewell discourse, that the Father is in fact greater than himself (14:28)!

Jesus Ascends First: His Priority in Time

In contrast to the triumphant note sounded by the opening "hymn" of the farewell discourse is the extraordinary emphasis, in the words which follow (13:33f.), upon the fact that the moment of glorification means separation between disciples and teacher:

> Little children, I am with you only a little longer.
> You will look for me, and, just as I told the Jews,
> "Where I go you are not able to come," I tell you
> the same thing now.

Jesus' followers are told they will not be able to follow him. The *teknia* are explicitly placed in the same position as "the Jews," that is, the outsiders, non-followers.

The unqualified, harsh statement that the disciples will be unable to follow Jesus is qualified in a second interchange between Jesus and Peter (13:36-38). In answer to Peter's question, *kurie, pou hupageis*: Jesus replies, "Where I go you are not able to follow me *now*, but you shall follow *afterwards*" (13:36). Though the force of the reply is softened by the qualification that "afterwards" Peter will be able to follow Jesus, this does not take away from the primary emphasis on the real separation which occurs in the meantime.[12] Jesus goes through "his hour" alone. There will be a period of time between Jesus' ascent (now) and the time when Peter will be able to follow him.

What is the reason for the interval? That is Peter's next question, "Lord, why is it not possible for me to follow you now?" Two answers are, in effect, given to this question. The first answer is given in terms of Peter personally. He will deny Jesus (13:38). But this answer is placed within a larger explanatory framework by Jesus' words in 14:1-3, which offer another reason for the interval between the ascent of Jesus and the subsequent ascent of the disciples.[13] Here we learn that while he is away Jesus will "prepare a place" for the disciples (14:2 *hetoimaso topon humin*). It is not necessary to speculate on the exact mythological sense of the term *hetoimazein topon* in order to grasp the main point of the passage, which is that the disciples cannot ascend with Jesus because while he has a "place" for himself in his Father's house already, the disciples do not. Their "place" in heaven depends upon his prior ascent and preparation.

The delay in time between the ascent of Jesus and the subsequent ascent of the disciples expresses a difference in the heavenly status or rank of the disciples and Jesus, a difference between original and derived status. In support of this thesis, we would note that frequently in John priority in time is correlated with superiority in rank. In John 1:15 the Baptist testifies that Jesus, though he comes "after" the Baptist chronologically (cf. Mk 1:7) ranks ahead of the Baptist (*empros- then mou gegonen*) because of his pre-existence (*hoti protos mou en*).[14]

In John 1:15 the author is unambiguously adressing the question of relative rank between Jesus and the Baptist.[15] The subject of rank is even clearer in the Baptist's reply to the question of the authorities as to the basis for his baptism (1:25ff.). John's answer is to refer to Jesus: "I baptize in water. In your midst stands one whom you do not know. Though he comes after me, I am not worthy to loose the thongs of his sandals." Again the Baptist brings up the fact that Jesus follows him chronologically and then testifies to Jesus' superior worth.[16] The emphasis which the question of rank receives in the Baptist's testimony as this is recorded by the author of the Fourth Gospel is evident already in the fact that it is the single point of the Baptist's testimony in the author's first summary of that testimony (1:15). The emphasis is all the clearer in the fact that this same summary is repeated almost verbatim in 1:30.

The importance of these three texts (1:15; 1:27; 1:30) is that they deal directly with the question of rank in relation to temporal sequence. The Baptist's testimony in each case is directed against the assumption that the Baptist is *superior* to Jesus because he appeared *first*.[17] The *point* of the testimony is to refute this view. What is crucial is that *the refutation assumes the correlation between rank and priority in time*. Jesus is superior to the Baptist because he is, in fact, *prior to him*. That is the explicit argument in 1:15, 30, and it is assumed in 1:27.

If we cast the principle on which the argument of the Baptist in 1:15 is based in general terms we could say that the first person in a sequence to perform a given action is the highest in rank. It is not clear how general this principle is in the author's thought. The example of the relative rank of Baptist and Jesus is not isolated. We find exactly the same thing in the case of Abraham and Jesus in chapter 8. The dispute involves directly the question of the relative rank of Abraham and Jesus, as is evident from the Jews' questions, "Are you greater than our father Abraham?" (8:53). Jesus' final answer to this question is his appeal to his pre-existence: "Before Abraham was born I am" (*prin Abraam genesthai ego eimi*, 8:58).

What is demonstrated by these texts is that the opposite correlation cannot be assumed in the Gospel of John. We may not take for granted that there is a correlation between *last* in time and superiority in rank. G. Bornkamm, in his article on the Paraclete, has assumed exactly this in applying the "forerunner-fulfiller" pattern from the Baptist-Jesus relationship to the Jesus-Paraclete relationship.[18] The "forerunner-fulfiller" relationship assumes the superiority of the one who comes *last*. One of the major difficulties with Bornkamm's argument is that, in applying this pattern to the Jesus-Paraclete sequence, he is forced to concede that this major feature of the pattern is reversed.[19] The Son, who comes first (hence the "forerunner"), is superior to the Paraclete, who comes last (hence the "fulfiller").

Jesus' Priority of Place

If we analyze the language of movement and place in the Gospel we find two main overall patterns. One, which we have been looking at, has to do with the movement *of* Jesus. The primary movements of Jesus are between heaven and earth. His comings and goings on earth, to and from Galilee and Judaea, are secondary.

The second main pattern of movement in the Gospel has to do with the movement of others *in relation to* Jesus. In this pattern Jesus is the *centre* towards which others in the Gospel move. It is a centripetal pattern. Jesus "draws" all men to himself (12:32), an "attraction" in which the Father also is active (6:44).

The fixed point of reference in the first pattern, the movement of Jesus, is "heaven," the place of the Father, or the Father himself. Jesus comes from heaven, goes back to heaven. Heaven is his home, the place where he "abides." By contrast Jesus is an outsider on earth, an alien, the "Stranger par excellence," in Wayne Meek's phrase. He is an enigma. He does not fit the categories of the cosmos. He is *out of place*.[20] His stay is temporary. He "encamps" on earth (1:14). He does not come to remain (8:23).

The primary expressions of Jesus' origin are to be found in the language of Jesus' unity or oneness with the Father. What is Jesus' original place? He is *eis ton kolpon tou patros* (1:18). Jesus not only has a place in the "father's house." His place is directly next to the Father. His place is in fact "in" the Father (10:38). In contrast to the disciples, to all others in fact, there is no one *between* Jesus and the Father, no mediator. Jesus has direct access to the Father on the authority of his original place in and with the Father.

Jesus' claim to an original place in heaven is supported by a look at other language used of Jesus' movements. Jesus bases his claim to recognition, to faith, over and over again upon the fact that he is sent *from the Father*. This claim appears for example in the sterotyped formula used in Jesus' speech to refer to the Father as "the one who sent me" (*ho pempsas me*) which occurs in this way some twenty-six times on Jesus' lips. "I am not alone, but I and him who sent me" is Jesus' claim to legitimacy (8:16).

The "sending" cannot be understood as a reference to a commission received at some point in Jesus' earthly sojourn, say at baptism. It refers to a heavenly commission to descend into the world. God "sends" (*apostellei*) Jesus "into the world" (3:17; 10:36; 17:18). Jesus "descends" from heaven. He is "sent" into the world. He "comes" into the world as "the light" (1:9; 3:19; 12:46), for judgment (9:39). Hence the departure of Jesus is a *return* to "my Father's house," to the place where he was "before" (6:63 *to proteron*). To understand the ascent of Jesus we are compelled to take into account the descent. The farewell discourses must be placed within the larger context of the pre-existent origin of Jesus. The correlation between descent and ascent is found in the deliberate utterance in the secondary farewell material: "I came forth from (*ek*) the Father and I came into the world. Again I depart from the world and go to the Father" (16:28). This correlation is also found in short form in the opening words of the foot-washing scene. Jesus' actions are performed, with the knowledge that "he came forth from God and is going to God" (13:3). In 3:13 the correlation is insisted upon in a polemically exclusive statement: "No one has ascended into heaven except the one who

descended from heaven, namely, the Son of Man.[21] Ascent is
conditional upon prior descent. There is only one who can
ascend, because there is only one who is originally from
heaven.

Jesus' place in heaven, then, is original. The place
of the disciples is derived, mediated, dependent upon the
"preparation" of a place for them in heaven. One of the striking
features of the Johannine use of the word *hetoimazein* in 14.2
is the use of the future tense. In apocalyptic usage, such as
Mk 10:40 par., and Enoch 25:7, it is past perfect. In Hebrews
11:16 reference is made to the "city" which God "has prepared"
for the martyrs. The use of the future tense in John 14:2
emphasizes the secondary status of the disciples' place in
heaven.

The *mediated* position of the disciples in relation to the
Father is a basic structural feature of the thought of the
Gospel as a whole. This is evident from a closer look at the
second pattern of movement in the Gospel, the centripetal
pattern of movement of men in relation to Jesus. In this
pattern of movement Jesus occupies the fixed point of reference,
the centre. Nicodemus (3:2), the Samaritans (4:30), the
centurion (4:47), the large crowds (6:5; 10:41) "come to"
Jesus. The complaint is voiced twice that everyone, the whole
world, is going after him (3:26; 12:19). He is "sought" throughout the Gospel, both by those who want to know where he "lives"
(1:38) in order to live with him, as well as by those who seek
him in order to put him to death (7:1; 10:39; 11:8). The
language of "seeking," "finding," "coming," "following" Jesus
must be placed in the context of the incredibly rich vocabulary
which the author uses with reference to the responses of men
to the Son: hearing, seeing, believing, receiving, honoring,
knowing, loving, obeying, indwelling, serving, bearing witness
to, eating of, drinking of, him.

In all of this Jesus functions as the sacred centre, the
place where heavenly reality--light, life, the bread of heaven,
etc.--is made available to the disciple. The Son represents
heaven, the Father, on earth. There is no direct, independent
access to the Father on the part of anyone other than Jesus.
One of the strongest statements of the strictly *mediated* access

of the disciples to the Father occurs in the very next section of the farewell discourse, 14:4-11, to which we turn in our next chapter.

To summarize, I maintain that the note of comfort in the introductory section of the farewell discourse is secondary in importance to the motif of separation and subordination.

CHAPTER III

THE CONCENTRATION OF AUTHORITY
IN THE SON (14:4-11)

We turn, in this chapter, to consider the second section
of the discourse, vss. 4-11. There is a tone of reminder and
even rebuke in this section, which contrasts with the words of
comfort in 14:1,[1] an appeal to what the disciples know and
believe or ought to have known and believed.[2] The disciples are
cast in the familiar role of ignorant and uncomprehending
listeners by the author's use of misunderstanding. "You know
the way" (vs. 4); "If you had known me . . ." (vs. 7); "This
long you have been with me and yet you do not know me, Philip?"
(vs. 9); "Do you not believe that . . .?" (vs. 10); and, finally,
the appeal, "Believe . . ." (vs. 11). In their concern over
the departure of Jesus the disciples are portrayed as having
lost sight of who he is, that is to say, his position of unity
with the Father, expressed in the formula, *ego en to patri kai
ho pater emoi estin*.[3] The fundamental importance of this
formula as the ground for Jesus' claim to be the exclusive "way"
is evident from the fact that it is repeated twice, verbatim,
in vss. 10 and 11. The introductory words, *ou pisteueis
hoti* . . . (vs. 10), and *pisteuete moi hoti* . . . (vs. 11), as
well as the use of the formula in the argument (as something
Philip was expected to believe already), suggest the possibility
that the formula, *ego en to patri kai ho pater en emoi*, may
have had confessional status in the Johannine community.

There is a clear structure to this section of the discourse. The focal point is the "I am" pronouncement in 14:6,
around which vss. 4-11 are organized.[4] The exchange between
Jesus and Thomas in vss. 4-5 leads up to the "I am" saying by
introducing the theme of "the way." Vss. 6-11 are a commentary
on the saying.[5] According to vs. 6b it means that Jesus is the
exclusive means of access to the Father.[6] According to vss. 7-9,
it means that to know Jesus is to know the Father, to see him
is to see the Father.[7] According to vss. 10-11 it means that

47

Jesus is one with the Father. Vss. 10-11 do more than paraphrase the meaning of Jesus' claim to be "the way." They are
cast in the form of a defense of that claim. The unity of
Jesus and the Father ("I am in the Father and the Father is
in me," 14:10,11) is the basis for Jesus' claim to exclusive
authority over access to the Father. His *exercise* of
authority (vss. 6-9) is grounded in his *position* of authority
(vss. 10-11).

A new motif, "the way," is introduced into the discourse
in vs. 4.[8] At first glance, the motif fits naturally into the
farewell. Nothing would seem more appropriate than for Jesus
to make clear to the disciples, in the hour of his departure,
the "way" they are to take in order to follow after him. However, such an understanding of the "way" motif stands in sharp
contrast to what Jesus has emphasized up to this point, namely,
the fact that the disciples will *not* be able to follow Jesus,
and will be reunited to him only after he comes back to get
them. Jesus has made it clear that reunion will be the result
of his return, not the ascent of the disciples. Thus it has
been established that there will be a period of separation
between Jesus and the disciples. But this leaves a vital
question unanswered. What about the fate of the disciples
while Jesus is gone? What will be their condition during this
period? Particularly dangerous is the inevitable corollary
question: Will someone *take the place of Jesus*? If so, who?

It is precisely the latter question, the question of
succession, posed in this way by the outline of the farewell
situation in 13:31-14:3, which is addressed in what follows.
This will become especially evident when we consider the role
assigned to the disciples and to the Spirit-Paraclete in vss.
12-17. It is already addressed, however, in Jesus' words in
14:4ff.[9]

"Where I am going, you know the way," Jesus tells his
disciples (14:4).[10] This remark seems to invite the idea that
a "way" will be needed *to Jesus* when he is gone, that is to say,
a mediator *other* than Jesus himself. Thomas's bewildered confession of ignorance of such a "way" reveals that he is thinking
along these lines (14:5). To be sure, the suggestion no sooner

occurs before Jesus' emphatic reply to Thomas categorically
denies that his departure has created the need for another
mediator outside of himself. "I *remain* the way, the truth,
and the life," is, perhaps, the best way to translate the
particular force of this "I am" pronouncement. There can be
no "successor" to Jesus. Vss. 6b-11 emphasize the exclusive
mediatorial role of Jesus, which is grounded in his unique
relationship of direct union with the Father. Three aspects of
this role will command our attention in the rest of this chapter:
first, its exclusivity, second, its legitimating basis, and
third, its function.

The Exclusive Sovereignty of the Son

The concentration of authority over access to the Father
in the Son is expressed in the series of "I am" sayings in the
Gospel, of which 14:6 is an example. It is also expressed,
formally, in the predominance of self-testimony which marks
Jesus' discourse in John. It is expressed, thirdly, in the
direct testimony to the investiture of authority in the Son,
which provides the context for interpreting the "I am" sayings.

The Language of Investiture

There is a rich vocabulary of investiture in the Fourth
Gospel. By investiture I mean the act of "giving" authority,
judgment, life, and glory to the Son. The investiture of the
Son with "all things" is explicitly attested in 3:35 and again
in 13:3. "The Father loves the Son, and has given all things
(*panta dedoken*) into his hand (3:35). In chapter 13 Jesus
washes the disciples' feet "knowing that the Father had given
(*edoken*) all things into his hands" (13:3). According to 16:15
"all that the Father has" belongs to Jesus. The Son shares
possession of all with the Father (17:10). The phrase *en te
cheiri auto* in 3:35 and *eis tas cheiras* in 13:3 is vivid
investiture imagery.

The central importance of the notion of investiture is
evident from the author's repeated use of the verb *didomi*.
According to 3:34 the "spirit" has been "given" (*didosin*) to
Jesus "without measure" (*ou metrou*). According to 5:22,23 the
Father "judges no one, but has given (*dedoken*) all judgment to
the Son, so that all might honor the Son even as they honor
the Father. In 5:26 it is "life in himself" which the Father
gives the Son: "For even as the Father has life in himself,
so also he gave (*edoken*) to the Son to have life in himself."
The Father has given to the Son *ta erga* (5:36; 17:4), the
commandment as to what he should say (12:49; cf. 14:10,24,31;
15:15), the words which he in turn gives to the disciples (17:8),
his name (17:11), his glory (17:22,24) whatever he asks for
(11:22). Jesus has, in a certain sense, been "invested" with
the company of believers, according to one of the typical
Johannine expressions for "the church," namely, "All those whom
the Father has given me," or variations on this use of the verb
didomi (6:37, 39; 10:29; 17:2,6,9,11,12,24; 18:9).

Twice it is explicit that "authority" (*exousia*) is what
is granted to the Son. In 5:27 it is "authority to judge"
(*exousian edoken auto krisin poiein*). In 17:2 it is universal,
sovereign authority, "authority over all flesh." In 17:2 Jesus
appeals to this authority as the basis for his request for
glorification, and then goes on to specify the purpose of the
grant of authority: to bring eternal life to the elect. Eternal
life is defined as knowledge of "the one true God" and of the
one sent by God. The authority is to issue in honor, worship,
knowledge of Father and Son. (It is worth noting in this connection, the even more explicit connection between investiture
and access to Father and Son in the two Synoptic texts, Mt.
11:27 and Luke 10:22. Mt. 11:27 reads, "All things have been
delivered to me by my Father [*paredothe*] and no one knows the
Son except the Father, and no one knows the Father except the
Son and any one to whom the Son chooses to reveal him.")

The primary text having to do with the investiture with
authority is the first part of Jesus' speech to the Jews after
the Sabbath healing miracle in chapter 5. In 5:17-29 Jesus

testifies, in third person self-testimony, to the basis upon
which he performs his works. He does nothing on his own
authority, independently. Everything that he does he has seen
the Father do first: *Amen amen lego humin, ou dunatai ho huios
poiein aph heautou ouden, an me ti blepe ton patera poiounta*
(5:19). Jesus' works are done in imitation of the Father's
works. This is how (in light of 5:19) we must understand the
simple conjunction between Jesus' working and the Father's
working in 5:17.

> *ho pater mou heos arti ergazetai*
> *kago   ergazomai.*

Jesus' commission with all authority is described, in 5:20, as
the Father's *disclosure* to him of all that he does: "The Father
loves the Son and shows him (*deiknusin auto*) all that he does
himself." The Father's disclosure of all things is equivalent
to his giving all things into the hand of the Son in 3:35, as
the parallelism suggests:

> 3:35 *ho pater agapa ton huion, kai panta dedoken en te*
> *cheiri autou*
> 5:20 *ho gar pater philei ton huion kai panta deiknusin*
> *auto ha autos poiei*

Jesus' vision of what the Father does as the basis of
what he does himself adds a feature to the Johannine idea of
Jesus' "witnessing" which is not always noted. Jesus tells
Nicodemus, "we speak what we know and we bear witness to what
we have seen" (3"11). The one who is above all bears witness
to what he has seen and heard (3:32). What he has seen according to 5:20, is all of the works which the Father does. His
witness, then, includes imitating the works which he sees the
Father perform:

> *ha gar an ekeinos poie*
> *tauta kai ho huios homoios poiei* (5:19).

The idea that the Son does what the Father does is
elaborated in the speech in chapter 5 in a series of correlative
sayings which specify the works performed by Father and Son.
The giving of life:

> *hosper gar ho pater egeirei tous nekrous kai zoopoiei*
> *houtos kai ho huios hous thelei   zoopoei* (5:21).

The possession of "life in himself":

hosper gar ho pater echei zoen en heauto
houtos kai to huio edoken zoen echein en heauto (5:26).

The correlative pattern is broken by the explicit statement
regarding judgment to the effect that the Father judges no one,
having given all judgment to the Son, but the author adds,
significantly, that this is "in order that all might honor the
Son even as they honor the Father who sent him" (5:22,23).

The author can use language which carries the idea of
investiture a step further. Not only does the Father give to
the Son life, glory, authority, his name, the spirit, etc.
Not only is the Son said to imitate all that the Father does.
The Father himself is said to be "in" the Son. This language
is found in the formula of reciprocal indwelling of Father
and Son in 10:38 and 14:10 and 11. It is also found, however,
independently of the formula, in 14:10 where after the reciprocal
indwelling formula, Jesus adds, "the words which I say to you I
do not speak on my own; *The Father who dwells in me* (*ho de pater
en emoi menon*) is doing his works." Here the indwelling of the
Father in the Son is cited as the source of the Son's power to
do the works of God. The "works" of God, in this context, refer
to the mediating role of Jesus as the way to the Father, as the
means of knowing the Father, and as the means of seeing the
Father (14:6-9). The indwelling of the Father in the Son
expresses the basis of the authority of the Son, and in this
sense is to be understood in relation to the language of
investiture.

The "I am" Language

The concentration of "authority over all flesh" in the
Son is expressed most strikingly in the series of "I am"
sayings.[11] Jesus makes the claim, in these sayings, to *be*, in
some sense, the way, the truth, the life (14:6), the resurrection
(11:25), the bread of life (6:35,48,51), the light of the world
(8:12), the door of the sheep (10:7,9), the good shepherd
(10:11), the true vine (15:1,5).

In three of the "I am" sayings the emphasis is on the copula, on the fact of identification between the "I" and the predicate object. In the Bread discourse (ch. 6), the request for a sign such as the manna miracle, is the occasion for Jesus to contrast the manna with "the true bread from heaven" (*ton arton ek tou ouranou ton alethinon* (6:32) also called "the bread of God" (*ho artos tou theou*) which "comes down from heaven and gives life to the world" (6:33). This leads his hearers to ask for this bread, in a sentence which has a remarkable liturgical ring to it: "Lord, give us this bread always" (*kurie, pantote dos hemin ton arton touton*). Jesus' answer is, "I *am* the bread of life . . ." In other words, I do not just *give* the bread, I *am* the bread.

Likewise, in the narrative of the raising of Lazarus, Jesus' promise to Martha that Lazarus "will rise again" is misunderstood by Martha to be a reference to the resurrection "at the last day." In response, Jesus says, "I *am* the resurrection and the life . . ." (11:25). Martha has misunderstood the relationship between Jesus and resurrection. She confesses her faith in Jesus' intercessory power, even to the point of his ability to petition to God to raise the dead (11:22). But the relationship between Jesus and resurrection is not so indirect. Jesus does not bring resurrection by interceding with the Father. He himself *is* the resurrection and the life. This recalls the important qualifying phrase added to the "life" which the Father gives to the Son: it is "life *in himself*" (*zoen en heauto*), just as the Father has life in himself (5:26).

The third place where the "I am" saying is used in a context which places the accent on the copula is in 14:6. The question of Thomas shows a misunderstanding concerning the relationship between Jesus and "the way," as we have seen. The purpose of the "I am" pronouncement of Jesus is to state that Jesus and "the way" are not separable entities, or rather, will not be, in the future. Jesus remains the way.

An important role in the discussion of the "I am" sayings has been played by a fourfold classification of the sayings, introduced by Rudolf Bultmann. Bultmann classified the "I am"

sayings according to the kind of question answered. The
"presentation formula" answers the question "Who are you/"
The "qualification formula" answers the question "What are you?"
The "recognition formula" answers the question "Who is the one
who is expected, asked for, spoken to?" In the recognition
formula, the "I" functions as the predicate object, in contra-
distinction to the other forms: It is *I* who am. . . . For the
"identification formula" Bultmann failed to formulate the
question which is answered. He defined the identification
formula as the form "in which the speaker identified himself
with another person or object."[12] There is a difficulty with
this definition. In a sense all of the forms can be said to
identify the speaker with "another" person or object unless the
adjective "another" is taken in a very literal sense. It would
appear that Bultmann intended the strict sense on the basis of
the examples he gives. He cites the Egyptian god Re's claim
to be Chepre, for example: "I am he who arose as Chepre."[13]
However, the scholarship making use of Bultmann's fourfold
classification reflects a considerable amount of confusion on
this point. According to Raymond A. Brown, in the identification
formula "the predicate sums up the identity of the subject."[14]
According to K. Schaedel, the "I am" sayings in John identify
Jesus as the fulfillment of eschatological promises and hence
are identification formulae.[15] If Jesus is the fulfillment of
these promises, they are not "another" object! What criteria for
"otherness" can be used when the formula itself intends to
proclaim identity? Even in Bultmann's own use of the classification scheme there is some confusion. In his initial discussion
of the I-am formula he suggests that 11:28 and 14:6 may be
identification formulae.[16] On what basis? Bultmann suggests
none. When we turn to the commentary on these two specific
texts we find that he has concluded that 14:6 is a recognition
formula.[17] We suggest that in keeping with the criteria by
which Bultmann has defined the other three formulae, the
identification formula be defined in terms of the question that
is answered, and suggest, further, that the question answered
in the identification formula is, "What is the relationship
between you (the speaker) and x?" On this understanding, 6:35,
11:28, and 14:6 are identification formulae.

Another issue involving Bultmann's classification may be noted here. Bultmann argued that most of the "I am" sayings in John are recognition formulae because "in the context of the Gospel the *ego* is strongly stressed and is always contrasted with false or pretended revelation."[18] In subsequent scholarship there has been a tendency to conclude from this that the recognition formula is the only one which expresses a polemic.[19] It is clear, however, that stressing the *ego* is not the only way in which a polemic can be expressed. The pronouncements in 6:35, 11:28, and 14:6 correct false understanding by stressing the copula, as we have suggested. There is also a polemic in several of the "I am" sayings which is expressed in the adjective used with the predicate object. In the Shepherd discourse the self-predication of Jesus, "I am the good shepherd" is preceded by reference to the "hireling" who "cares nothing for the sheep" (10:13,14). Here the stress is on the adjective "good" which characterizes Jesus over against *false* "shepherds." Thus the question of whether a particular "I am" saying is to be classified as a recognition formula is not determined by the absence or presence of a rhetorical contrast or polemic. The "I am" sayings in 6:35, 11:28, and 14:6 express a contrast or polemic but are nevertheless to be classified, if we use Bultmann's scheme, as identification formulae.[20]

What the identification formulae in John express most pointedly is that whatever is referred to by the predicate object coincides with the person of the speaker. Outside of him "the life," "the truth," "the resurrection" are not available.[21] No one comes to the Father outside of Jesus (14:6b). The language of spatial concentration in the sacred person of the Son is taken to its logical conclusion further on in the discourse in the idea that the believer is given a place "in" Christ (14:20).

The centering structure of the self-testimony of Jesus has an ordering, or mapping function. More accurately, it has a *re*ordering function. The symbols applied to Jesus in the "I am" sayings are those commonly associated with the traditional cult and with the traditional sacred centers, temple, king,

meal. In John these traditional symbols have been taken over
and applied exclusively to the central speaker. The application
of the temple saying to the body of Jesus is only the most
vivid illustration of this process. What is crucial is the
fact that the new center, the new sacred figure is from the
outside, from above, from heaven. He is not known to the
traditional authorities. They do not recognize him (7:47,48).
He represents, therefore, a break with the traditional ordering
of society by placing himself above all traditional criteria of
legitimacy. This does not mean that Jesus bears no relationship of any kind to tradition. He appeals in fact to Moses,
that is to say, the law, as witness to his claims (5:39,46,47).
But in his appeal he is not subordinating himself to the law.
On the contrary, he does the exact opposite, subordinating the
law to himself. Jesus is speaking to the Jews, those who in
fact "searched the scriptures" and placed their hope of life
in the study of scripture. But Jesus rejects the legitimacy of
their appeal to scripture because it has not led them to believe
in Jesus. Thus recognition of Jesus' claims becomes the
criterion for testing appeals to scripture. The scriptures,
properly understood, are the Father's witness to Jesus (5:37).

Jesus in this way relativizes all traditional sources
of legitimation, and is left with nothing but his appeal to the
Father as the one who sent him. But that is precisely the claim
which is under attack. The defence of the claim is identical
with the claim itself. Bultmann has correctly emphasized this
as the central feature of Jesus' defence. Commenting, for
example, on 5:36,37a, Bultmann points out,

> Apart from his (Jesus') witness he offers no other
> proof of his authority which might provide a man
> with a *means* of believing in that witness. The
> hearer who asks can be referred only to the very
> thing whose validity he is questioning, to the
> object of faith itself.[22]

What Bultmann does not notice is that this is a typical feature
of charismatic authority.[23] In the second part of this chapter
we turn our attention to the issue of legitimation in order to
look more closely at the self-authenticating structure of Jesus'
claims.

Concentration and the Problem of
Legitimation: Autodoxology?

Jesus' claim to be the exclusive way, the truth, and the
life is met by misunderstanding on the part of the disciples
(14:6-9), and this leads, in turn, to Jesus' defence of his
claim: "The words which I say to you, I do not say on my own
authority (*ap emautou*); rather (*de*), the Father who dwells in
me is doing his works" (14:10). If charismatic authority in
its pure form is understood as the relativization of all
traditional authority by the claim to *direct* access to the
divine source of all authority, then one of the central problems
which the charismatic figure faces is how to prove the truth
of his claims.[24] There is no authority to which he can appeal
outside of the divine source which possesses him. But it is
precisely the claim to divine possession (cf. 3:34) which is
the subject of dispute. The unlimited concentration of all
authority in the person of Jesus means, as we noted above,
that the only defence which he can make on behalf of his claims
to authority is the reiteration of the claims in question. The
result is that Jesus, like other charismatic figures, appears
inevitably to be acting on his own authority.

There is, it is true, an appeal by Jesus to other witnesses, the testimony of John the Baptist (5:33), and the
writings of Moses (5:39, 45-47). However, it is clear, as we
have argued above, that Jesus is not subordinating himself to
the Baptist, or even to Moses. In the farewell discourse, as
well as earlier, Jesus appeals to his "works" as evidence of
the truth of his claims: "Believe me that I (am) in the Father
and the Father (is) in me; otherwise believe because of the
works" (14:11, cf. 5:36, 10:38). The works of Jesus are his
miracles. But the miracles do nothing to reduce the independence
and isolation of Jesus from the prevailing structures of
legitimation recognized by his opponents.

In the last analysis, the only authority which Jesus
acknowledges as superior to himself is that of the "one God"
who is known only by those who recognize him as the Father, in
a unique sense, of Jesus, the Son. Consequently, time and time

again we find Jesus defending himself against the charge
of acting and speaking on his own authority, of self-seeking,
of boasting. "I am not able to do anything on my own," Jesus
says emphatically, in 5:30, thus reiterating in first person
self-testimony what he has said of himself as "the Son," in
the third person (cf. 5:19). When he is lifted up, Jesus tells
the Jews, then "you will know that *ego eimi*, and do nothing on
my own (*ap emautou*)" (8:28). "I have not come on my own (*ap
emautou*)" Jesus says earlier (7:28), an apologetic repeated in
8:42. "I say nothing on my own (*ex emautou*)," he says again in
12:49. The criterion of legitimacy is whether or not a teacher
is speaking on his own (*aph heautou*): "The one who speaks on
his own authority seeks his own glory" (7:18). The author
associates autonomy with self-aggrandizement. Accordingly
John's Jesus acknowledges that if he were to seek his own glory
his glory would amount to nothing (8:54). He likewise acknowledges that if he were to "bear witness" (*marturein*) to himself,
his witness would not be true (5:31). By the same token, the
accusation which Jesus makes against his opponents is that they
would accept one who came "in his own name," that is to say,
one who came on his own authority and was not sent by God.
Their failure to recognize Jesus testifies to their utter lack
of discrimination. To be sure, they form a group which "receives
honor from one another" (5.44) in relation to which Jesus is the
one who appears to be on his own. But in fact it is Jesus who
stands with the Father, and in this sense is not alone, whereas
his opponents have cut themselves off from any standing with
"the one God" (5.44)

Jesus denies bearing witness concerning himself--in a
Gospel which is stamped by his unceasing self-testimony! The
flagrant contradiction between claim and form, however, does not
go unrecognized by the author. In 8:12 Jesus proclaims to the
public in Jerusalem, "I am the light of the world; he who follows me shall not walk in darkness, but shall possess the light
of life" (8:12). In an obvious allusion back to Jesus' denial
that he offers self-testimony the "Pharisees" respond: "You
are testifying concerning yourself; your witness is not true"
(8:13, cf. 5:31). This time Jesus says, "Even if I am bearing

witness concerning myself, my witness is true." The apparent
contradiction between this statement and 5:31 is deliberate and
constitutes only one of the more graphic examples of the
author's love of riddle, paradox, and esoteric language.[25] We
are therefore invited to resolve the paradox by interpreting
the two references to self-testimony in two different ways.
The comments by Jesus which follow the claim in 8:14 point the
direction. Jesus' self-testimony is true, he says, "because
I know whence I have come and where I am going." In other
words, Jesus knows that his self-testimony is not delivered
autonomously. "I am not alone," (8:16). That is the ground on
which Jesus stands. We must understand the kind of self-testimony referred to in 5:31 as illegitimate, therefore, because
it is understood as autonomous.

In resolving the paradox represented by the disclaimer
in 5:31 and the claim in 8:14, however, it is essential to go
on to ask why the author has chosen to express himself in such
deliberate paradox. What is demonstrated by the paradox is, I
suggest, *the author's* acute awareness of the problem of legitimation posed by a figure who claims the kind of authority Jesus
claims, who concentrates all authority in himself, the problem,
namely, that there is nothing by which to distinguish, outwardly,
between the independent and therefore illegitimate agent and the
only legitimate Son.[26] Hence the author's appeal to the "will"
of the hearer in 7:17. "If any one wants to do his (God's)
will, he shall know concerning the *didaches*, whether it is from
God or whether I am speaking on my own authority (*ap emautou*)"
(7:17).

The problem of legitimation faced by the author can be
brought into sharper focus by looking again at the "I am" form.
It is Jesus' "I am" pronouncement in 8:12 which provokes the
accusation that he is bearing self-witness. It is clearly
because of his continual self-testimony that Jesus is accused
repeatedly in the Gospel of boasting, of "making himself a god"
(10:33), or "equal to God" (5:18), of "making himself a son of
God" (19:7), of "making himself a king" (19:12).

Eduard Norden, in his pioneering form-critical study of
the "I am" sayings in John concluded that the discourses of
John's Jesus were in a class with the "pompous" claims of

conventional Hellenistic religious propaganda.[27]. The author
of John, said Norden, clothed "die schlichte Lehre Jesu" in
words whose content and form stemmed from the "high-sounding
phraseology" of those prophets who, drawn from city to city
and village to village, stepped forward with the claim to be
Saviours.[28] The church did this, he concluded, under the
pressure of competition from older salvation religions.

Norden argued that the origin of this "soteriological
speech type," epitomized by the speech attributed by Celsus to
the wandering prophets of his day, was to be found in the
ancient Babylonian and Egyptian literature where the "I am"
formula of self-predication was originally reserved for the
gods and later adopted by rulers as the earthly representatives
of the gods.[29]

Norden's view of the origin and character of the "I am"
discourses in John was attacked by Karl Kundsin who argued that
the "I am" sayings in John were Christian creations and had
their origin in the sort of prophetic visions of the risen Lord
found in the book of Revelation where Jesus likewise speaks in
the "I am" form (Revelation 1:8,17).[30] Proof of their Christian
origin is, according to Kundsin, the "soteriological clause"
attached to the "I am" sayings in John, as in John 6:35: "I
am the bread of life; *he who comes to me shall not hunger, and
he who believes in me shall never thirst*." This soteriological
addition is not found, according to Kundsin, in the propaganda
forms cited by Norden.[31] Similarly, Raymond E. Brown, in his
summary discussion of the Johannine "I am" sayings concludes
that the predicates attached to the "I am" form in John (bread,
light, shepherd, vine) "are not static titles of autodoxology
but a revelation of the divine commitment involved in the
Father's sending of the Son."[32] Thus we find that the scholarly
discussion of the "I am" form mirrors exactly the controversy
found within the Gospel itself as to whether Jesus is merely
boasting, seeking his own glory in the highly competitive
marketplace of Hellenistic religion, or whether he is in fact
sent by "God" and seeking God's glory.

This is not the place to attempt a review of the subsequent course of the debate over the origin of the Johannine

"I am" sayings, as important as this is for an understanding of the Gospel.[33] I must, however, call attention to one glaring weakness in the scholarly discussion. The *Gospel's own* treatment of the issue of "autodoxology," to use Brown's useful phrase, has not been brought into relation with the discussion of the origins and function of the "I am" form. The fact that the Johannine Jesus is so anxious to defend himself against the charge of seeking his own glory is evidence of how acutely sensitive the author is that Jesus sounds like other divine or prophetic claimants to authority.

It goes without saying that the author's own point of view is unambiguously clear: Jesus is unique, the only savior, son of god, and mediator. But in the way that he deals with the question of legitimation, it is equally clear that *the author recognizes no outwardly visible difference between the "boasting" of Jesus and the "boasting" of other prophets, divine men, or saviour figures,*[34] since the difference is recognized only by those whose "eyes" are opened by the Father (cf. John 3:3; 6:44). The "I am" form is an example of this outward resemblance. The distinction which Brown tries to draw between soteriological and autodoxological uses of the "I am" form is not one that can be made on the basis of external criteria. In the Gospel of John autodoxology and soteriological speech coincide.[35] That is to say, Jesus presents himself as a saviour figure, as *the* saviour of the world, and the salvation which he brings consists in himself. It is understood in the Gospel that "salvation" means ultimately the vision of the Father, the "high god." Jesus' self-testimony is that to see him is to have this vision of the Father (14:9). In his self-testimony Jesus does in fact "make himself a god" (10:33), equal to 'God' (5"18). He offers salvation by pointing to himself as the place of salvation. He offers salvation by "boasting."

Dieter Georgi in his study of the opponents of Paul contrasts the missionary or apostle who proclaims an eschatological message concerning the imminent end of the world and the missionary who proclaims the presence of divine power in himself.[36] The latter type is represented, for example, by Simon "the magician" who proclaimed himself to be someone great (*legon einai tina heauton megan*), and was accepted by the Samaritans as "the power of God called Great" (Acts 8:9,10), just as their fellow-Samaritans had accepted Jesus as "the saviour of the world" (John 4:42). The parallel between the two confessional formulae is worth noting:

Acts 8:10 *houtos estin he dunamis tou theou he kaloumene megale*
John 4:42 *houtos estin alethos ho soter tou kosmou*

Georgi draws a profile of *Christian* missionaries who conceived of themselves as "divine men," that is to say, as possessing in themselves the divine pneuma, and who saw their mission to consist in the demonstration of this divine power in themselves. Their mission could be said to consist in the responsibility to "boast," to proclaim themselves as bearers of the divine spirit.[37] Proving their powers in competition with other claimants was an important responsibility.[38] Triumph in competition could even be said to be the content of their message.[39]

The "boasting" of John's Jesus reflects the profile drawn by Georgi. It has been argued that the Johannine "critique" of faith based on miracles alone shows that John's Jesus in contrast to that of his "Signs Source," does not belong to the class of typical Hellenistic prophets, and saviour figures.[40] I suggest the opposite. The author's ambivalence regarding miracles is due to his recognition that outwardly Jesus looks like the sort of Hellenistic prophet, described by Georgi, who lays claim to divine powers.[41] The author's ambivalance is indirect evidence of the common ground since, although he makes it clear that Jesus is not just another miracle worker, he is aware that Jesus' self-presentation in miracle and divine claim opens the door to misconceptions based on popular images of charismatic figures. This does not, however, lead him to downgrade the role of the miracles, as has frequently been maintained.[42]

*Concentration as Polemic: The
Question of Opponents*

Verses 4-11 form a capsule summary of the Johannine
"creed."[43] Why is it included in the farewell discourse?
What is its specific function at this point in the narrative?
The transitional dialogue in 14:4 and 5 links the claim and its
exposition in vss. 6ff. to the theme of the farewell. It is,
specifically, the one who is going away who proclaims himself
to be the exclusive agent of access to the Father. In the
context of the farewell, as we have argued, the reiteration of
this claim has the force of extending its jurisdiction to the
time following the departure. Jesus' claim is that he continues
to be the only way to the Father. No one can take his place
after he goes away. The departure does not alter the exclusive
jurisdiction of the Son over access to the Father.

The pronouncement of Jesus, "I am the way, the truth,
and the life," is addressed to the specific issue of the
boundaries of the Son's authority. It is a statement about
the extent of the Son's jurisdiction. It is, in effect, which
is to say, in context, an assertion that the departure of Jesus
does not constitute a limitation on his mediatorial authority.

Vss. 4-11 have the force, then, of countering negative
implications which might be drawn from the fact of the departure.
They correct a fallacy about the departure. The fallacy implicit
by negation is that the departure creates the need for a replace-
ment.

To whom is the author speaking when he insists that the
authority of Jesus is not limited by the departure? Against
whom is he speaking? The claim takes polemical form in the
statement, "No one comes to the Father outside of me" (14:6b).
Is this polemic merely formal, a stylistic device? Or does the
author have in mind actual opposing points of view? Whether or
not the Gospel of John as a whole is a polemical work is a much
debated question, which I would answer in the affirmative.[44]
The Gospel *contains* some of the most violent polemic in the
New Testament in the controversy in ch. 8:31ff.

Those who have held the view that John is polemical have been unable to agree on who the postulated opponents are. John 8 on its face suggests that they were "the Jews." Some have argued, accordingly, that the Gospel of John represents a polemic directed against the synagogue.[45] Others have suggested the disciples of John the Baptist as opponents on the basis of the rivalry explicitly described in 3:26.[46] Still others have suggested the Qumran community,[47] or, more generally, "gnostic" revealers or saviours.[48] According to E. C. Colwell, the Fourth Gospel is directed against the three Synoptic Gospels.[49]

According to Rudolf Bultmann the polemic of John is not directed primarily against any particular concrete rival, but rather has "fundamental significance."[50] Jesus' attack upon all pretended predecessors in 10:8 ("All who have come before me are thieves and robbers") expresses, according to Bultmann, *the exclusiveness and the absoluteness of the revelation.*[51] Which particular historical figures are referred to here is a purely secondary question, says Bultmann. He continues:

> The saying is of fundamental significance and refers to all pretended revealers, all pretended saviours who have ever called men to them, who have ever been followed by men. Thus there is no allusion here to rival revealers of the Evangelist's time (although of course the saying judges them also), nor to the religious authorities of that time.[52]

On the other hand, Bultmann does not deny that the author had a particular rival in mind, whether "the heathen religions in general," or "the revealers and saviours of the Hellenistic Gnostic world," whose followers still existed in John's day, or "the Gnostic doctrine that the Revealer incorporated himself in different persons in different ages."[53]

A new approach to the polemical language of John is suggested by Wayne Meeks's article on the descent/ascent motif in John, "The Man from Heaven in Johannine Sectarianism."[54]

Focusing attention not just on the polemical language, but also on the riddling, paradoxical, esoteric character of Johannine language as well, Meeks raises the question of the social function of this language. The social function of the book, he argues, is reflected in its "structural characteristics, on the basis of which Meeks concludes that one primary function of the Gospel was to reinforce the esoteric identity of the Johannine community.[55] In writing about Jesus the author is, in an important sense, writing about his social group. "In telling the story of the Son of Man who came down from heaven and then re-ascended after choosing a few of his own out of the world," Meeks says, "the book defines and vindicates the existence of the community that evidently sees itself as unique, alien from its world, under attack, misunderstood, but living in unity with Christ and through him with God. *It could hardly be regarded as a missionary tract, for we may imagine that only a very rare outsider would get past the barrier of its closed metaphorical system. It is a book for insiders, . . .*"[56]

If, following Meek's lead, we ask concerning the social function of the language of polemical exclusivity we may note that the answer is already indicated in Meeks's portrait of the Johannine group. According to Meeks, the Johannine community is characterized above all by its sectarianism, its isolation from the larger society. It is a "counter-cultural group."[57] Faith in Jesus is for the Johannine community "a change in social location."[58] Joining the community involves removal from the "world" and entry into another "world." The word "world" is defined by Meeks, following the approach of the sociology of knowledge, as "the symbolic universe within which one functions."[59] Faith in Jesus involves being "quite literally taken out of the ordinary world of social reality" and being transferred to a community "which has totalistic and exclusive claims."[60] What is suggested by Meeks's approach is that the polemical exclusivity with which authority is concentrated in the figure of Jesus serves the function of reinforcing the community's social boundaries over against the larger society. Meeks's argument raises the questions of what community, what boundaries, what larger society are in view.

We have considered three approaches to the polemical language of the Gospel. First, attempts to identify the particular object or objects of the polemic. Second, recognition of the total or absolute sense in which the polemic is intended. Third, the question of the social function of the polemic. It should be noted that these three approaches are not by any means mutually exclusive. Particularly important is it to note that the polemic has totalistic sense when viewed as a function of the sectarian consciousness of the community.

A fourth question must now be addressed, namely, to what extent the polemic is directed against other "Christians." If we have interpreted the thrust of 14:6 correctly, it is directed against a view which holds that Jesus is *replaced* by successor figures. The inference is that Jesus was acknowledged as a legitimate prophet but not as a unique, pre-eminent authority. From the author's point of view, I suggest, those who held such a view were illegitimately placing themselves on a level with Jesus and were thus setting themselves up as rivals to Jesus. Judging from the insertion into the farewell discourse of the contentious reiteration of what should have been, on the basis of the earlier discourses, truths well known to the disciples (14:4-11), it would appear that the author approached the issue of succession with an eye to a threat coming from those who recognized the legitimacy of Jesus, and were, in this sense, "Christians."

I am suggesting that what is reflected in this text is a conflict between what we may consider as two understandings of succession. The author understands the successor as a subordinate to Jesus. He takes issue with a view according to which the successor is an equal to Jesus and hence, in the author's view, a *rival* to Jesus. Anticipating the argument we shall make below (Chapter VI) that both the author and his opponents considered themselves prophetic figures and hence charismatic, it could be held that the opponents were, in one sense, more consistently charismatic than the author. There is no subordination, no hierarchy, no appeal outside of themselves to Jesus for their own legitimation. From the author's point of view they would be considered guilty of precisely the charge of acting independently, on their own authority, against which the author has had to defend Jesus.

The hypothesis I have developed here on the basis of an understanding of the function of Jesus' claim to pre-eminent singularity in 14:4-11 is supported by the analysis of the rest of the discourse, where what comes to the fore is the role of

the believer as agent of the works of Jesus (14:12ff.), and
as the earthly locus of the presence of Father and Son (14:20,
23). In other words, the rest of the discourse is concerned
with succession, which lends support to the interpretation of
vss. 4-11 as addressing the same issue. The astonishingly high
view of the role of the believer which is unfolded in the
discourse from vs. 12 on is protected from misunderstanding by
the unqualified statement of the Son's sovereignty which
precedes.

Summary Remarks on 14:4-11

It is worth pausing to compare our results thus far with
Jürgen Becker's formal analysis of the discourse. There is, to
begin with, significant formal agreement on the function of the
"I am" pronouncement of Jesus as the theme statement of the discourse. Moreover, Becker also regards the "I am" saying as a
polemical statement directed against a Christian viewpoint which
the author considers false. Here the agreement ends since in
our analysis the issue involved is not alternative views on
eschatology but conflicting views of the authority of Jesus.[61]
A second point of disagreement has to do with the formal
structure of the discourse. According to Becker, the idea of
the second coming of Jesus, which the author intends to correct,
is formulated in the discourse itself, in 14:2,3, so that not
only is the discourse from vs. 4-26 an interpretation of the
"text" in 14:2-3, it is intended by the author as a *correction*
of the viewpoint expressed in the "text."
Our understanding of the relationship between 14:4-11 and
the first part of the discourse, in 13:31-14:3 is quite different. There is, as we have indicated above, a shift in perspective which occurs between 14:3 and 4. But underlying this
shift there is a consistent position, contrary to Becker. Up
to 14:3 the departure of Jesus is viewed as the expression
of the authority of the Son to ascend, to be lifted up, to
claim heavenly glory. Departure is triumph, the demonstration
of access to heaven. In 14:4ff. the departure is viewed from
the perspective of the actualization of that ascent authority,

the exercise of the ascended one's authority on *earth*. The
departure of Jesus does not leave a vacuum which must be filled.
It means, rather, that Jesus may now exercise authority on
earth from his position in heaven. Thus the controlling point
of view which brings together the parts of the discourse is one
which sees things from the standpoint of heavenly authority.
The situation of the disciples on earth is viewed from the
perspective of heaven. The author's standpoint is heaven.
Such a proposition formulates the logical inference of prophetic,
charismatic self-understanding for the question of place or
authorial point of view. The standpoint of prophetic author-
ship is heaven.[62]

CHAPTER IV

THE PLACE OF THE DISCIPLES IN RELATION TO
THE SON, THE WORKS (14:12-24)

The Paraclete

In the scholarship on the farewell discourses, the figure
of the Paraclete has naturally commanded a great deal of
attention. The first of the Paraclete promises occurs in
14:16,17. We shall begin our discussion of the third section
of the discourse, 14:12-24, by a review of the scholarship on
the Paraclete figure, focusing attention on those issues
especially pertinent to the question of the place of the
Paraclete promise in 14:16,17 within the structure of the discourse as a whole.[1]

The problem may be posed in terms of the relationship
of the Paraclete figure to the Son. Within the framework of
the first farewell discourse the problem has a twofold aspect.
On the one hand, the Paraclete is described as a figure who
will *take the place of* the departing Son. Interpreting the
promise in vss. 16, 17 in relation to what has *preceded* in the
discourse it seems clear that the Paraclete is a figure *distinguished* from Jesus, a figure who succeeds Jesus in a
chronological sequence of appearance. Jesus is going away
(14:12) and promises to petition the Father for "another
Paraclete" to be with the disciples for ever. On the other hand,
immediately following vss. 16, 17, Jesus promises that he himself
will return to the disciples soon, to dwell in them and be seen
by them exclusively, and not by the world (14:18-24). It is
generally recognized that this return of Jesus cannot be the
final Parousia of Jesus at the end of the age, since that event
will be visible to all.[2] There is, then, a promise that the
Paraclete-Spirit will come to dwell in the disciples and take
the place of Jesus who will be gone, and immediately juxtaposed
to this a promise that Jesus will come back again soon (*eti
mikron*) after all, to dwell in the disciples himself. How are

69

these two indwelling figures related? Why two indwelling
figures? A number of scholars have concluded that they
cannot be understood as two distinct figures but must, in some
sense, be identical. Yet we have just pointed out that in
relation to the prior context, the Paraclete and the Son are
distinguished ·from one another.

The question of the unity and coherence of the first
farewell discourse is posed in its most acute form by this dual
aspect of the Paraclete figure in relation to the Son.[3] Is
the Paraclete distinct from the Son, or identified with the
Son? After reviewing the scholarly discussion of this issue,
we shall suggest that, as regards the purpose and structure
of the farewell discourse, insufficient attention has been paid
to the position of the *disciples* and the relationship of the
promises of Paraclete and returning Son to the disciples' role
as agents of the Son.

Wellhausen

Julius Wellhausen published two literary-critical studies
of John in quick succession. In the first, *Erweiterungen und
Änderungen im vierten Evangelium*, he treated 13:31-14:31 as a
unified discourse, distinguished from the secondary farewell
material in chapters 15-17.[4] In his second, more comprehensive
study, published a year later, however, Wellhausen draw
attention to what he now regarded as a deep division *within*
chapter 14.[5] On the one hand, some parts of the discourse
(Part A: vss. 1-4, 16, 26) depict Jesus as one who after his
departure does *not* return to earth but sends his substitute
(Ersatz), the Paraclete. In other parts (Part B: vss. 5-15,
18-24) Jesus remains as "the life principle of the community"
united to the disciples.[6] According to Wellhausen the two parts
of the discourse offered two logically incompatible solutions
to the problem posed by the departure of Jesus, and on this
basis he drew the conclusion that they represented different
literary sources, the Paraclete sayings (Part A) being regarded
as more original.

Windisch

Hans Windisch, in his 1927 study of the Paraclete sayings, took the same position as Wellhausen, that the promise of the Paraclete and the promise of the returning Son were incompatible. He, too, proposed a literary-critical solution. Where Wellhausen suggested that the Paraclete sayings belonged to the original stratum, however, Windisch concluded that the Paraclete sayings were secondary.[7]

Windisch stressed the fact that the Paraclete represents a successor figure to Jesus, one who takes the place of the departing Jesus. Jesus' last deed on behalf of the disciples, says Windisch, "is to provide a successor."[8] What marks out the Paraclete sayings is the representation of the Spirit's coming "as a sending of a new heavenly messenger." "The decisive factor," he says, "is the expectation and sending of a new helper from heaven who takes over the function of the earlier emissary."[9] The Paraclete promise is incompatible with "the mystically reinterpreted parousia of Jesus" in 14:18ff. because the idea of the Paraclete presupposes the *absence* of Jesus: The idea underlying the Paraclete sayings is "that the Paraclete represents Jesus who is absent and will remain absent."[10]

Commenting on the question of the intercessory function suggested by the Paraclete title and by the reference in 1 John to Jesus as a "*parakleton*" (1 John 2:1), Windisch concludes that both Jesus and the Paraclete, in the *Gospel* in contrast to the epistle reference, function primarily as prophets. What we have, he suggests, "is more the image of a prophet who, after the departure of the chief prophet, substitutes for him and now stands at the side of the orphaned church as witness, helper, counselor, and teacher."[11] He goes on to cite parallel cases: Joshua as Moses' successor (Windisch cites Deut. 18:15 and Acts 7:37 as references to Joshua); and Elijah and Elisha. As a successor figure to Jesus, the Paraclete is also his "double" in the sense that he *functions* in the same way.[12] "Like him, he witnesses and teaches. He is his successor (14:16), and his witness, like the witness of Jesus, deals with the Son of God. Like Jesus, he is, on the one hand, Paraclete and Intercessor, and on the other hand, preacher of judgment and accuser."[13]

Thus, Windisch stresses the fact that the Paraclete and the figure of Jesus are alike in function but distinguished from one another in time of appearance. He points out that an organic structure is possible in the discourses "only if one identifies the sending of the Spirit with the promised return of Jesus. However," he adds, "this would do violence to the original sense of both promises."[14] Therefore, the Paraclete sayings are secondary.

Though Windisch argues that the Paraclete promise is secondary because it presupposes the absence of Jesus, he, at the same time, accepts the rest of the farewell discourse as belonging to the "first stratum of the chapter."[15] Yet the farewell discourse from 13:31 to 14:3, as well as 14:12-15, also presupposes the departure or absence of Jesus. In particular 14:2-3 makes it clear that Jesus will go away and remain away until he comes back *to take the disciples to heaven*. If the Paraclete sayings are secondary then 14:2-3 must also be secondary. Likewise the promises to the disciples in 14:12-15 are based explicitly upon the fact that Jesus is going away (14:12) and that they will take his place. In other words, the figure of the Paraclete is not, as Windisch argues, isolated from its context. On the contrary, it fits in very well to the farewell situation.

What Windisch has to say about the *rank* of the Paraclete relative to the departing Jesus also calls for comment. According to Windisch, the evangelist, in setting forth the idea of a figure who takes the place of the Son, "takes the greatest pains to stifle any idea that this last sending might be--as it actually should be--the highest and most eminent."[16] This statement raises fundamental questions which, unfortunately, Windisch does not pursue. In fact, the statement assumes without argument a debatable position on the question of the rank of the successive sendings. Why "should" the last sending be the highest and most eminent? This was certainly not the case with the Moses and Joshua pair or the Elijah/Elisha pair

which Windisch has earlier cited as parallel examples. Behind
Windisch's statement is the assumption of an *eschatological*
structure in which "last" is "highest." Windisch in earlier
remarks alludes to an eschatological scheme behind the fourth
Paraclete saying (16:5-11) in which Jesus states that unless
he goes away the Paraclete will not come. There is here,
according to Windisch, "a faint gleam of the succession of two
reigns or two ages: the reign of Christ comes to an end so that
the reign of the Paraclete can commence."[17]

There is one other reference to the issue of rank. In
the fifth saying (16:12-15), according to Windisch, "there is a
sudden glimpse of a thought which ascribes a certain superiority" to the Paraclete. He is presumably referring to the
statement, "When the Spirit of truth comes, he will guide you
into all the truth" (16:13). Windisch adds immediately that
this hint of superiority is qualified in the same passage, since,
in the Gospel, the Paraclete's sending "had to be subordinated
to that of the Christ."[18]

In sum, the issue of rank does not receive much attention
in Windisch's discussion of the succession relationship. Nevertheless, it does intrude. In the remarks he does make, two
points emerge. On the one hand, he assumes that there "should"
be an eschatological ranking, and finds at least one glimpse
of such. On the other hand, he recognizes that in the Gospel
the rank must be the reverse. The later sending of the Paraclete must be subordinated to the earlier sending of the Son.

Bornkamm

In Günter Bornkamm's discussion of the Paraclete,
originally published in the 1949 Festschrift for Bultmann and
subsequently revised, the issue of rank is posed in a provocative
way.[19] We referred to Bornkamm's position above, in the
introduction. It will be necessary to examine it more closely
here. Bornkamm focuses sharply on the relationship of the Son
and the Paraclete as the key to the religio-historical background of the Paraclete figure. It is a relationship of
succession, but in place of an indefinite series of figures
succeeding one another, there are only two figures involved.

They are "exclusively related to one another," parallel figures
in many respects, but at the same time "sharply distinguished
as far as the time of their working and their respective
functions."[20]

In seeking to characterize this relationship more
precisely and find sources for it, Bornkamm turns to the
forerunner-fulfiller motif known from Jewish eschatology and
introduced into early Christianity in connection with the
relationship of John the Baptist and Jesus. In Bornkamm's
opinion the closest analogy to the relationship of Jesus to
the Paraclete is to be found in the relationship of the Baptist,
as forerunner, to Jesus. The Paraclete sayings, according to
Bornkamm, depict the earthly Jesus as paving the way, by his
departure, for the sending and working of the Paraclete. "That
means, in other words, that the departing Jesus appears here,
astonishingly enough, as a sort of 'forerunner' and 'precursor,'
while the Paraclete appears as a 'fulfiller' who brings the
consummation (16:7, 12)."[21]

It is astonishing indeed that the author of the Fourth
Gospel would make use of a tradition which might suggest that
Jesus is subordinated to anyone. To be sure, Bornkamm proceeds
to argue that in taking over the Paraclete tradition, the
author has made drastic changes. Essential to Bornkamm's
position is his insistence that two especially significant shifts
occur. In the first place, Jesus and the Paraclete are ultimately one and the same for the author, not distinct figures, as in
the tradition taken over. The extensive parallelism between
Jesus and the Paraclete in John points in this direction. The
forerunner-fulfiller scheme is applied by the author to a single
saviour figure in order to distinguish between his two forms of
existence.[22] The Paraclete becomes, for the author, "funda-
mentally nothing more than the Son of Man in a state of
glorification!"[23]

The second change which occurs in the author's appropri-
ation of the Paraclete tradition is that the hierarchical
relationship implicit in the forerunner-fulfiller scheme is
reversed. In his initial statement on how the rank aspect of
the relationship is affected, Bornkamm seems to say that it

becomes an *irrelevant* feature. The new meaning given to the
forerunner motif is such that "the idea of a rank differentiation between the forerunner and fulfiller so important in the
Baptist sayings has in truth no place here."[24] However, he
immediately qualifies this by noting that in 16:7 the notion
of rank does intrude in the fact that "before his end, the
earthly Jesus had a temporally limited function anticipating
the consummation."[25] And he subsequently points out that the
Paraclete is "subordinated" to Father and Son.[26]

The question which naturally arises is: Why did the
author make use of a tradition running so contrary to the
exclusivity and primacy of the Son? Bornkamm of course
recognizes the problem and poses the question himself quite
explicitly."[27] His answer, however, is not entirely clear.
What it boils down to is that the Paraclete tradition expresses
the author's insistence that the earthly Jesus can only be
understood retrospectively, that is, from the perspective of
the new age inaugurated by the "hour" of Jesus' death and
glorification. In other words, the Paraclete sayings give
expression to the view that the eschatological age, the
"Äonenwende," began with Jesus' death and exaltation.[28]

This so-called explanation of the reason for the inclusion
of the Paraclete sayings is not an explanation at all. It offers
no solution to the problem posed by the Paraclete figure in
relation to the Gospel's prevailing christocentricity. In
fact, it simply poses the issue in an even more acute form since
now the hierarchy which subordinates the time of Jesus to the
time of the Paraclete is attributed to the author, not just to
the tradition used by him. If the eschatological age begins
with Jesus' departure, then the time of his "earthly" appearance
is anticipatory and subordinate, despite the claims of the
revelation discourses, the claims of the "I am" sayings.

We suggest that the basic problem with Bornkamm's discussion is that, despite his starting point, he has treated
the issue of rank only in passing. As a result, his conclusions
on the issue are contradictory. Though he says that there is no
room for the idea of a rank differentiation in the Son-Paraclete
relationship, he cannot escape it in his eschatological model.

There were, in fact, *two* ways of understanding the relationship of the time of Jesus to the time which followed as regards their respective rank. Bornkamm has failed to give serious consideration to the possibility that the time *before* the departure is superior to the time after the departure. In support of this possibility two observations are worth noting. In the first place, in addition to the forerunner-fulfiller relationship in which the first of the two figures is inferior to the second, there are examples in Jewish tradition involving two figures in which the relationship is reversed, as in the case of Moses and Joshua, or Elijah and Elisha. In the second place, in the Johannine version of the tradition concerning the Baptist, there is evidence that the author *rejects* the forerunner-fulfiller understanding of the relationship of the Baptist to Jesus. In 1:15 and 1:30, as we have seen, there appears to be a polemic against disciples of John the Baptist who interpreted the temporal priority of the Baptist as an argument for his superiority to Jesus. In other words, the author is in dispute with a group where priority = superiority. Instead of appealing to the forerunner-fulfiller understanding, the author *accepts* the premise that priority = superiority and applies it in a radical way. Jesus is superior to the Baptist because, in fact, he was before him: "he who comes after me ranks before me, because he was before me." There is every reason to think this kind of model, the "protological," lies behind the *author's* understanding also of the Son-Paraclete succession. The evidence Windisch and Bornkamm appeal to suggests only that the alternative view, the eschatological (last = highest), had a formative influence on the traditions of the community to which the author belongs. Indeed, such a view, according to which the Spirit was elevated above Jesus, either because the eschatological age was viewed as having been inaugurated with the coming of the Spirit, or without the eschatological overtones, seems to have been widespread in early Christianity.[29] This leads to a further suggestion. If, as seems probable, the titles "Paraclete" and "Spirit" reflect two originally distinct figures, it is possible that the eschatological hierarchy may have been associated with the "Spirit" whereas the protological hierarchy may have been originally associated with the "Paraclete."[30]

We may put the issue in pointed fashion by acknowledging that Bornkamm is correct in stressing the retrospective point of view explicitly adopted by the author but incorrect in interpreting this as evidence of the preparatory, limited nature of the epiphany of the Son. It is, rather, to be interpreted as evidence of the subordinate, limited status of the *disciples* over against the Son. Whereas the Son was in possession of full knowledge always, the disciples were at first ignorant, bewildered, full of misunderstanding, and had to await the coming of the Spirit for their eyes to be opened. The delay in their achieving understanding contrasts with the full knowledge possessed by the Son from the beginning. The retrospective point of view, as we shall argue below (Chapter VI), expresses the dependence of the disciples, as successor-agents of Jesus, on the prior work and words of the Son. In this way, it also expresses the subordination of the time of the Spirit-Paraclete, which is the time of the disciples' agency, to the prior time of the Son's epiphany.

Betz

In 1963 Otto Betz published a monograph on the subject of the Paraclete. Although the central question addressed by Betz was the question of the origin of the Paraclete figure in John, Betz did address directly the issue of the relationship between the coming of the Paraclete and the return of Jesus, claiming, in fact, that his particular solution to the problem of origin was confirmed by the fact that it solved the exegetical problem.[31]

Following Windisch and Bornkamm, Betz focused attention upon the function of the Paraclete as a successor figure to Jesus. He rejected, however, Bornkamm's appeal to the apocalyptic idea of a succession of two ages as the background for the Johannine conception.[32] Betz drew attention instead to biblical traditions concerning the succession of prophets, teachers, "witnesses," and "protectors." But these traditions are useful only as general background to the Johannine figure of the Paraclete, who combines in himself the four offices named. To

explain the particular phenomenon represented by the Johannine
Paraclete, Betz turns to Jewish traditions concerning Michael
the archangel.

The solution which Betz proposes is as original and daring
as that proposed by Bornkamm. It is also the exact reverse,
formally. Whereas Bornkamm suggested that what was originally
attributed to two figures (the forerunner and the fulfiller) was
fused together in John in the one person of the Christ-Paraclete,
Betz proposes that one figure, the archangel Michael, has served
as the prototype for two distinct persons in the Gospel, the Son
and the Paraclete. Michael, so Betz argues, played a dual role
in Jewish apocalyptic tradition. He acted as intercessor in
heaven before the throne of God, and as the "Spirit of truth"
on earth in the souls of the righteous. These two roles are
divided, in the Gospel of John, between the exalted Christ, who
takes the role of heavenly intercessor (14:14, 15), and the
Paraclete on earth, who functions as the "Spirit of truth."

Betz's solution is based upon a great deal of speculation
and imaginative reconstruction and combination. It requires our
attention because, as noted, he offers it explicitly as a
solution to the exegetical problem of the relationship between
the coming of the Paraclete and the return of Jesus according to
14:18ff. Betz begins the section in which he introduces the
Michael hypothesis by calling attention to the problem posed by
the juxtaposition of the two comings.[33] He rejects Wellhausen's
and Windisch's attempts to assign the two promises to separate
literary strata. He also rejects the view that the two comings
can be fused together as the coming of Christ in the Spirit.
Instead, he suggests, one should ask whether or not both figures,
the Paraclete and the returning Son, can be understood as
working "*neben- und miteinander*."[34]

It is difficult, however, to see how Betz's Michael
hypothesis solves the problem of the two comings. According to
his hypothesis, Christ is specifically assigned to *heaven* where
he exercises the functions of Michael before the throne of God.
The *location* of Christ is a basic element in Betz's proposal
since the point of his appeal to Michael is that the two offices
carried out by Michael are distinguished by where they take
place, the one in heaven, the other in the souls of the faithful.

The Christ who is in heaven before the throne of God is *not* the Christ who has returned to indwell the faithful. It would seem as if Betz's proposal has simply posed the problem in extreme form. Astonishingly, though Betz starts by claiming to offer a solution to the problem of the two comings, he never returns to the subject to explain why, if Jesus goes to heaven to serve as intercessor and sends the Paraclete to indwell the disciples, Jesus then promises to come himself also to indwell the disciples![35]

Summary

Stepping back to see what conclusions we may draw at this point as far as the Paraclete's relation to the Son is concerned, we find that in the four scholars we have looked at the picture is dominated by the differentiation between the Paraclete and the Son as successor figures.[36] In Wellhausen, Windisch, and Bornkamm emphasis on this feature of the Paraclete promise leads to distinctions between strata of the tradition. Windisch acknowledges that as the text stands the sending of the Spirit and the promised return of Jesus must be identified or there is no "organic structure" possible, but cannot seem to bring himself to ascribe such an intention to the author.

> That the sending of the Spirit may be his (Christ's) mystical parousia is only later speculation, but the fourth evangelist indeed plays a role in its development. By interposing the promise of the Paraclete between the promises of the parousia (14:1ff.; 14:18ff.; 16:16ff.)--both are originally mutually exclusive and cancel each other out--he suggested the view that the parousia takes place in the sending of the Spirit.[37]

Bornkamm attributes such an identification to the author, but then qualifies this in such a way that it is not clear in the end just what the relationship is. Betz does not seriously address the problem.

If we were to turn now and look at studies dealing with the farewell discourse rather than studies focusing primarily on the Paraclete figure, we would find a startling contrast. In a large number of modern studies some sort of identification of the indwelling Son and the indwelling Spirit is recognized.[38] On the other hand, the succession relationship is either not recognized, or it is de-emphasized in most of these cases.

On the one hand, then, scholars who have focused attention on the Paraclete figure have emphasized the succession structure, but have been unable to show how this is integrated into the context of the farewell discourses. On the other hand, scholars who have focused attention on the returning Son in 14:18ff. within the framework of the discourse have tended to sacrifice the idea of succession to the identification of Son and Paraclete.

We may pose the problem in terms of the relationship of vss. 12-17 to vss. 18-24.[39] In vss. 12-17 the idea of succession predominates. In vss. 18-24 the idea of the Son's return predominates. Or, to put it another way, in vss. 12-17 the Paraclete and the disciples succeed Jesus. In vss. 18-24 Jesus becomes his own successor! This formulation suggests that we cannot escape Windisch's conclusion: "an organic structure is possible only if one identifies the sending of the Spirit with the promised return of Jesus."[40] It also suggests that a unifying theme of both sections is the idea of succession. In support of this suggestion we would call attention to the role of the disciples. It is they who are the visible successors of Jesus. It is their role as successor-agents of the works of Jesus which constitutes the unifying subject underlying both sections. We turn then to an analysis of the text focusing on the role of the disciple-believers. Our discussion will be divided into two parts. We will look first at the extraordinarily high view of the disciples evident in vss. 12-24. We will then look at the subordinate status of their office.

The Disciples

The main theme of vss. 12-24 is announced at the outset, in vs. 12: "I solemnly say to you, he who believes in me, he shall do the works which I do; he shall in fact perform even greater works, because I am going away to the Father." When Jesus goes away, the believer will take the place of Jesus as agent of the works Jesus has been doing. The stature of the disciples as successor-agents of the works of Jesus is underscored by the promise that the disciples will do "greater"

works than those Jesus has done. In a Gospel which pays as much
attention to questions of rank as does John, this anomalous
promise must be taken very seriously. The authority of the
believer as successor is reinforced by the promise which follows,
of full intercessory powers (14:13, 14). As in the promise
that the disciples will be agents of "greater" works, it is
important not to overlook the full force of what is being
promised, in this case unlimited intercessory powers: "whatsoever you shall ask in my name, I will do" (vs. 13).[41] The
authority of the disciples is grounded, finally, in the promise
that "another Paraclete" will be sent to dwell in them (14:15-17).

What is new in vs. 12 is the introduction into the discourse of an active role for the disciples. Up to this point
they have figured as observers of the "works" of Jesus (14:10).
The formal words *amen amen lego humin* underscore the importance
of the new theme.[42] Where vss. 4-11 were cast in the present
tense and had to do with the response of the disciples to Jesus
and the Father, with the disciples' knowledge, faith, and vision,
vss. 12-17 return to the future tense and have to do with the
future activity and authority of the disciples. Formally, vss.
4-11 are an exhortation to believe, whereas vss. 12-17 are a
promise, almost an investiture. The point of view in vss. 12-17
is, once more, unambiguously, the farewell situation in which
the disciples are left behind by the departing Jesus. This too
marks off vss. 12-17 from vss. 4-11, where the farewell situation is blurred (though still in view). But the major contrast
between vss. 4-11 and vss. 12-17 lies in the fact that the point
of vss. 4-11 has been to insist upon the exclusive claims of
Jesus as mediator and agent of the works of God, whereas in
vss. 12ff. Jesus turns around and appoints the believer to be
his successor as agent of his works: "the works which I do that
one will do also.[43]

In analyzing what the author here has to say about the
believer-disciple as a successor to Jesus, we must begin with
the notion of "works." The disciples are characterized as
agents of the works of Jesus. What are the "works" performed
by Jesus? In the first place, the "works" are an expression of
power. The element of power is not foreign to the farewell
scene. The first farewell discourse is, in fact, framed by a

conflict over power between Jesus and Satan. The last event
recorded before Jesus begins the farewell discourse is an act
of Satanic possession. The betrayal by Judas is announced,
and then, the narrative goes on, "Satan entered into him"
(13:27). Commentators have frequently noted the dramatic
symbolism of the comment, after Judas departs, "and it was
night" (13:30). What calls for emphasis is what the darkness
symbolizes, the act of possession. The first farewell discourse
concludes with Jesus' announcement that "the ruler of this world
is coming" (14:30). And this is followed, if we attach 14:31
to 18:1, by the arrival of Judas and the strange scene in which
Jesus demonstrates his power over what is happening by the
effect of his words. Jesus' *ego eimi* causes the soldiers to
draw back and fall down (18:6).[44]

The conflict of Jesus' last hour is a conflict with Satan,
the *archon tou kosmou* (14:30). Satan's demonic possession of
Judas on the one side of the conflict is to be contrasted with
the cosmic "exorcism" of Satan by Jesus on the other side. The
moment of glorification, of exaltation, is the moment of judgment. "Now is the judgment of this world, now shall the ruler
of this world be cast out" (*ekblethesetai exo*, 12:31).[45]

The glorification of Jesus demonstrates his power over
Satan. In announcing the "coming" of the archon of the cosmos,
Jesus adds the assurance, "and he has no authority over me"
(14:30). Literally, "and he has nothing in me" (*en emoi ouk
echei ouden*). *Echein* may be taken either in the sense of
"having a claim," or in the sense of "having power to do something." Both senses would be true in this instance, so that the
best translation would be one which conveys both aspects as is
the case with the term "authority."

In talking about power it is essential to recognize
that what is involved is a type of magical power, understanding
the term "magical" to include "miracle." It is, as we have
already seen, a conflict which involves demonic possession
(Satan's entering into Judas). In this connection it is worth
underlining the exact words of Jesus' rejection of the authority
of Satan: "*in me* (*en emoi*) he has nothing." By contrast, Satan
enters into Judas (*eiselthen eis*, 13:27). It would be wrong to
overemphasize the literal rendering of an idiomatic expression.

It would also be wrong to overlook the associations made possible by idiomatic expressions.[46] It is significant that the author calls attention to the internal conflict which accompanies Jesus' announcement of the impending betrayal "After saying these things, Jesus was stirred (*etarachthe*) in the spirit and bore witness and said . . ." (13:21). The verb *tarasso* is the same one used earlier by Jesus in his own testimony to the inner conflict of the final hour (12:27). It points without question to an inner activity. We would suggest that it is to be understood as a conflict involving the assertion of Satanic power and authority over Jesus (14:30), a conflict over the attempt of Satan to "possess" Jesus.[47] Jesus' "glorification" is the vindication of his claim to be "possessed" by the "one God," to be indwelt by him (cf. 10:38).

We will come back to the notion of "indwelling," which is so crucial to the Johannine understanding of power. In passing, however, we may note that we have talked about three kinds of space in the Gospel. First there is the space of sacred geography, the distinction between "heaven" and "earth," "above" and "below," a dualistic map. Second, it has been necessary to talk about "social" ranking, involving "place" or "position." Jesus is above all, in the sense of a social hierarchy, because he "comes from above" (3:31). Thirdly, there is the interior space of the Father (who is indwelt by the Son), of the Son (who is indwelt by Father and believer), and of Judas (who is entered into by Satan).

Turning to the term "works" itself (*ta erga*), it is necessary to insist that the works include *miracles*. In 7:21, for example, the healing of the lame man on the sabbath is referred to as an *ergon*. Again, in 9:3,4, Jesus explains to the disciples that the man born blind is to be an occasion for manifesting *ta erga tou theou*. The restoration of sight is "the works of God." The miracles are generally referred to in the Gospel by the term *semeion* (2:11,19,23; 3:2; 4:48,54; 6:2,14, 26,30; 7:31; 9:16; 10:41; 11:47; 12:18,37; 20:30). But the term *erga* is also used frequently, particularly where Jesus cites the miracles as legitimating evidence of his claims, as in 14:10,11 (cf. 5:36; 7:3; 10:25,38).

The miracles, in other words, are a clear display of power in the Gospel. Yet even in connection with the miracles, there has been a tendency in the scholarly literature to understate the aspect of power. This has frequently taken the form of a redaction-critical argument that the author appropriated a miracle source (the so-called "Signs Source"), but "demythologized," or "downgraded," or "countered" the "divine man" christology of the miracle source.

Perhaps the most radical denial of the moment of power in the miracles is found in Bultmann's position that the miracles may not have been regarded by the author as actual events.[48] According to Bultmann John's Jesus offers no outward display of his heavenly origin. The difference between Jesus and other saviour figures of the Hellenistic world is his refusal to offer miracles, his refusal to appear outwardly as anything other than a man like other men.[49] This, according to Bultmann, is the fundamental legitimating claim of the author's Jesus.

To reach this conclusion, in the face of the Gospel's repeated appeal to the "works" for legitimation, Bultmann must argue that the "works" refer to the words of Jesus, and not to the miracles as independently visible demonstrations of power.[50]

Few have followed Bultmann to the radical conclusion that the author may not ascribe historical reality to the miracles. Jürgen Becker, for example, explicitly takes issue with Bultmann's doubts regarding the historical reality of the miracles in the author's mind.[51] At the same time, Becker concludes that the miracles, as historical events, are "superfluous" for the believer, and even "empty of meaning."[52] In the narrative of the resurrection of Lazarus, according to Becker, the author "degrades" the miracle to a position of "nachhinkenden Sinnlosigkeit."[53]

A more balanced discussion has been published recently by Robert Fortna, who starts by recognizing the possibility that the canonical gospels may have been moving toward a *heightening* of a divine man theology, rather than away from such a christology.[54] Fortna concludes that in the case of John there is evidence on both sides. He concedes that "John has *heightened* some aspects of the portrait of Jesus that can be

considered appropriate to the divine man," such as the fore-
knowledge, the sovereignty, the persuasive speech, and the
epiphanic self-disclosure of Jesus.[55] Fortna goes so far as
to say that the author's Jesus is, in some ways, "more nearly
a *theios aner* than his source's!"[56] On the other hand, in
regard to the miracles, and the christocentrism of the source,
Fortna concludes that the author is moving away from the divine
man image.[57]

Such conclusions fly in the face of the emphasis of the
Gospel on the miraculous, one might even say, the exaggerated
emphasis on the miraculous. Whatever the Johannine "critique"
of miracles may mean, it cannot be interpreted as robbing them
of their historicity, or their significance as expressions of
the heavenly power and authority of the Son. The author does
not downplay the miracles. He does counter the view, of those
who are "blind," that Jesus' miracles are like those of any
other miracle worker (just as he counters the view that Jesus'
claims in the "I am" discourses are like those of any other
magician).[58] He does this, in part, not, so to speak, by
turning the volume *down* on the miraculous as such, but by
turning the volume up. In Käsemann's words, "there is no
reductionism about the miracles in the Fourth Gospel."[59]

The "works" which Jesus does, and which the disciples
will do, include not only miracles, however, they include also
giving life and condemning to death (5:21-23). As we have seen,
these are the works which Jesus sees the Father doing, and does
also himself (5:19ff.). This is the exercise of the authority
of Jesus over access to the Father, described in 14:6-11. There
is no sharp distinction drawn in the Gospel between these works
and the miracles. The power demonstrated in turning the water
into wine is the same divine power exercised by the Son in
"making alive" (*zoopoiein*) and passing judgment.[60]

The disciples, therefore, succeed not only to Jesus'
authority to do miracles but also his authority over life and
death! This conclusion is supported by the comissioning scene
in John 20:21-23. What is promised in the farewell discourse
is enacted in this post-resurrection scene. The relationship

between the two texts is suggested by the benediction of peace in each case (14:27, cf. 20:21). More importantly, the Spirit promised in the discourse is imparted by Jesus directly in the commissioning scene.[61] The disciples succeed to Jesus' power in the most direct form imaginable: "he breathed on them, and said to them, 'Receive the Holy Spirit'" (20:22). They received his Spirit directly, and are thereby granted authority over access to heaven: "If you forgive the sins of any, they are forgiven, if you retain the sins of any, they are retained" (John 20:23). This commission recalls the promise of authority in 14:13, 14. Together, these texts indicate that included in the "works" which the disciples are empowered to perform is the "forgiving" and "retaining" of sins.[62]

This promise of intercessory power, made in 14:13 and repeated in vs. 14 supports the initial characterization of the successor position of the disciples in terms of authority and power. The disciples are promised access to power in the "name" of Jesus. According to Barrett "John's thought is by no means magical," because the intercessory powers presuppose the love and obedience of the disciples.[63] In the magical literature of the Hellenistic world, however, the use of a name for magical purposes typically presupposes that the one who invokes the name knows the deity, and is in union with the deity.

This is well illustrated, for example, in the love charm of Astrapsoukos.[64] In lines 6-14 the petitioner claims knowledge of the names, the forms, the plant, the wood, and the city of Hermes, "I know you, Hermes, who you are and whence you are and which is your city, Hermopolis (line 14). The petitioner also knows the foreign names of Hermes (ll. 20-21, 41-49). The petitioner, in fact, claims union with Hermes as the basis for the intercessory authority which the petitioner claims:

I know you Hermes, and you me.
I am you and you me.
Therefore (kai) do for me all
And descend with Agathe Tuche and Agatho Daimoni,
Now! now! quick! quick!

Our purpose in citing the magical papyri is to underscore the fact that in talking about miraculous and intercessory powers in the Hellenistic period, we cannot ignore the world of

Hellenistic magic. It is striking that in so much of the discussion of the "background" of the Gospel of John little or no
mention is made of the magical literature, which offers insight
into basic understandings of access to heavenly forces.[65] Too
often comparison between the magical aspects of Hellenistic
religion and early Christian literature, particularly the New
Testament, has been foreclosed by citing alleged differences
between "religion" and "magic." According to Festugière, for
example, there is an essential difference in attitude with
respect to the deity in each case, expressed in the way the
deity is addressed. In religion one petitions the deity. In
magic, the deity is summoned.[66]

In drawing on magical literature to illumine the Gospel
of John we are not intending to imply that there are no differences. Some differences are obvious, especially those related
to the fact that when talking about the magical papyri collected
by Karl Preisendanz, for example, we are dealing with a different kind of *literature* from the Gospel of John. What we would
maintain, however, is that the differences which have been cited
by various scholars are not such as to make comparison illegitimate or useless for purposes of illuminating the Gospel. One
of the most important features shared by both literatures is a
concern with heavenly power and authority, and with problems
of transmission and succession of power and authority.[67]

The promise of the Spirit in 14:15-17 points in the same
direction, to a concern with extraordinary powers. What is
emphasized about the Spirit is that it will be visible only
to the disciples, not to the world. The world will not be able
to "receive" the Spirit, will not be able to "see" it, or "know"
it. It is the disciples alone who will receive, see, and know
the Spirit, because the Spirit will be "*in*" them. The disciples
will be "possessed" by the Spirit. In terms of the immediate
context, the Spirit is the power which will enable the disciples
to do the "works" of Jesus. To be united with a spirit in order
to accomplish extraordinary actions is a commonplace of magic.[68]

The language of "possession" continues in vss. 18-24 in
the description of the return of Jesus. The promise of the
Paraclete is followed immediately, with no formal break, by

Jesus' promise that he will return. The return is described in almost the same words that have just been used by the Paraclete: "the world will no longer see me, but you will see me" (vs. 19). The visual aspect is emphasized by repetition in vs. 21: To the one who "loves" him Jesus promises reciprocal love and epiphany: "I will love him and will manifest myself to him." The split between the world and the disciple occasioned by the selective visibility of Jesus upon his return is the subject of the question of Judas-not-Iscariot: "Lord, how is it that you are about to manifest yourself to us and not to the world?" (vs. 22). The answer of Jesus is that the coming he is speaking of is in the nature of an act of possession. Father and Son will "come to" the disciple and will make their home with him (14:23). The disciples will know that they are indwelt by Jesus even as they indwell him (14:20).

Just as the Spirit will be invisible to the world and visible to the disciples because he will be *in* the disciples, so Jesus will be invisible to the world and visible to the disciples *because he will be in the disciples*. Jesus returns to the disciples in the same way that the Spirit comes to them. He returns as Spirit. The parallelism suggests the identification between Jesus and the Spirit, and this identification is supported by the commissioning scene referred to above where the Spirit is conferred by Jesus' breath! Jesus returns to the disciples in the form of the Spirit.

The true disciple, thus, stands in contrast to Judas Iscariot. Judas is possessed by Satan who "enters in" to him (13:27). The obedient disciple is possessed by the Spirit of Christ who enters into him (14:20, 23).

The succession structure continues to apply after vs. 18. As the place where the Father, with the Son, comes to make his *mone*, or dwelling-place (14:23), the disciple assumes the role of the temple. In this additional sense the disciple takes the place of Jesus as the center of access to heaven, with powers to forgive or retain sin. Whereas the parallels between the sending of the Paraclete and the return of Jesus (invisibility to the world, indwelling) have often been noted, the connection between the promises in vss. 18-24 and the appointment of the disciples to the work of Jesus in vs. 12 has been generally overlooked, so that vss. 18-24 have seldom been interpreted in terms of the active role of the disciples as agents of heavenly power in the world.

To summarize our discussion so far, we have found that the disciples are depicted in the discourse as successors to the powers and place of Jesus by virtue of their possession of Jesus himself in the form of the Spirit. One of the few who has emphasized that succession applies not just to the Spirit but also to the disciples in the discourse in Louis Martyn, who draws upon our text, from verse 12 on, in support of his notion of the Christian as the "double" of Jesus, just as Windisch earlier had described the Spirit-Paraclete as the "double" ("*Doppelgänger*") of Christ.[69] According to David Aune, likewise, "an amazing correlation" can be found especially in chapters 13-17 of the gospel: "the character and function of Jesus is identical with the character and function of the followers of Jesus."[70]

This brings us to the promise that the disciples will do "greater works" than Jesus. It is not clear in what way the author understands the works of the believer to be greater than the works of Jesus. Scholars agree generally that the reference is not to more marvellous miracles.[71] A traditional opinion was that it referred to the missionary expansion of the church after the resurrection, a position which Schnackenburg, for example, accepts, though warning against a merely external understanding of the missionary success.[72] Bultmann rejects this meaning and argues that the point of comparison between the works of Jesus and that of the disciples is the potential for misunderstanding. In the work of the church, the work of Jesus is "protected from the misunderstanding that it is simply a historical phenomenon. Jesus' word is word of revelation in its continual newness on every occasion when it is present. Only when it is effective in this way in the community does Jesus' work come to its fruition. Thus there is no question here of supplementing or surpassing Jesus' work in any quantitive way."[73] The eschatological character of Jesus' work,

that is to say, its unlimited, final, significance becomes
clear in the work of the church.

What cannot be avoided, regardless of the interpretation
proposed, is that, taking the promise by itself, the agency of
the disciples is ranked, in some sense, above the agency of
Jesus. In order to gain perspective on the issue it is essential
to ask after the possible contexts and circumstances in the
early church in which the question of the relative ranking of
the work of Jesus and the work of the disciples might have
been raised.

One point on which there was comparison in the early
church had to do with just the issue touched on by Bultmann,
the relative clarity or freedom from misunderstanding in the
work of Jesus and the work of the disciples. James M. Robinson
in his article "On the *Gattung* of Mark (and John)" cites Wrede's
observation that common to Mark and John is the idea that "for
the disciples the resurrection separates two times, the time of
blindness and that of full knowledge."[74] Robinson suggests that
the so-called "messianic secret" in Mark was only one manifestation of this broader contrast, which Robinson prefers to describe
in hermeneutical terms as a contrast between "the obscure text
and its clarifying exposition."[75] According to Robinson, the
relative importance of the two times and two levels of teaching
became an issue dividing gnosticism and orthodoxy. "Gnosticism,"
he says, "preferred the exalted Christ, no doubt because he has
seen the heavens and is freed from a body, and hence is more
qualified to give gnostic revelations than was the earthly
Jesus."[76] This preference showed itself in the gospel form typica
of gnosticism, which consisted of revelations of the resurrected
or glorified Christ to his disciples.[77]

This gnostic position preserved a very early viewpoint
according to which the resurrection or exaltation meant a basic
shift from the situation prior to Easter:

> Early Christological fromulae such as Rom 1:3-4,
> Phil 2:6-11; Acts 2:36 reflect a change in Jesus'
> status, and the gift of the Spirit at this time
> (Acts 2:33; John 20:22) indicates a comparable
> change in the disciples' status. The location
> of the latter two references at the conclusion

of two of the Gospels (Luke and John), together
with the comparable conclusion of Matthew (28:18-
20), in which Jesus' new status of authority is
correlated with the disciples' new status as
missionaries, indicates that this basic awareness of primitive Christianity was constitutive
of the *terminus ad quem* for the canonical
Gospels. However the same basic awareness of
primitive Christianity could, differently
developed, become constitutive of the *terminus
a quo* for the gnostic Gospels.[78]

What is important for us in Robinson's discussion is the
inference that the contrast in "gospel" forms reflects a conflict over the relative rank of the revelations of the earthly
and the heavenly Jesus. This issue is suggested by Robinson's
observation that in Luke the "Easter shift is insured against
the possibility--exploited by gnosticism--of relegating to
insignificance the earthly life of Jesus, as just a lower and
hence irrelevant prelude."[79]

A *Sitz im Leben* for the ranking issue similar to that
derived from Robinson's analysis of orthodox versus "gnostic"
gospel forms can be reconstructed if we take the "greater works"
promise as the reflection of a community with a "charismatic
tradition of origin."[80] The portrait of the disciples which
can be drawn from the discourse in vs. 12ff. is a portrait of
charismatic figures. Their authority is derived from the
indwelling Spirit, and it is manifested in miracles and acts
of salvation and judgment. It is typical of charismatic
authorities to place themselves above tradition, to relativize
traditional authority. It is to be expected therefore that in
the Johannine community there may well have been charismatic
leaders who considered themselves on a par with Jesus or even
superior to him. The earthly Jesus would have become, for them,
a figure of the past, a voice of tradition. While acknowledging
his legitimacy, they would have, as charismatic authorities,
considered themselves to be representatives of new manifestations
of heavenly power and revelation.

Charismatic authority is inherently competitive and
divisive, not only in relation to traditional authorities, but
also in relation to other charismatic figures who are readily
perceived as rivals.[81] We suggest that the picture of the disciples as agents of greater works than those performed by Jesus

derives from the self-understanding of the leadership of such
a community.

On the other hand, having drawn from the discourse the
high view of the Johannine community and its leaders portrayed
above, it is necessary to observe that this is only one side
of the picture. In drawing that picture, we have been deliberately selective. The other side of the picture to which we now
turn our attention is the fact that the context of the promise
of "greater works," the discourse as a whole, clearly understands the disciples to be *subordinate* to the authority of Jesus.

The Subordination of the Disciples to
Jesus in vss. 12-24

The subordination is evident, in the first place, in the
language used to describe the successor-agent. He is "the one
who believes" in Jesus (14:12). Belief in Jesus, in John's
Gospel, means recognition that Jesus is the exclusive and pre-
eminent authority. The Spirit is given to those who "love"
Jesus and keep his commandments (14:15). "He who has my commandments and keeps them, that one loves me, and he who loves me
shall be loved by my Father . . ." (vs. 21). Again, in vs.
23 the promise of union with Father and Son is preceded by the
words, "If you love me you will keep my word," and is followed
by the negative formulation of the same truth: "the one who
does not love me does not keep my words" (vs. 24).

The successor is one who believes in Jesus, and loves
him, demonstrating his love by keeping his commandments. Four
times from vs. 15-24 the author reiterates the fact that the
successor-agent is the one who loves Jesus in the sense of
keeping his word or his commandments. The word *terein*, used
consistently (vs. 15,21,23,24), has not only the sense of "obey,"
but also the sense of submission to and preservation of a
tradition.[82] That the latter sense is present is evident from
the fact that according to 14:25, 26, the task of the Spirit
will be to "teach you all things and bring to your remembrance
all that I said to you."[83]

In the second place, the way in which the author describes the intercession of the disciple places remarkable stress upon the role of Jesus. In the first form of the promise (v. 13), the disciples pray in the name of Jesus and he, himself, answers their petition. In the second statement of the promise (vs. 14), the petition is in the *name* of Jesus, the petition is directed *to* Jesus, and Jesus, himself, *answers* the prayer: "if you ask *me* anything *in my name*, *I* will perform it!" According to Bultmann, "the wording, whereby the Father is so to speak by-passed has the effect in this context of guarding the promise of the *meizona erga* from the misunderstanding that the disciples stand alongside of Jesus, *independent* of him, on the grounds of their own relationship to God. God remains for them mediated by Jesus, and the point is made emphatically by stating that it is he who will hear their prayer."[84]

The mediated status of the disciples' authority is, in fact, the central point of the whole section of the discourse under discussion. In vss. 12-17 it is expressed by the very fact that they are appointed to their position as successors by Jesus himself, and by the fact that their work is to continue to do Jesus' work (vs. 12). The Spirit which they receive is sent because of the intercession of Christ. In vss. 18-24 it is expressed by identifying the Spirit that is sent as, in fact, Christ himself in the form of the Spirit. The very life of the disciple, understood as the life of heaven, new life, is based upon the prior possession of life by Jesus: "Because I live, you also shall live" (v. 19). Likewise, the union of the disciple with the Father is mediated by the Son: "In that day you shall know that I (am) in the Father and you (are) in me and I (am) in you" (vs. 20).

This last statement recalls the earlier claim made by Jesus on behalf of himself in vs. 10, repeated in vs. 11, concerning his exclusive position of union with the Father. Jesus' claim in these two verses was made as the basis for his prior claim, in vss. 6-9, to be the exclusive agent of access to the Father. The connection between Jesus' union with the Father and his performance of his works is explicit in Jesus' statement, in vs. 10, that "the Father who dwells in me does his works."

Two verses later Jesus tells the disciples that they will do the works which he, Jesus does, which means, in light of vs. 10, the Father's works, since Jesus' works are the works of the Father. If, however, Jesus' performance of the Father's works depends upon his position of union with the Father, how can the disciples do his works unless they share in Jesus' relation to the Father. And if Jesus' position in relation to the Father is unique, how can they be said to share it?

What we find in vs. 20 is that the disciples do in fact share in Jesus' union with the Father, but their union with the Father is *mediated* by Jesus. Verse 20 expresses a *hierarchy*, in which the disciples, while clearly drawn into union with the Father, are subordinated to the Son, who alone stands in *direct* relation to the Father. The Son occupies the central place between Father and disciple.[85]

One of the fundamental structural elements of the first farewell discourse is to be found, I suggest, in the extension of the formula of reciprocal indwelling of Father and Son, in vss. 10 and 11, to include the disciples, in vs. 20. This movement should be accorded the same attention, in future discussions of the discourse, as the movement from the *monai pollai* in 14:2 to the *mone* in 14:23. It pulls together the agency of Jesus, set forth in vss. 4-11, with the agency of the disciples, set forth in vss. 12-23.

The Conflict Over Authority

The disciples appear in vss. 12-24 in a double light. On the one hand, they are clearly placed in a subordinate position to the Son, the speaker. On the other hand, they are accorded a remarkably high position, as successors to Jesus. The high status accorded the disciples stands out in stark contrast to the prevailing christocentrism of the Gospel which allows no possibility of a rival to the exclusive position of the Son. What calls for explanation in particular is the author's inclusion of the promise that the disciples will do greater works, a statement which at a minimum was in danger of being misunderstood as assigning to the disciples a higher rank than that accorded

Jesus. Why would the author have included a statement which suggested the exact opposite of that which the rest of the discourse clearly intends to say?

An answer is suggested in the question. That is to say, the author regarded the statement as safe from misunderstanding by the very fact that it was placed in a context which was intended to preclude such a misunderstanding. This suggests, however, the further inference, that the author regarded it as impossible to leave out the promise of greater works, and the promise of the Spirit as another Paraclete. We are suggesting, in other words, that these promises were *a given* of the author's community and were too important a part of the self-understanding of the community to be left out. The author had no choice but to address the highest boast of his own community, because of what he regarded as dangerous misunderstandings to which it had given rise, in order to counteract such misunderstandings by his own critical interpretation of the boast. The purpose of the discourse was to counter what the author preceived as a misunderstanding of the relationship of the community leadership to Jesus by making it clear that the leadership of the community was subordinate to Jesus.

It will be helpful to continue to use Jürgen Becker's analysis as a foil with which to compare my analysis. According to Becker, the purpose of the discourse is to counter what the author regarded as a false eschatology which looked for Christ to appear in the future leaving the present "empty" of his presence. This false future eschatology was understood by Becker to be the *given* tradition of the author's community which he intended to correct by the farewell discourse. The given tradition was, according to Becker, included in the discourse, in 14:2-3.

According to the understanding of the discourse which I am proposing, there is, as with Becker, a critical or polemical edge against a given tradition of the community. However, the tradition which the author is interpreting or reinterpreting comes to expression not in 14:2-3, but in 14:12-17, the boast of the believer-prophets to be Jesus' successors, performing

"greater works," by the power of the Spirit, the successor to
the figure of Jesus past.

The author's answer to the charismatic "boasting" of
his opponents is to interpret the Spirit as the returning Jesus,
so that the earthly Jesus in effect becomes his own successor
working in his followers, who thereby become subordinate agents.
The Jesus who comes in the Spirit is inescapably identified with
the past figure of Jesus. Within the context of the discourse
as a whole, in fact, the author has taken what the opponents
have boasted of, their possession of the Spirit, and turned it
into evidence of their subordination to and dependence upon the
Son. The authority of the Son is based upon his direct and
original access to the Father, to the heavenly world from which
he alone has descended. The authority of the disciples, by
contrast, is derived from the descent of the Son, in the form of
the Spirit, not from their own ascent to heaven. Looking back
from this vantage point to the beginning of the discourse, the
sharp logion in 13:33 appears to be evidence of such a polemic,
perhaps directed against ascent claims on the part of Christian
prophets similar to the polemic which has been proposed in
Jn 3:13.[86] According to 13:33, Jesus alone ascends. The
disciples do not. The ascent of Jesus which, according to some,
rendered him a figure of the past and therefore cf less importance than the contemporary figures through whom the power of the
Spirit was manifested, is interpreted by the author as the
triumphal demonstration of the unique authority, power, and
rank of the Jesus of the tradition, who is identical with the
Jesus present in the Spirit.

It should not be overlooked that the discourse sets forth
the subordination of the believer-disciple to Jesus along two
dimensions, vertical and horizontal, so to speak. It is not
sufficient to understand the hierarchy as simply vertical, the
dimension which is to the fore in vs. 20, for example. The
succession relationship into which the disciples are so explicitly brought constitutes a horizontal hierarchy, in which
the disciple-believer is subordinated to the Jesus of the
tradition. This aspect comes to the fore especially in vss. 25,
26 of the discourse, to which we turn in the next chapter.

CHAPTER V

THE PLACE OF THE DISCIPLES IN RELATION
TO THE SON, THE WORDS (14:25, 26)

The final two verses of the discourse, before the
benediction of peace in 14:27, form a sort of coda.[1] The
author returns to the subject of the Paraclete with the promise
that the Paraclete "will teach you everything and recall to you
everything I have said to you" (14:25, 26). The promise as a
whole consists of two main clauses. Jesus is the subject of
the verb in the first clause: "I have said these things to you
while abiding with you." The Paraclete is the subject of the
two main verbs in the second clause: "But the Paraclete, the
Holy Spirit the Father will send in my name, he will teach
you everything and recall to you everything I have said to you."

The focus of attention is upon *the words* spoken by Jesus,
recalled by the Paraclete. The contrast between Jesus as the
one who will soon be gone and the Spirit who will then come to
remain "forever" (14"16) is stark, deliberately underscored by
the qualifying phrase *par humin menon*, which recalls the wording
of the promise of the Paraclete in 14:17 (*par humin menei*).
Jesus' stay, his *menein* on earth, is temporary. It comes to an
end.

"I have spoken these things while dwelling with you."
"These things" refer in the first place to the farewell discourse, but cannot be limited to that discourse. The author has
in view the whole of the now completed testimony of Jesus: "all
that I have said to you." The promise has to do with the fate
of Jesus' testimony after he is gone. His words will not be
forgotten and left behind in the past without effect. After he
is gone the successor figure of the Paraclete will keep his
words alive in the memory of the disciples. Just as the *works*
of Jesus will continue to be performed after he is gone by the
disciples, according to vs. 12, so the *words* of Jesus will
continue to be remembered (and spoken, we may infer) by them.
Succession remains the subject in these two verses.

97

The importance of this second Paraclete promise lies
in the reference to the remembering activity of the Spirit.
The explicit ascription of a remembering role to the Spirit has
no parallel elsewhere in the New Testament,[2] which suggests
that it should be taken into account as evidence of a distinctive concern in the Johannine conception of the Spirit.[3] The
focusing of the role of the Spirit, the symbol par excellence
of charisma, on the activity of recalling an authoritative
tradition (all that Jesus has said) makes this promise a crux
for understanding the point of view of the author on the
question of authority.

The Remembering Motif in the Gospel

The remembering motif occurs three other times in John,
twice in the account of the cleansing of the temple (2:17, 22),
and again in the story of the triumphal entry (12:16).[4] It is
noteworthy that in each of these three occurrences there is a
reference to the Jewish Scriptures. In 2:17, after Jesus'
violent action in driving out the money-changers from "my
father's house," the author makes the following observation:
"his disciples remembered (*emnesthesan*) the words of Scripture:
'The zeal of your house will consume me.'" According to
Schnackenburg, the reference is to Jesus' death.[5] The quotation
is from Ps 68:10 (LXX) with the verb changed to the future
tense. The Synoptic accounts have Jesus' quoting from Scripture
the words, "Is it not written, 'My house shall be called a house
of prayer for all the nations?' But you have made it a den of
robbers" (Mark 11:17). And this is followed, in Mark, by the
report that "the chief priests and the scribes heard it and
sought a way to destroy him" (Mk 11:18, cf. Lk 19:47).

John does not have Jesus quoting from Scripture explicitly.
Instead he has the disciples *remembering* Scripture, in the sense
of understanding that the Scripture word is fulfilled in Jesus'
action. It becomes clear, in the hostile dialogue which follows,
that the remembering and understanding occur later, after Jesus
departure.

The Jews demand a sign, as evidence of Jesus' authority
to act as he has done in the temple. Jesus replies, "Destroy
this temple and in three days I will raise it up." The Jews
"misunderstand" the saying as a reference to the actual temple
built by Herod. The author adds an interpretive comment to the
reader; Jesus was referring to "the temple of his body." The
author goes on to add another editorial comment which appears
to mean that the disciples did not understand Jesus until after
the resurrection: "When therefore he was raised from the dead,
his disciples remembered that he had said this; and they
believed the scripture and the word which Jesus had spoken"
(2:22). It is clear that after the resurrection the disciples
"remember" Jesus' saying *as a prophecy of the resurrection*.
Only then do they realize *what Jesus meant*. The hostile Jews
never understand what Jesus meant. The disciples, like the
Jews, do not understand at the time Jesus' words were spoken,
but they "remember" and understand later. The reader is let in
on the meaning as he reads.

In this second reference to the remembering motif (2:22),
it is again connected to the Scripture. The result of the disciples' post-resurrection illumination is faith: "they believed
the Scripture and the word which Jesus had spoken." The conjunction between the Scripture and the word of Jesus is noteworthy. It is not clear whether *te graphe* refers to the specific
citation in vs. 17 or to the whole of the Old Testament.[6]
Certainly the specific citation in vs. 17 is included. Thus
after the resurrection the disciples remember the Scripture
(cited in vs. 17), and the word of Jesus (vs. 19), realize
that they refer to Jesus' death and resurrection, and find in
this understanding a confirmation of the truth of both. But it
is events of Jesus' life which confirm Scripture, according to
the author, not vice versa.

The third remembering text, 12:16, exhibits the same
elements. The author observes explicitly that Jesus' entry into
Jerusalem, seated on a young ass, was in fulfillment of prophecy:
"even as it is written" (12:14). The disciples' failure to
understand the connection with the Old Testament prophesy at
the time is even more pointedly underscored in this case.

"These things his disciples did not understand (*egnosan*) at
first (*to proton*), but when Jesus was glorified, then they
remembered that these things had been written about him and that
they did these things to him." The author's point of view on
the fulfillment of Scripture comes into clear focus. The fact
that the Old Testament bears witness to Jesus' coming and his
departure is taken for granted (cf. 5:46; 12:41), so that what
the historian understands as the process by which the early
church, following the resurrection, *came to interpret* the Old
Testament in a new light is viewed by the author as something
quite different. From the *author's* point of view the act of
(re)interpretation of Scripture as prophecy of Jesus is an act
of *remembering. The early church acquired a new memory of
Scripture*, one shaped by their experience of Jesus' appearance.

The reference to the remembering motif in 14:26 differs
from the three earlier occurrences in certain respects. In the
first place, it differs formally in that it is not an editorial
comment by the author explaining what happened later, but a
promise placed on the lips of Jesus foretelling what is going
to happen. It does not refer to a particular event together
with the Scripture which is fulfilled thereby but is general in
nature. The Paraclete will remind the disciples of everything
Jesus has said. Thirdly, there is no reference to the Old
Testament Scriptures as that which is remembered. Finally, the
remembering is specifically attributed to the agency of the
Spirit.

These differences should not, however, obscure the fact
that the specific instances of "remembering" noted earlier in
the narrative are to be understood in light of the general
promise in the farewell discourse, so that the earlier references
may be used to understand the farewell promise. With this in
view we may understand the teaching and remembering to be
closely related, in fact, as aspects of one and the same
activity. In *reminding* the disciples of all Jesus has said,
the Spirit at the same time causes them to *understand* what "at
first" (12:16) they did not understand.[7]

The Function of the Remembering Motif

What is the function of the remembering motif within the Gospel? Why does the author underscore the fact that the disciples did not understand until after the resurrection? Why at the end of the farewell discourse does he refer again to the Paraclete and describe the Paraclete's function as teaching and recalling Jesus' words?

Some have found in the remembering motif the expression of the inferiority of the time of the earthly appearance of Jesus. On this view the words of the earthly Jesus were obscure, open to misunderstanding, and dependent upon the coming of the Spirit after the resurrection for full illumination. This point of view appears to be expressed in such a promise as 16:25: "I have said this to you in parables; the hour is coming when I shall no longer speak to you in parables but tell you openly of the Father."[8]

In evaluating this interpretation of the remembering motif we must first ask what is in fact the issue being addressed by the author. Focusing our attention on the most general, programmatic reference to the remembering motif, in 14:25,26, we must look back to the farewell discourse as the immediate context, to identify the issue. We have attempted to show that the central issue of the discourse is the relationship between the authority of Jesus and the authority of the disciples. We have argued that Jesus is depicted as occupying a position and rank which is exclusive and supreme, and that the disciples are depicted as successor-agents of Jesus, subordinate to him, and dependent upon him.

If we read the promise in 14:25,26 in this light, we must conclude that the issue being addressed is, in fact, the status and rank of the message of the disciples in relation to the tradition of Jesus. But it is also clear that the point of the promise is not the inferiority of the earlier, obscure, tradition to the later, interpreted and inspired teaching, but the opposite, namely, the subordination of the post-resurrection teaching of the disciples to the Jesus tradition. *The obscurity and misunderstanding encountered by Jesus' teaching is a sign,*

not of its inferior, earthly character, but of its heavenly,
other-worldly origin. The fact that the disciples do not understand what he is saying "at first," but must await the coming
of the Spirit is evidence of their subordinate status in relation to Jesus, who, from the beginning, knows all things. The
life of Jesus has become, in this Gospel, an account which
begins "in the beginning." The time of Jesus' earthly appearance has become invested, in this way, with the absolute
primacy of cosmogonic time.[9]

In 14:25,26 the subordination of the disciples to Jesus
is expressed in the fact that for the disciples truth is
mediated by means of the words spoken by Jesus in the past.
The disciples have access to the truth by means of the indwelling Spirit, the Spirit of Jesus himself, but the Spirit teaches
them all things by reminding them of all that the departed Son
has said. Verses 25, 26 in this way develop the motif of
obedience to the "commandments" of Jesus and faithfulness to the
"words" of Jesus which occur in the farewell discourse from
vs. 14 on.[10]

In speaking of the subordination of the word of the
disciples to the Jesus tradition, particular care must be taken
in understanding the word "tradition."[11] The words *hupomnesko*
and *mimnesko* involve an explicit looking back, a "retrospective"
point of view.[12] But, as we have pointed out before, a distinction must be made between using the past and ascribing to
tradition a binding, overriding authority. We have found a
looking back to the past on the part of John's Jesus which
relativizes its authority, as is the case with Jesus' references
to Abraham in 8:58 and to Moses in chapter 5. We have found a
retrospective appeal on the part of Jesus which constitutes one
expression of his claim to charismatic authority; that is,
Jesus' claim to pre-existence with the Father is the basis of
his claim to unique authority, as we have seen. It would be
altogether misleading to call this appeal to "traditional"
authority. The past typically influences the present, in John,
in the form of the predetermining role of paternity. In the
controversy in John 8 over freedom the Jews make the claim, "We

are descendants of Abraham, and have never been in bondage to
any one" (8:33). Jesus acknowledges the principle, "If you
were Abraham's children, you would do what Abraham did" (39),
but proceeds to argue that their deeds prove them to be of
different paternity: *humeis ek tou patros tou diabolou este.*
Nils Dahl has marshalled convincing evidence that the reference
here is to Cain as the "father" Jesus is speaking of.[13] Cain
was regarded in Jewish and early Christian circles not only as
the first murderer but also as the arch heretic. Dahl suggests
that Jesus is here accusing the "Jews" of belonging to an
heretical tradition.[14] Similarly, the epithet, "you are a
Samaritan," which Jesus' opponents apply to him, also signified
"heretic."[15] John 8, in other words, reflects a controversy
between conflicting traditions. The word "tradition" cannot
be used abstractly. We must ask, *Which* tradition? There are
"false" traditions and "correct" traditions.

The conflict addressed (according to this paper) in the
farewell discourse is to be understood, similarly, as a conflict
between alternative traditions. In this case, however, the
conflicting traditions are both Christian, in contrast to what
is ostensibly the case in John 8.[16] What is in view in John
14:25,26 is not "tradition" in general, "tradition" as an
abstract principle, but, quite specifically, the Jesus
tradition of the community as interpreted by the author, in
contrast to the alternative interpretation of the tradition
which he views as usurping prerogatives which belong only to
Jesus. What is in view in 14:26 is, in other words, the record
in the Fourth Gospel itself.

That the author has in view his own work as a product
of the Spirit's recollecting agency was suggested by Windisch.[17]
Bultmann follows Windisch, noting that "it is also correct to
see this as the Evangelist's justification of his own work."[18]
Ulrich B. Müller argues likewise that the Fourth Gospel itself
fulfills the function of remembering the words of Jesus and
that by attributing the remembering function to the Spirit the
author is legitimating what he is doing. "He wrote the Gospel,
but in doing so recalled, with emphasis, the words of Jesus.
This happened, we must conclude, in full consciousness of doing
something that, according to 14:26, was a function of the Spirit.

Therefore his book has become the Spirit-gospel (*Geistev-angelium*), the legitimated form of the revelation of Jesus."[19]

Müller attempts to show, in support of this interpretation, that in Jewish literature, the farewell discourse functioned typically for the purpose of legitimating sacred writings.[20] He overstates his case, however, by formulating it too narrowly in terms of a form critical comparison which does not hold up. For instance, 4 Ezra 14, which he cites as an example of a farewell speech, is, rather, a narrative account of Ezra's commission to write ninety-four books. What is narrated is, to be sure, a farewell scene. It even includes a farewell speech by Ezra to the people (4 Ezra 14:27-36). As a narrative record of Ezra's farewell, however, it cannot be cited as a formal parallel to a farewell *discourse*. On the other hand, one central purpose of this narrative of Ezra's commission by God and inspiration by the Spirit is, in fact, the legitimation of his writing(s).

A second example cited by Müller is 2 Peter.[21] Here, as in John 14:26, the concern is explicitly with "remembering" a tradition (2 Peter 1:13-15; 3:1-2). The "letter" is in fact the "testament" of Peter, since its purpose is to provide a lasting body of teachings and exhortations which will be available after Peter's departure (2 Pet. 1:15).[22] Again, however, 2 Peter cannot be taken as a formal parallel to the farewell discourse in John. The reference to his departure does not make "Peter's" letter a farewell address. He in fact refers to an earlier letter which served the same purpose of "reminding" the brethren of his teaching. Both cannot be farewell addresses or letters. At the same time, the reference to the departure does contribute to the legitimation of the letter as a record of sacred teaching by indicating that this function was in view in "Peter's" mind when he wrote the letter.

The parallels Müller cites do show a connection between departure situations and the legitimating of sacred writings. The departure of a figure of authority was often cited as the occasion for the recording of his teachings, and, as in the case of 4 Ezra, the description of the farewell scene could include explicit details of the circumstances of the writing down of the record to prove its divine source.

There is reason, therefore, to consider one function of the farewell discourse to be the legitimating of an author's work by appeal to the Spirit. It would be unwarranted to *restrict* the reference to the author's work alone, as if it were the *only* expression of the Spirit's reminding work. It is likely that the author viewed his work as a faithful record of the tradition of his community. At the same time, however, I suggest that he viewed his work as something more, namely, as an authoritative, *controlling* record of the tradition over against false interpretations of it.

To summarize, John 14:25,26 completes the teaching on succession, which has been the central theme of the discourse, by making it clear that the disciple-successor is subordinate to the Jesus of the "tradition" *as that tradition is understood by the author*.

PART II
THE FIRST FAREWELL DISCOURSE AND
JOHANNINE CHRISTIANITY

CHAPTER VI

THE CHARISMATIC COMMUNITY AND THE
PARADIGMATIC PAST

The central issue which has been raised by the analysis of
the first farewell discourse presented above is the plausibility
of the conflict over authority postulated as the *Sitz im Leben*
of the discourse. In the concluding part of this study I wish
to focus directly on this issue. In doing so I am attempting
to say something about the Christian community or group represented by the Gospel. The difficulties attending such an
enterprise have been sadistically emphasized by practically
every scholar who has addressed the matter. Yet, as has been
equally emphasized, it is an issue which cannot be avoided. It
is "the great unsolved problem in Johannine studies with which
almost all other problems are closely linked."[1] If not
addressed directly, it is addressed implicitly by anyone who
attempts to interpret the Gospel.

The need to address the issue explicitly has been
increasingly acknowledged in recent years. According to Charles
Scobie, "the quest for the Johannine community has become central
in Fourth Gospel studies."[2] Among the most important recent
works engaging in this quest we may note the articles by Wayne
A. Meeks, D. Moody Smith Jr., James M. Robinson, Charles
Scobie's own unpublished paper, the dissertation by Richard
Culpepper on *The Johannine School*, monographs by Ernst Käsemann,
Oscar Cullmann, Louis Martyn, and, somewhat earlier (1959), the
study by Alv Kragerud.[3]

This is not the place to review in detail all of this
literature. Some of the scholars referred to are concerned
with tracing the sequence of stages from which the Johannine
form of Christianity emerged.[4] Others are more concerned with
describing its particular character in contrast to other forms
of early Christianity.[5] D. Moody Smith's article is a judicious
attempt to point to "significant patterns and points of coinci-
dence" in what seems to be a "trackless morass" of scholarship.[6]

109

Scobie's article, like Smith's, draws on a wide range of approaches and methods to produce a coherent, detailed view of the development of the Johannine community. In what follows we must confine ourselves to noting only those points most pertinent to the present argument.

In the first place, a number of scholars writing recently have emphasized the "sectarianism" reflected in Johannine literature. According to D. Moody Smith, "it can probably be agreed that on any reading of the Gospels and Epistles there appears a sectarian consciousness, a sense of exclusiveness, a sharp delineation of the community from the world."[7] However, as Smith goes on to point out, it is not as clear what the "roots, causes and social matrix" of this sectarianism are. "What thereby comes to expression? A Christian sense of alienation or separation from the world generally? From the Synagogue? From developing eccesiastical orthodoxy?"[8] Herbert Leroy, for example, argues that the Gospel is characterized significantly by the use of in-language, a *Sondersprache* belonging to a closed, esoteric circle.[9] For Wayne Meeks the sectarian consciousness means, as we have seen, "transfer to a community which has totalistic and exclusive claims."[10] It is also not clear what "sectarianism" means with reference to the social organization of the Johannine community, its understanding of leadership and authority.

In the second place, many scholars emphasize in various ways the importance of the "prophetic" or "charismatic" or "pneumatic" or "enthusiastic" element. J. Ramsey Michaels, in a paper entitled "The Johannine Words of Jesus and Christian Prophecy,"[11] calls the Johannine circle "a prophetic community," and "a pneumatic community," though acknowledging that "whatever 'prophetic' characteristics may be associated with Jesus' disciples in the Fourth Gospel are carefully limited and qualified."[12] According to Ernst Käsemann, the author of John, "at the very centre of his proclamation, is dominated by a heritage of enthusiasm against which Paul had already struggled violently in his day and which in the post-apostolic age was branded as heretical."[13] "It is not at all sufficiently emphasized," Käsemann says, "that John must be seen in the historical and theological context of a Christian prophecy whose characteristic feature, according to 1 Cor. 14, is the actualization of the Christian proclamation."[14] While "tradition is absolutely necessary" in John, nevertheless, "the peculiar feature of the Johannine use of tradition . . . is that he deals with what he has received more freely and more vigorously than anyone else in the New Testament."[15]

D. Moody Smith suggests that "charismatic prophetic activity likely played a significant role in the development of Johannine tradition,"[16] and was probably one of the elements "constitutive of the Johannine Eigenart."[17] The discourses of Jesus in John were "obviously spoken from the standpoint of a spirit-inspired post-resurrection community," he observes, citing also the Paraclete promises as evidence in this connection.[18] Smith points to the demand in 1 John to test the spirits in the face of false prophets as evidence that the First Epistle of John faces "a situation in which spirit-inspired prophets uttering words of the risen Lord have become a distinct problem in the church." If this is the case "this would be exactly the development one might have anticipated" on the basis of the Gospel evidence.[19] Smith also points to the miracles in John as evidence of charismatic origins. Citing the work that has been done by D. Georgi and others on the opponents of Paul in II Corinthians 10-13, Smith concludes, "When all cautions and reservations are allowed for . . . it is still tempting to see in Paul's Jewish-Christian Corinthian opponents, with their charismatic excesses, their interest in miracles, and possibly their conviction that the heavenly world was already opening out before them close relatives of these early Christians responsible for the miracle tradition of John's Gospel."[20]

Smith's emphasis on the charismatic origin of the community is all the more significant in light of the fact that his purpose, in the article cited, is to adduce evidence of a community (or communities) "with some stability, with which it has been endowed in part by its continuity with the past."[21] In other words, Smith's purpose is to show that the Johannine literature reflects a community with a tradition. Smith

properly sees no contradiction between the charismatic activity
which appears to be characteristic of this community and the
notion that it had its own tradition. Smith acknowledges that
the Johannine Jesus is "in large part a Jesus distilled from
the confession and controversies of the Johannine church,"
but points out that this does not necessarily militate *against*
the traditional nature of the material "*since the questions of
historical authenticity and traditional character are altogether
distinct.*"[22] In this connection it is particularly important to
note Smith's conclusion regarding the Paraclete sayings in
14:15f. and 16:12-15. He sees in them "the enunciation of a
theory concerning the phenomenon of spirit-inspired utterance
intended on the one hand to ground it in Jesus' own historic
ministry, and thus to validate it (14:26), and on the other to
set some control over it by placing it within the context of a
portrayal of Jesus who was not only the word become flesh, but
one who spoke words with the irrevocable status of divine
commandments."[23]

The Charismatic Tradition of Origin

At this point we must ask how useful the term "charismatic"
is in describing the Johannine group. Our particular interest
is in what can be said about the social organization of the
group and the dynamics of the social situation reflected in the
Gospel. The term "charismatic" draws attention to the aspect
of authority, together with the related issues of power,
legitimation, rank, and prestige. We shall draw upon the sociological literature on authority relations within groups to bring
into focus the way we are using the term "charismatic authority,"
and the related terms. One of the advantages of using a category like "charismatic authority" is the amount of effort which
has been devoted by sociologists to its conceptual clarification
For the non-specialist this creates in its turn a problem of
critically evaluating the alternative positions put forward by
sociologists. We shall take the recent discussion of Michael
Hill in *A Sociology of Religion* as a guide in what follows.[24]

Three features of charismatic authority will be emphasized. In the first place, charismatic authority is understood to be innovative, revolutionary. According to Max Weber, "the genuine prophet, like the genuine military leader and every true leader in this sense, preaches, creates, or demands *new* obligations." "From a substantive point of view," Weber observes, "every charismatic authority would have to subscribe to the proposition, 'It is written . . . ., but I say unto you. . . .'"[25] The newness is described by Weber, in the first instance, over against what is *routine* and *profane*. "Charismatic authority is . . . specifically outside the realm of every-day routine and the profane sphere. In this respect, it is sharply opposed both to rational, and particularly bureaucratic, authority, and to traditional authority, whether in its patriarchal, patrimonial, or any other form. Both rational and traditional authority are specifically forms of every-day routine control of action; while the charismatic type is the direct antithesis of this."[26] The contrast with the routine involves, further, an opposition to rules and precedents. "Charismatic authority is specifically irrational in the sense of being foreign to all rules. . . . Within the sphere of its claims, charismatic authority repudiates the past, and is in this sense a specifically revolutionary force."[27]

Michael Hill underscores this feature of charismatic authority. "Above all," he says, "charisma is a source of new ideas and obligations."[28] Hill illustrates this by the vivid example of the career of Jan Bockelson, the messianic leader of the Anabaptists of Münster in 1534. Bockelson's first important act was to run naked through the town of Münster in a frenzy, after which he fell into a silent ecstasy which lasted three days.[29] Hill comments: "Bockelson's tactic of establishing a charismatic claim included denuding himself--the pun is not entirely inappropriate--of all other symbols of authority. The anti-institutional character of charismatic leadership is well demonstrated in this case by the initial break with traditional channels of authority."[30]

Hill's interpretation of Bockelson's nudity needs to be modified in light of the fact that his nudity was a very archaic symbol wholly in the public domain.[31] It is therefore misleading to suggest that the nudity symbolized the discarding of all symbols of authority. On the other hand, Bockelson's act did signal a claim to direct divine inspiration as the authority for his subsequent legislation.[32] It represented a claim to authority outside of the routine, officially recognized channels of authority *of his day*. The innovative character of charismatic authority has to be defined *in relation* to the specific social and cultural context in which the prophet appears, and in relation to the specific time he appears.

We may clarify this point further by drawing on a distinction which Peter Brown makes in his article, "Sorcery, Demons and the Rise of Christianity: From Late Antiquity into the Middle Ages." Brown distinguishes between two "systems of power," articulate and inarticulate. "Articulate" power is "power defined and agreed upon by everyone (and especially by its holders!): authority vested in precise persons; admiration and success gained by *recognized* channels."[33] Over against such power "there may be other forms of influence less easy to pin down--*inarticulate* power: the disturbing intangibles of social life; the imponderable advantages of certain groups; personal skills that succeed in a way that is unacceptable or difficult to understand. Where these two systems overlap, we may expect to find the sorcerer."[34] Using Brown's language, I would suggest that the charismatic figure stands outside the system of power "defined and agreed upon by everyone," either because he does not occupy recognized office, or because he has gone beyond the recognized and accepted boundaries of his office.

The charismatic figure claims direct, unmediated authority from the divine source of power and authority. Such a claim may be seen as one form of "inarticulate" power since it bypasses the channels of authority which belong to the system of power defined and agreed upon by everyone. It constitutes, so to speak, a "short circuit," from the point of view of articulate power. It is a usurpation of powers of access which is potentially threatening. Typically, the charismatic figure's claim to authority is, as we have seen, on behalf of new obligations, new *in relation to the prevailing structure of order*, so that there is a challenge to the direction or limits of the officially recognized system of power. The claim to direct inspiration

from "god" or the gods, or the Spirit is, to be sure, an act
which acknowledges the basic traditional source of authority,
namely, the divine. But it is independent of the routine
mediators of tradition and therefore also typically takes the
form of reviving archaic, unfamiliar or esoteric traditions.

A second feature of charismatic authority stressed by
Weber is the focus on the individual person. Charismatic
authority, he says, rests on "devotion to the specific and
exceptional sanctity, heroism or exemplary character of an
individual person, and of the normative patterns or order revealed or ordained by him."[35] Weber points out that in the
traditional authority type, obedience may be owed to the person
of the chief who occupies the traditionally sanctioned position
of authority and the obligation of obedience is a matter of
"personal loyalty within the area of accustomed obligations."
In the case of charismatic authority, however, "it is the
charismatically qualified leader *as such* who is obeyed by virtue
of personal trust in him and his revelation, his heroism or his
exemplary qualities so far as they fall within the scope of the
individual's belief in his charisma."[36] Michael Hill likewise
notes that "traditional authority *shares* with charismatic
authority the feature of a personal capacity on the part of the
leader to define for himself the limits of the obligations owed
to him by his followers--the difference between tradition and
charisma being that in the former the leader's scope in this
respect is *limited* while in the latter, theoretically at least,
it is not."[37]

In a classic passage Weber uses the word "personality"
("*Persönlichkeit*") in defining "charisma":

> The term "charisma" will be applied to a certain
> quality of an individual personality by virtue of
> which he is set apart from ordinary men and treated
> as endowed with supernatural, superhuman, or at
> least specifically exceptional powers or qualities.
> These are such as are not accessible to the ordinary
> person, but are regarded as of divine origin or as
> exemplary, and on the basis of them the individual
> concerned is treated as a leader.[38]

This passage has been the basis for the popular use of the term
"charisma" which essentially reifies the notion of charismatic
qualities or the charismatic personality. According to Peter

Worsley, however, charisma is "*not* an attribute of an individual personality or a mystical quality." It is a social relationship, a "function of recognition" on the part of followers, who follow not simply because of some abstract "mystical" quality but because the leader evokes or plays upon some strand of intellectual or emotional predisposition in the followers, and because he purports to offer the realization of certain values in action. The leader is followed "because he embodies values in which the followers have an 'interest.'"[39]

Michael Hill takes issue with Worsley's view that the original attribution of charisma is largely determined by the interests of the followers, seeing in this a restricted notion of charismatic innovation.[40] However, Hill agrees with Worsley on the essential point, the *relational* character of "charisma."[41] Charisma, in other words, does not exist apart from the recognition and acceptance of followers. Worsley's statement that the charismatic leader "is singularly dependent upon being accepted by his followers" is echoed in Hill's view that "no leader can be labelled charismatic unless he is accredited with the possession of such a quality by his followers."[42] "Recognition," says Hill, "is the relational aspect of charismatic authority, because what one 'population' may recognize as a charismatic qualification (epilepsy, for instance) another may recognize as an illness that required treatment."[43]

Hill goes on to argue that Weber himself intended the term charisma to be used as a category of sociological analysis rather than as a reference to an inherent psychological trait. Hill's remarks must be quoted in full. In "his most rigorous formulation of the concept of charisma, says Hill,

> Weber made an even more explicit step away from the individualistic conception when he referred to it as the "quality of a personality" (*Qualität einer Persön-lichkeit*), indicating an abstract category rather than a "person," a concrete individual. He also qualifies his definition by stating that charisma is a quality "believed to be extraordinary" (*als ausseralltäglich* [sic!] *geltend*). The emphasis in these phrases is clearly towards a sociological construction rather than to some vague, quasi-mystical conception of "Great Men" in history.[44]

What is involved, to put it another way, is the difference between the viewpoint of the insider and the outsider. From the point of view of the insider it is precisely the extraordinary quality, attribute, or "gift" of the charismatic leader which is all important. From the point of view of the outside observer, on the other hand, it is the *attribution* which is definitive of the charismatic leader.

In talking about charismatic authority, then, we are talking about a particular type of social relationship, situation, and group. The charismatic situation is one in which, for a particular group, authority is concentrated in a single individual who stands outside the dominant, articulate system of power, or who has gone beyond the recognized boundaries of his position.

The third feature to which we wish to call attention is the crisis of succession and routinization that follows the death or departure of a charismatic leader if the followers are to continue as a group. The process "through which an *audience* becomes a *following*, then a *movement*, and finally an *organization*" is, it should be noted, only one possible outcome of the disappearance of a prophet.[45] The focus of Weber himself and much subsequent scholarship on the process of routinization has tended to obscure, perhaps, the fact that a variety of other outcomes are possible. For one thing, the followers of the prophet may disperse. Michael Hill points out that the charismatic power may be "blocked" by the cult of the dead leader, for example, or by other events such as the restriction of charismatic power to the original group of disciples."[46]

What comes to expression in the crisis of succession are, in Weber's words, "the ideal and also the material interests of the followers in the continuation and the continual reactivation of the community."[47] It is true of course that succession can be problematic in the case of traditional and legal or rational types of authority. In the case of charismatic authority, however, succession is inevitably a problem, since charisma involves the attribution of *exceptional* powers or qualities to one person as an individual. Any provision made for transferring that authority to another individual or group modifies, to that extend, the exceptional quality of that authority, and tends to transform it from an authority received directly from the divine to an authority *mediated* by the original figure. The nature of charismatic authority seems to militate against succession, whereas the interests of the group formed by the leader require succession.

This paradox may be illuminated if we distinguish between the relationship of the charismatic leader to the larger society and his relationship to the group of followers. On the one hand, the prophet has stepped outside of the routines of the larger society by which authority is transferred. His claim to authority is exceptional in relation to the prevailing structure of power. On the other hand, if the new group is to continue a means of transferring authority must be instituted within the group.

It should be clear that the first and third features to which we have called attention, namely, innovation and succession crisis may be viewed as expressions of the second feature, the concentration of extraordinary authority upon an outsider. The innovative aspect expresses this concentration over against the articulate system of power. The succession crisis is an expression of the same in relation to the group of followers. If we follow the logic of this conception a step further we can say that charismatic authority tends to stand in *exclusive* association only with the original prophet. We take this to be a legitimate inference from Weber's statement that in its pure form charismatic authority may be said to exist "only in the process of originating."

At the same time, it is, perhaps, even more important to emphasize that the charismatic concentration of authority *occurs within the context of a process of social change and conflict.*[48] The focus of attention on the appearance of a charismatic leader and the outcome of his appearance must be balanced by equal attention to the social milieu in which he emerges.

Kenelm Burridge locates the emergence of a prophet within a broad pattern of millenarian activities which begins with members of a community becoming aware of being "disenfranchized" and "separated from the mainstream of power and its associated activities."[49] This first phase is followed by "an attempt to give overt and active expression to the problems and their solutions."[50] But these activities are "merely probings," says Burridge. "Until a prophet emerges to symbolize the new man by concentrating these probings in himself and giving them coherence, the activities remains (sic!) inchoate and disorganized."[51] This second phase is followed by a third and last phase in which, as in each of the other two phases, a variety of developments are possible:

> Sometimes, as organizational skills are deployed and the new assumptions begin to be firmly established, a sect develops. In other cases there follows a period of anticlimax and disillusion which then tends to redevelop into the first phase of intellectual probing, rumour-mongering and heightening emotional tensions. Failure to bring about the overt ends of the activities tends to restart the cycle: we recognize those outstanding figures we call precursor prophets. . . .[52]

Returning now to the Gospel of John, I wish to point out that, in the way it depicts the Son, it conforms, in an extreme way, to the three features of the charismatic type of authority we have described above. First, in relation to the official systems of authority of his time, the Son appears as *an outsider*, the "Stranger par excellence."[53] Second, he claims an unheard of *concentration* of power and authority based upon direct access to the Father, an access which bypasses all of the mediating channels of authority, an access which elevates him above all of the official channels of authority, an access which relativizes all officially accepted legitimating procedures. Third, his departure creates a crisis of succession.

Not only does the Johannine Jesus conform to the charismatic type of authority, but, I suggest, this charismatic Jesus reflects a charismatic group, a group with a "charismatic tradition of origin."[54] Such a picture of the Johannine group is consistent with the near consensus description of it as sectarian.[55] Sectarianism is characterized above all by its stance over against and outside of the "world," which is equivalent to the system of power recognized and accepted by the society at large. This matches the first feature of charismatic authority noted above. The directness of the relationship to the divine

source of power and authority is also matched in sectarianism.
This is emphasized in Peter Berger's description of sectarian-
sim.[56]   Berger suggests that the distinguishing mark of the
sect, as distinct from the church, is to be found in the kind of
relationship to the "spirit" characteristic of each.   "The sect,"
he says, "may be defined as a religious grouping based on the
belief that *the spirit is immediately present*. And the church,
on the other hand, may be defined as a religious grouping based
on the belief that *the spirit is remote*."[57]   The spatial imagery
is underscored by Berger as the basic criterion in this typology
of religious groups.   "Social groupings that are religiously
based can be understood as forming themselves *around* the location
of the sacred. The area near the sacred is that which is
specifically religious; outside lies the world, in the religious
sense of the word. Figuratively, one may speak of the sociology
of religion as an ecology of the sacred."[58]   The sect, standing
immediately next to the spirit on this schema, requires no
mediation.   "The church, on the other hand, sees the spirit as
remote, having to be brought near by its apparatus of mediation."[59]   Berger qualifies this by observing that in some sects
there is a "mediating apparatus" required by particular religious
conceptions.   This suggests that the important thing is not
whether an apparatus of mediation as such exists, "but what it
means in the total religious gestalt."   Citing the example of
the Roman Catholic church, on the one hand, and the Christian
Community originating in the Anthroposophist movement, on
the other, Berger points out that both "possess a priesthood
and an elaborate sacramental system, yet the latter is filled
with a constant sense of the *immediacy* of the spiritual world
it seeks to contact."[60]

It is a short step from Berger's characterization of the
sect, in terms of a group separated from the world and standing
in direct proximity to the sacred center, to our definition of
charismatic authority in terms of the concentration of power
and authority in an outside figure--or group.

The Beginning As Norm

The christology of the Gospel, read as a projection of the community's self-understanding, points to a charismatic, sectarian group. On the other hand, the christology, read in relation to the author's intended message in the Gospel,[61] appears as a step in the direction of the routinization of authority. These two conclusions are not contradictory, if understood as aspects of a social process. On the contrary, they are mutually confirming. On the one hand, charismatic groups tend to issue in conflicts over authority which in turn issue in attempts to establish an ordered, routinized hierarchy of authority. On the other hand, the explicitness with which the author of the Fourth Gospel marks off the time of Jesus from the subsequent time of the disciples and elevates the former over the latter in the "remembering" motif is, in my opinion, evidence that he is consciously addressing a threat arising from charismatic claims. In the final part of this dissertation I wish to focus attention once more on the "remembering" motif in order to locate it within the context of the charismatic social process described above, and, in so doing, to locate the whole first farewell discourse in this process.

I have argued that the purpose of the farewell discourse is to subordinate the disciples to the Son. In the last two verses of the body of the discourse, vss. 25, 26, it is unmistakably clear that the author understands the vertical hierarchy of Son and disciples to apply "horizontally," that is, temporally, to the relationship between the time of the disciple's agency and the prior time of the Son's agency.

This temporal hierarchy is implicit in the promise in 14:12, where it is the works of the departing Jesus which the disciples will do, where, in other words, it is a matter of two parties who stand in a succession relationship which is also hierarchical.

The temporal framework, which is so pointedly expressed in the promise that the Spirit will recall all the words which were spoken by the departing Jesus, is, in fact, present throughout the discourse in its very *form* as a farewell discourse. It is the departing Son who is speaking, whom the reader

is hearing. The author has cast his work in the form of words
spoken by a departing (and, for the reader, departed) figure.
He has chosen "historical" narrative as the form of his work,
thereby identifying the Son in terms of past time. This statement is not contradicted by the fact that the Son transcends
time. The author has chosen to identify the Son in terms of
his "work" *finished*, in some sense, in the past, and his words
spoken in the past, and has explicitly subordinated the
disciples, and the Spirit, to the Son *in this role*.

To say that the disciples are subordinated to the Son in
his role as a figure of the past is not enough, of course. It
is necessary to go on to ask what "the past" means *in the Gospel*,
more specifically, what *this* past means. It is not simply
"history." It is not the "center of time" in a linear chronol-
ogy. The problem is how to talk about kinds of time. We do not
have a systematic vocabulary for talking about temporal quality
since we are not used to thinking systematically about time as
something that has varying qualities. The embarrassment of
scholars in the face of this problem as it occurs in connection
with the Gospel of John, for example, may be illustrated by
looking at various attempts to describe the author's point of
view on the time of Jesus' earthly life, what Günter Bornkamm
calls the "retrospective" point of view of the author.[62]

W. Nicol, in *The Semeia in the Fourth Gospel*, speaks of
"a strong anchor in history" which was necessary "in order to
keep the Johannine Christology from being blown away." Nicol
is concerned to argue for the unity of "event" and "meaning" in
John. He faults Ernst Käsemann for attributing to John a
docetic view of history in which "the unity of event and meaning"
are situated "above the sphere of historical reality." Against
such a view, Nicol holds that for John there had to be a "unity
of meaning and *real* history."[63] This formulation begs the
fundamental question as to what is "real history." For John
the time of Jesus' appearance belongs to the "past," a "past"
marked off from the present by a real line of differentiation.
This sort of sequence in time is what Nicol seems to mean by
"real history," since he says that in order for there to be
real history John "needed two phases for it."[64] But we must go

on to ask whether the two "phases" of this history are qualita-
tively the same. We are suggesting that they are *not*, that the
first "phase" has been ascribed a quality of uniqueness and
absoluteness which marks it off from all ordinary "history."

Ernst Käsemann poses the question of John's conception of
history directly.[65] Käsemann rightly insists that "history"
does not exist as a kind of independent entity whose meaning
and reality can be taken for granted by the interpreter. The
same is true if, as in Käsemann's discussion, one invokes the
term "incarnation" in order to get at the particularity of the
Son's appearance in time. According to Käsemann "incarnation"
does not refer to "merely a miraculous event within history."
"Incarnation rather means, as the prologue unmistakably indicates, the encounter of the Creator with his creature. This,
however, implies that history and the world must be understood
in this light and from this perspective. . . . In the confrontation with the Creator, history ceases to be what we imagined it
to be. John placed this idea at the very centre of his presentation and developed it with many variations. This idea is the
perspective from which he composed his Gospel and therefore it
is the hermeneutical key to its interpretation."[66]

Attention to Käsemann's ascription of a naive docetism
to John has led some interpreters to overlook the central insight of Käsemann's work, namely, the assigning of decisive
significance to the perspective of creation. The Creator-
creature perspective to which Käsemann here refers is a further
development of the idea of "protology," to which we have made
reference above (pp. 40ff).[67] Käsemann, I would insist, is
perfectly correct in designating the perspective of creation as
"the hermeneutical key" to the Gospel. I suggest, however, that
there are serious problems with the way in which he has applied
that key.

The initial clue to the problem is Käsemann's use of the
term "incarnation" in addressing the question of temporality.
The use of this term leaves room for an evasion of the germane
fact, namely, the *specific time frame* of the "incarnation."
Käsemann thus can define "incarnation" in essentially timeless

terms as "the encounter of the Creator with his creature" and on this basis go on to show how the author, from this perspective, relativizes all temporal boundaries.[68]

But the author has *not* relativized all temporal boundaries. If we have interpreted the farewell discourse correctly, the author has, in marking off so sharply the period in which the events narrated occurred from the subsequent time in which the narrative is being written, extended the hierarchical relationship of Son and disciples *to time*. The author has introduced a hierarchical division into time, a division which is no more to be blurred or relativized than is the hierarchical boundary between the only-begotton Son and his disciples.

In part, therefore, I agree with Bornkamm's criticisms of Käsemann's statements. According to Käsemann, the Gospel's presentation of Jesus is so dominated by the glory that the passion becomes problematical, so problematical, in fact that "one is tempted to regard it as being a mere postscript which had to be included because John could not ignore this tradition nor yet could he fit it organically into his work."[69] Over against this preposterous statement, Bornkamm makes the highly pertinent observation that, despite the fact that Käsemann's study is based upon the farewell prayer in chapter 17, the farewell discourses play a remarkably minor role in his argument.[70] By contrast, Bornkamm emphasizes the place of the farewell discourses in the Gospel in a way that few other scholars have done. According to him, the farewell is "the actual birth-hour of faith." Jesus' departure constitutes "the ground and beginning of a new day which has no end."[71] In short, the farewell has, as we saw earlier, eschatological significance for Bornkamm. Furthermore, the Gospel was written from the standpoint of this post-departure faith. It is written from a *retrospective* point of view, a feature Käsemann has, according to Bornkamm, completely failed to do justice to.[72]

Bornkamm is surely correct in stressing, over against Käsemann, that the hour of death and departure plays a central role throughout the Gospel in marking off a division in time.[73]

On the other hand, Bornkamm has completely failed, himself, to do justice to the importance of the creation and pre-existence perspective emphasized by Käsemann. Bornkamm fails, as we have seen above, to address directly the crucial question of the status and rank of the periods of time, marked off by the departure of Jesus, relative to each other. As a result, only one aspect of the relationship comes into view in his discussion, the fact that the faith perspective on Jesus' earthly life is only possible after Jesus' departure. Viewed in terms of this aspect alone, the relationship of the two time periods shows a progression from a time of incomprehension and unbelief or immature faith to a time of faith and full vision. But this aspect, the growth of faith, has been placed by the author in a larger context, the overarching time frame of the pre-existent Son and the cosmogony (John 1:1-3). The way in which this larger framework alters the relationship of the two time periods is overlooked entirely Bornkamm as a result of his easy dismissal of the creation perspective stressed by Käsemann.[74]

According to Bornkamm, Käsemann has exaggerated the creation motif and lifted it out of its context within the thought of the Gospel. In Bornkamm's view the creation idea belongs within the framework of the "urjohanneischen Relation von Offenbarung und Glauben." "*Here* is where the creation motif has its proper place in John, that is to say, in the field of antitheses of light and darkness, truth and illusion, freedom and bondage, life and death as possibilities of man, which he grasps or rejects."[75] Bornkamm's critique here amounts to nothing more than a declaration, with no argument, that Käsemann is wrong. But Käsemann has not *isolated* the creation motif from the thought of the Gospel, as Bornkamm asserts. He has argued that it is the ultimate horizon of the "field of Antitheses" referred to by Bornkamm. Bornkamm has simply reiterated a position which Käsemann quite emphatically rejected. Furthermore, just as Käsemann's understanding of "incarnation" turns out to be a timeless abstraction, so with Bornkamm's understanding of the creation motif.

Käsemann and Bornkamm each have emphasized a piece of the whole picture. If we retain the division in time emphasized by Bornkamm, together with the creation emphasis of Käsemann, we arrive at the conclusion that the author has marked off the time of Jesus' visible presence, as belonging to the time of "the beginning," from the period of time after his departure. The time of Jesus' visible presence takes on the normative, paradigmatic character of cosmogonic time, normative and paradigmatic for the time of the Paraclete which follows.

How then does the creation perspective affect the relationship of the two time periods marked off by the departure of Jesus? Most importantly it places the motif of the incomprehension of the disciples prior to the coming of the Spirit followed by their retrospective illumination by the Spirit in a very different light. The disciples' incomprehension and misunderstanding stands now in primary contrast to the perfect knowledge of the Son from the beginning. Whereas the disciples must await the coming of the Spirit before they understand who Jesus is and therefore who the Father is (14:9), Jesus possesses perfect knowledge of the Father from the beginning. In light of the specific contrast between the prior, primary agency of Jesus and the subordinate, dependent agency of the disciples in the farewell discourse, I would argue that it is the contrast with the Son's perfect knowledge which is the determinative perspective for understanding the disciples' illumination by the Spirit. In other words, the contrast between the incomprehension and subsequent illumination of the disciples, which Bornkamm makes decisive, is overshadowed by the far more basic contrast between Son and disciple.[76] The epiphany of the Son is not any the less complete because of the blindness of the world or the disciples.

In this light, the remembering motif is to be understood as an expression of the paradigmatic, protological status of the words and works of the Son in his epiphany in the past. Furthermore, the remembering motif says something about the way the author views his own book. His work is clearly one expression of Spirit-inspired recollection of Jesus' words, and is therefore authoritative. Thus, by his Gospel, the author has elevated the charismatic tradition of origin into a controlling, paradigmatic channel of mediation for authority in the community. The writing of the Gospel is, in other words, a step in the process of the routinization and stabilization of authority.[77]

Conclusion

In conclusion it may be helpful to attempt a summary of the argument from the beginning. I began by calling attention to the promise of the Paraclete as a successor figure to Jesus in 14:16, 17 and noted the anomaly which it represents over against the radical christocentrism of the Fourth Gospel.

In the first part (Chapters I-V) we analyzed the promise of the Paraclete in terms of its function within the context of the first farewell discourse. The message of the first farewell discourse is that the authority of the disciples as agents of the works (14:12) and words (14:25,26) of the Son is mediated by and dependent upon the Son. The disciples are dependent upon the Son both for their eventual access (14:2-3) and their interim access to the Father (14:20). The disciples are appointed to be successors to the Son, but succession is understood hierarchically. The union of the Son with the Father (14:10,11) is extended to include the disciples (14:20), but the union of the disciples with the Father is mediated by the Son. In short, the message of the first farewell discourse is that the authority of the disciples is *not* charismatic, in the sense of *direct access* to the ultimate source of power and authority. It is *mediated* authority. The Paraclete-Spirit becomes, within the discourse, the form in which Jesus returns to his disciples to mediate their access to the Father.[78]

In the second part of this dissertation (Chapter VI) we have shifted attention from the specific literary context of the Paraclete promise to ask after the tradition behind the Gospel. Taking the attention given to the Paraclete and to the Spirit in the Fourth Gospel as a clue to the kind of group from which the Gospel emerged, we have suggested that it was an actively charismatic variety, defining "charismatic" in terms of direct access to the Spirit. Such a picture is supported by the christology of the Gospel, if the christology is likewise taken as a reflection, or projection, of the self-understanding of the community. The Son in the Fourth Gospel is a "charismatic" figure par excellence. He has direct, unmediated access to the Father. His authority is independent of all officially recognized, taken-for-granted channels of authority. In this respect,

then, the Paraclete promise, and the exclusive christology
of the Gospel are consistent as reflections of the kind of
Christianity which nourished the author.

On the one hand, then, the Paraclete promise and the
christology of the Gospel reflect a charismatic type of authority. On the other hand, the first farewell discourse locates
the Paraclete promise within a message of mediated authority.
This paradox can be explained on the hypothesis that the
occasion for the writing of the Gospel is a situation in which
claims to direct, independent access to divine authority have,
in the author's eyes, gotten out of control by becoming a threat
to the primacy of the Son. To counter this threat the author
draws on the traditions of his circle, which were profoundly
charismatic. As I picture it, the author and those he is
countering were very likely drawing on the same charismatic
tradition of origin. What was viewed by the author as an
illegitimate type of authority could be viewed as very consistent
with the traditions of Jesus drawn on by the author. In other
words, those who in the author's eyes appeared to be rivals of
Christ may very well have considered themselves to be the
rightful "followers" or "successors" of Christ *in the sense of
claiming the same kind of direct access which he claimed.*[79]
Against such a view, the author in the farewell discourse set
forth his own doctrine of a hierarchical succession.

Returning to the question of the reason for the inclusion
of the Paraclete promise in this Gospel, I suggest that the
author included it because it was just as important to him as
it was to his opponents. He understood himself to be a prophet,
speaking in the Spirit, and was invoking the Spirit to legitimate
his Gospel. On the other hand, his purpose was to take the very
doctrine that was being, in his view, misappropriated, and
interpret it correctly and safely. In its context in the farewell
discourse, its anomalous implications have been defused.

INTRODUCTION

[1]James M. Robinson, "Introduction: The Dismantling and Reassembling of the Categories of New Testament Scholarship," James M. Robinson and Helmut Koester, *Trajectories Through Early Christianity* (Philadelphia: Fortress Press, 1971), p. 4.

[2]Robert Kysar, *The Fourth Evangelist and His Gospel: An Examination of Contemporary Scholarship* (Minnespolis, Minn.: Augusburg Publishing House, 1975), p. 280.

[3]The increase in attention to the social world of early Christianity has brought with it an increase in attention to issues of leadership, authority, power and magic. The works of John Schütz, Gerd Theisen, Theodore Weeden, John Gager, Peter Brown, and Morton Smith illustrate this trend (see Jonathon Z. Smith's review article, "The Social Description of Early Christianity," *Religious Studies Review* 1 [1975]:19-25, for an influential analysis of what this trend might mean and for a bibliography). It is striking, however, to note what little effect this trend has had to date on Johannine scholarship. "Authority" as an interpretive category continues to be neglected by Johannine scholars, perhaps, in part, as a result of the dominating influence of "eschatology" as an organizing principle of interpretation. Bultmann, for example, has much to say on the subject of "legitimation" in John but interprets legitimation by means of his understanding of realized eschatology. One of the better discussions of authority and leadership in Johannine Christianity is to be found in chs. V and VI of Alv Kragerud's 1959 monograph on the "beloved disciple," *Der Lieblingsjünger im Johannesevangelium* (Oslo: Osloer Universitätsverlag, 1959). But Kragerud's monograph as a whole illustrates a typical feature of most discussions of leadership and authority in John in that he bases his conclusions upon peripheral, or subordinate texts, such as ch. 21, and those texts having to do with "the beloved disciple." What is needed is a study which relates the central texts of the Gospel to the picture, drawn by Kragerud, of the Johannine community as an itinerant prophetic group.

[4]The theme of succession is one which is, a priori, worth examining closely for clues to the social structure of Johannine Christianity. It is a motif which lends itself to those claiming leadership as a means of establishing the claim to authority. Max Weber pointed out that in the particular situation of the disappearance of a charismatic leader, and the problem of succession following upon his disappearance, the *interests* of his followers "become conspicuously evident" in attempts to maintain the group. (See S. N. Eisenstadt, ed., *Max Weber on Charisma and Institution Building: Selected Papers* [Chicago: University of Chicago Press, 1968], p. 55.) One way in which the political interests of a group may become evident is in its literary products, especially in those having to do with

succession. Thus, for example, appeal to the dying words of
a founder may become a significant propaganda instrument.
There are numerous examples of the use of farewell literature
for propaganda purposes. One of the most striking has been set
forth by James D. Purvis in a study of Samaritan traditions on
the death of Moses. Purvis points out that in the great fourth
century work, the *Memar Marqah*, there is a conscious attempt to
downgrade the significance of Joshua in the account of the death
of Moses (James D. Purvis, "Samaritan Traditions on the Death
of Moses," George W. E. Nickelsburg, Jr., Ed., *Studies on the
Testament of Moses: Seminar Papers*, Septuagint and Cognate
Studies, No. 4 [Cambridge, Mass.: Society of Biblical Literature,
1973], p. 111). According to the *Memar Marqah*, the time of
Apostasy and Disfavor which Moses foresees after his death will
come *because of Joshua* (p. 96). On the other hand, a later
abridgement of part of *Memar Marqah*'s account of the death of
Moses deviates most conspicuously from its source precisely in
its treatment of Joshua. The passage in the *Marqah* which says
that the time of Disfavor will come because of Joshua is omitted.
Purvis lists other points of contrast, and then goes on to
suggest that these contrasting accounts of Joshua's role in the
succession are to be understood within the context of lay-priest-
ly conflict in the Samaritan community (p. 112). The *Memar
Marqah* reflects "the anti-Joshua theology of the priestly
dominated orthodoxy," whereas the abridgment has its provenance
in lay-heterodox circles with a strong theology of Joshua (p.
112). In the case of the Gospel of John it is worth noting
Richard Culpepper's recent proposal that the event which is
reflected in the Paraclete texts is the death of the beloved
disciple, whom Culpepper regards as the founder of the Johannine
"school." According to Culpepper, this event causes the
Johannine community to reach back to traditions of the death of
Jesus and appropriate them in the new crisis of leadership
(Richard Alan Culpepper, The *Johannine School: An Evaluation of
the Johannine-School Hypothesis Based on an Investigation of
the Nature of Ancient Schools*, Society of Biblical Literature
Dissertation Series, Number 26 [Missoula, Montana: Scholars
Press, 1975], p. 269).

[5]*Allon parakleton* may be translated: "the Father will
give you another, a Paraclete," a pleonastic usage found in Luke
23:32, for example. Aside from the fact that this usage is not
typical Johannine style, which renders it less probable as a
translation, it does not remove the idea of the Paraclete as a
successor figure to Jesus. This is also true of the translation,
"and he will give to you as another paraclete . . . the spirit
of truth," taking *allon parakleton* as an adjectival phrase modi-
fying *to pneuma tes aletheias*. The latter translation is
adopted by George Johnston, *The Spirit-Paraclete in the Gospel
of John* (Cambridge: University Press, 1970), p. 84).

[6]Hans Windisch, *The Spirit-Paraclete in the Fourth Gospel*,
trans. by James W. Cox (Philadelphia: Fortress Press, 1968), p.
20. This book contains the translations of two articles by
Hans Windisch, "Die fünf johanneischen Parakletsprüche," first
published in *Festgabe für Adolf Jülicher* (Tubingen: J. C. B.
Mohr [Paul Siebeck], 1927), and "Jesus und der Geist in

Johannesevangelium," first published in *Amicitiae Corolla* (London: University of London Press, 1933).

[7]See below, Chapter III, for a discussion of Johannine christocentrism. One of the most striking expressions of this christocentrism is that noted by Rudolf Bultmann in one of his earliest articles on the Fourth Gospel, where he called attention to the fact that though the Johannine Jesus is depicted as one who has come from the heavenly world to reveal secrets, the only thing that he reveals, in fact, is that he *is* the revealer. This observation is, as Wayne A. Meeks points out, the starting point for Bultmann's interpretation of the Gospel (Rudolf Bultmann, "Die Bedeutung der neuerschlossenen mandäischen und manichäischen Quellen für das Verständnis des Johannesevangeliums," *Zeitschrift für die neutestamentliche Wissenschaft* 24 [1925]:102). Wayne Meeks's comment is in "The Man from Heaven in Johannine Sectarianism," *Journal of Biblical Literature* 91 (1972):47. There is no room in John's Gospel, it would seem, for other mediator figures besides the Son. "Jesus becomes the only mediator between God and man: voices, dreams, visions, angels, signs all disappear. All are absorbed within the glory of the one who is the sole channel of traffic between heaven and earth (John 1:51)." (John M. Hull, *Hellenistic Magic and the Synoptic Tradition*, *Studies in Biblical Theology*, Second Series, No. 28 [London: SCM Press LTD, 1974], p. 122.)

[8]Windisch, *Spirit-Paraclete*, p. 24, citing Oswald Spengler, *Der Untergang des Abendlandes* 2 (München: C. H. Becksche Verlagsbuchhandlung, 1924):277.

[9]Günther Bornkamm, "Der Paraklet im Johannes-Evangelium," *Geschichte und Glaube*, Part I, *Collected Essays* 3 (München: Chr. Kaiser Verlag, 1968):68-89.

[10]The tendency to overlook the successor role is even more pronounced in the case of the disciples than it is in the case of the Paraclete. Fortna illustrates this tendency in his comment that "Jesus is not one to be imitated, but on the contrary recognized as unique. While the initial disciples are said to 'follow' him (1:40), this leads not to a sharing in his divine power but only to *belief* in it (2:11c)." (Robert T. Fortna, "Christology in the Fourth Gospel: Redaction-critical Perspectives," *New Testament Studies* 21 [1975]:493).

[11]There is a large body of literature on the Paraclete. Two recent monographs are Otto Betz, *Der Paraklet: Fürsprecher im häretischen Spätjudentum, im Johannes-Evangelium und in neu gefundenen gnostischen Schriften, Arbeiten zur Geschichte des Spätjudentums und Urchristentum*, Vol. 2 (Leiden: E. J. Brill, 1963), and Johnston, *The Spirit-Paraclete in the Gospel of John*. Betz provides a useful review of the research in his opening chapter. Johnston's work is very disappointing. His critical review of Betz's argument, for example, is impossible to follow. Raymond E. Brown has a brief discussion of the Paraclete in Appendix V of *The Gospel According to John (XIII-XXI)*, The

Anchor Bible, Vol. 29A (Garden City, N.Y.: Doubleday &
Company, Inc., 1970), as well as in a longer earlier article,
"The Paraclete in the Fourth Gospel," *New Testament Studies* 13
(1967):113-32. An important article published subsequent to
Johnston's and Brown's works is U. B. Müller, "Die Parakleten-
vorstellung im Johannes-evangelium," *Zeitschrift für Theologie
und Kirche* 61 (1974):31-77. Two other recent discussions are
Rudolf Schnackenburg's excursus in *Das Johannesevangelium*,
Part III, *Herders Theologischer Kommentar zum Neuen Testament*
4 (Freiburg: Herder, 1975):156-73, and Kysar, *The Fourth
Evangelist*, pp. 234-40.

12
    Neither Betz, Schnackenburg, nor Müller touch on the
problem, except incidentally. The only reference to the problem
by Betz, for example, is in a brief footnote denying that the
Paraclete leads to a second stage of revelation "surpassing"
that of Christ (*Der Paraklet*, p. 189, n. 3). Brown does not
mention the problem, even though he sees in the Paraclete
"another Jesus." See *Gospel According to John (XIII-XXI*, p.
1141. Johnston apparently senses the problem, but deals with
it in summary fashion (*The Spirit-Paraclete*, p. 95). The same
is true of Bornkamm, despite the way in which his forerunner-
fulfiller thesis highlights the issue!

13See above, p. 2, no. 2.

14Müller points this out in his critical review of
scholarship ("Die Parakletenvorstellung," pp. 38-40).

15
    See below, chapter IV.

16Siegfried Schulz, *Das Evangelium nach Johannes, Das
Neue Testament Deutsch* 4 (12th ed.; Göttingen: Vandenhoeck &
Ruprecht, 1972):178. But Robert Kysar's recent review of
research has no separate treatment of the farewell discourses
as such, and only mentions them in passing (Kysar, *The Fourth
Evangelist*, pp. 137, 143). Likewise, Robert Fortna notes, on
the one hand, that the author's "principal structural alteration"
of his source was "the insertion of the farewell discourse into
the combined narrative," but then concludes that the farewell
discourse "is only a kind of massive parenthesis in the gospel"
(Fortna, "Christology in the Fourth Gospel," pp. 502-3).

17
    For a review and critical assessment of the Signs Source
discussion see Kysar, *The Fourth Evangelist*, pp. 13-37.

18There is no sustained critical treatment of the farewell
material from a form- and redaction-critical point of view
which asks why so much of the Gospel is cast in a form which
underscores the *separation* of Jesus from the disciples.

19The most striking example of this sort of thematic study
is the scholarship on the Paraclete sayings.

20

A good review of the discussion may be found in Jürgen Becker's article, "Die Abschiedsreden Jesu im Johannesevangelium," *Zeitschrift für die neutestamentliche Wissenschaft* 59 (1970): 215-46. See also Raymond E. Brown, *Gospel According to John*, pp. 581-604 for a general discussion of the farewell discourses.

21

Wilhelm Heitmüller, "Das Johannes-Evangelium," J. Weiss, ed., *Die Schriften des Neuen Testaments* 2 (2nd improved and expanded edition; Göttingen: Vandenhoeck & Ruprecht, 1908):829. Heitmüller's judgment has not found much support. Bibliographical data show that the first farewell discourse has not been a focus, as such, of scholarly attention. I have found only two articles devoted specifically to the first farewell discourse. One, which I was unable to obtain, has the title, "La Présence dans l'absence (Jean 13:31-14:31)," by *C. Charlier, Bible et vie chretienne*, no. 2 (May-July, 1953), pp. 61-75, referred to by I. de la Potterie, "'Je suis la Voie, la Verité et la Vie' (Jn 14:6)," *Nouvelle Revue Théologique* 88 (1966):907, n. 2. The second is Rudolf Schnackenburg's recent study, "Das Anliegen der Abschiedsrede in Joh 14," H. Feld and J. Nolte, eds., *Wort Gottes in der Zeit: Festschrift Karl Hermann Schelkle zum 65, Geburtstag dargebracht von Kollegen, Freunden, Schülern* (Dusseldorf: Patmos-Verlag, 1973), pp.95-110. Schnackenburg's focus on this discourse as a unity is in response to Jürgen Becker's excellent study (see previous note), which, though it is devoted to the farewell discourses as a whole, goes further than any work since the article by Heitmüller in treating 13:31-14:31, as a single literary unity with a coherent structure. Interpretation of the discourse has suffered from what could be called "atomistic exegesis," that is to say, particular pericopes, such as the Paraclete sayings, have been discussed endlessly, but seldom with a rigorous concern for the specific literary context. In addition, a great deal of the literature on the farewell discourses is accurately characterized by G. B. Behler's forthright comment on his own work. It "ist nicht--dies sei von vornherein mit aller Klarheit gesagt--als Beitrag zur wissenschaftlichen Forschung gedacht" (G. B. Behler, *Die Abschiedsworte des Herrn: Johannesevangelium Kapitel 13-17* [Salzburg: Otto Müller Verlag, 1962], p. 9).

CHAPTER I

1
For example, C.K. Barrett, *The Gospel According to St. John* (London: S.P.C.K., 1965), p. 392; Rudolf Bultmann, *The Gospel of John: A Commentary*, trans. by G.R. Beasley-Murray (Oxford: Basil Blackwell, 1971), p. 459; Schnackenburg, *Johannesevangelium*, 3:100.

2
Bultmann, *Gospel*, 459.

3
For example, B.F. Westcott, *The Gospel According to St. John* (Photolithograph reprint of the 1908 edition. Two Volumes in One; Grand Rapids, Mich.: Wm. B. Eerdmans Publishing Company, 1954), p. 197.

4
Brown, *Gospel According to John*, p. 583.

5
P. Corssen, "Die Abschiedsreden Jesu in dem vierten Evangelium," *Zeitschrift für die neutestamentliche Wissenschaft* 8 (1907): 125-42.

6
Heinrich Zimmermann, "Struktur und Aussageabsicht der johanneischen Abschiedsreden (Jo 13-17)," *Bibel und Leben* 8 (1967): 289. C.H. Dodd has a similar interpretation: "With the words of verse 31 the journey has begun. There is no physical movement from the place. The movement is a movement of the spirit, an interior act of will, but it is a real departure nevertheless. As we shall see, the next stage of the discourse takes definitely a standpoint beyond the cross" (*The Interpretation of the Fourth Gospel* [Cambridge: University Press, 1965], p. 409). This is an explanation which goes back to Cyril of Alexandria. See E.C. Hoskyns, *The Fourth Gospel*, ed. by F.N. Davey (2d ed., rev.; London: Faber and Faber Limited, 1961), p. 465.

7
Bultmann summarizes several proposals, *Gospel of John*, p. 460, n. 1.

8
Rainer Borig, *Der Wahre Weinstock: Untersuchungen zu Jo 15:1-10, Studien zum Alten und Neuen Testament* 16 (München: Kösel-Verlag, 1967):20.

9
Howard lists Moffatt, Macgregor, Bernard, F.W. Lewis as placing chapter 17 after chapter 14 (W.F. Howard, *The Fourth Gospel in Recent Criticism and Interpretation* [3d ed. rev. by C.K. Barrett; London: Epworth Press, 1955], p. 303).

10
Friedrich Spitta, *Das Johannes-Evangelium als Quelle der Geschichte Jesu* (Gottingen: Vandenhoeck & Ruprecht, 1910), pp. 297-301. Spitta's order is: 13:21-31a; 15:1-17:26; 14:1-31.

11
Gospel of John, p. 461.

[12] Bultmann's proposal is criticized by Dwight Moody Smith, Jr., *The Composition and Order of the Fourth Gospel: Bultmann's Literary Theory* (New Haven: Yale University Press, 1965), pp. 168-75. Smith argues for keeping chapter 17 after the discourses. Cf. also the sharp words of J. Schneider, who calls Bultmann's rearrangement theory "ein absurder Gedanke" since the prayer "nur den Abschluss der Abschiedsreden bilden" [kann]" ("Die Abschiedsreden Jesu: Ein Beitrag zur Frage der Komposition von Johannes 13:31-17:27," *Gott und die Götter: Festgabe für Erich Fascher zum 60. Geburtstag* [Berlin: Evangelische Verlagsanstalt, 1958], p. 104.

[13] J. Wellhausen, *Erweiterungen und Änderungen im vierten Evangelium* (Berlin: Reimer, 1907), pp. 7-15. Cf. Wellhausen, *Das Evangelium Johannis* (Berlin: Reimer, 1908), p. 79.

[14] Georg Richter, "Die Deutung des Kreuzestodes Jesu in der Leidensgeschichte des Johannesevangeliums (Jo 13-19)," *Bibel und Leben* 9 (1968):21-36. Cf. also Richter's monograph, *Die Fusswaschung im Johannesevangelium: Geschichte ihrer Deutung, Biblische Untersuchungen*, Vol. 1 (Regensburg: Verlag Friedrich Pustet, 1967). Richter finds evidence of the same two tendencies in the Bread discourse. See his article "Zur Formgeschichte und literarischen Einheit von Joh 6:31-58," *Zeitschrift für die neutestamentliche Wissenschaft* 60 (1969):21-55. This is a critique of Peter Borgen's analysis of the homily in chapter 6.

[15] Becker, "Abschiedsreden." Schnackenburg distinguishes two secondary speeches; ch. 15 containing the first, ch. 16 the second (*Johannesevangelium*, 3:102-3).

[16] Cf. for example Dodd, *Interpretation*, p. 407 and Barrett, *Gospel*, p. 379. Raymond Brown holds that there were "several independent last discourses" (p. 586). He suggests that 13:31-14:31 represents "substantially the discourse that stood in the early written form of the Gospel" and that the material in chs. 15 and 16 was added later by the final redactor (p. 594). However, he holds that both parts contain earlier and later material.

[17] Namely, 13:31-14:31 and 16:4b-33. Raymond Brown sets out the parallels in a synoptic chart on pp. 589-593 of his commentary.

[18] Cf. Rudolf Schnackenburg's conclusion that "in der neu einsetzenden Diskussion über Schichten im Johannesevangelium . . . wird die Herkunft der Abschiedsrede in Kap. 14 vom Evangelisten selbst nicht bestritten" ("Das Anliegen der Abschiedsrede in Joh 14," p. 95).

[19] Brown, *Gospel According to John*, p. 623.

[20] This is true of J.H. Bernard, Hoskyns, Leon Morris, Westcott, and Lindars. See J.H. Bernard, *A Critical and Exegetical Commentary on the Gospel According to St. John, The International Critical Commentary* (New York: Charles Scribner's Sons, 1929); Hoskyns, *The Fourth Gospel*; Leon Morris, *The Gospel According to John, the New International Commentary on the New*

Testament (Grand Rapids, Mich.: Wm. B. Eerdmans Publishing Co., 1971). Barnabas Lindars, *The Gospel of John, New Century Bible,* ed. by Ronald E. Clements and Matthew Black (London: Oliphants, 1972).

[21]Adolf von Harnack, "Zur Textkritik und Christologie der Schriften des Johannes," *Sitzungsberichte der preussischen Akademie der Wissenschaften,* Phil.-his. Klasse, 1915, p. 551, n. 2. Cited by Bornkamm, "Der Paraklet," p. 86, n. 38.

[22]See below, pp. 24ff.

[23]We are here speaking only of the rearrangement aspect of such theories. Source critical theory has not treated chapter 14 so kindly.

[24]See above pp. 17-18.

[25]Brown, *Gospel According to John,* p. 609.

[26]Cf. Brown's discussion, ibid., pp. 608, 609.

[27]*Gospel,* p. 612. Cf. Schneider, "Abschiedsreden," p. 107 and A. Wikenhauser, *Das Evangelium nach Johannes, Das Neue Testament,* ed. Alfred Wikenhauser and Otto Kuss 4 (Regensburg: Verlag Friedrich Pusted):221. But Gächter, followed by Ibuki, holds that the theme of "believing" in 14:1 and 11 form an "inclusio," which defines 14:1b-11 as a unified piece (see P. Gächter, "Der formale Aufbau der Abschiedsrede Jesu," *Zeitschrift für katholische Theologie* 58 [1934]: 176, 177; and Yu Ibuki, *Die Wahrheit im Johannesevangelium, Bonner Biblische Beiträge* 39 [Bonn: Peter Hanstein Verlag GMBH, 1972]:213).

[28]Gospel *According to John,* p. 623.

[29]Ibid., p. 624

[30]See Bernard, Bultmann, Brown, Schulz, *Evangelium;* Wikenhauser, *Das Evangelium nach Johannes,* and Dominic Crossan, *The Gospel of Eternal Life: Reflections on the Theology of St. John* (Milwaukee: The Bruce Publishing Company, 1967).

[31]Bernard, Lindars, Crossan, and Friedrich Büchsel, *Das Evangelium nach Johannes, Das Neue Testament Deutsch, Neues Göttinger Bibelwerk,* ed. by Paul Althaus and Johannes Behm, Vol. 4 (4th ed.; Göttingen: Vandenhoeck & Ruprecht, 1946).

[32]With Bernard, Büchsel, and Wilhelm Heitmüller.

[33]With Bultmann, Wikenhauser, Westcott, Crossan.

[34]Dominic Crossan has followed this principle most consistently, outlining chapters 13-17 as a whole, on the basis of the disciples' questions, as follows: 1) Dialogue with Betrayal (13:1-35); 2) Dialogue with the Apostles (13:36-16:33); 3) Dialogue with God (17:1-26). There is, of course, no "dialogue" in chapter 17. It is a monologue. Crossan divides the second

division up according to the disciples' questions (Crossan, *Gospel of Eternal Life*).

[35]Brown recognizes that the questions do not introduce new motifs, but obscures the consistency with which they are used to develop a theme (Cf. *Gospel According to John*, pp. 624, 643). Schnackenburg recognizes the function of the questions. Philip's request in vs. 8 "hat, ähnlich wie die Einrede des Tomas, vor allem eine literarische Funktion. Sie ermöglicht es Jesus, in seiner Antwort noch schärfer den Kerngedanken zu formulieren" (*Johannesevangelium*, 3:76).

[36]Dodd, *Interpretation*, p. 403; Bultmann, *Gospel*, p. 598; Becker, "Abschiedsreden," p. 221; Schneider, "Abschiedsreden," p. 106.

[37]*Interpretation*, p. 403.

[38]Ibid., p. 404.

[39]J. Becker, "Abschiedsreden," pp. 219-28. See the critique of Becker offered by Rudolf Schnackenburg in his article on the first farewell discourse (Rudolf Schnackenburg, "Das Anliegen der Abschiedsrede in Joh 14"). Schnackenburg goes even further than Becker in emphasizing the theme of the presence of the Son, arguing that the promise in 14:2-3 already refers to the return of Jesus at the resurrection. My criticism of Becker, that he overlooks the emphasis on distance and separation in the discourse, applies all the more to Schnackenburg.

[40]It is not clear what Becker means when he calls this piece of tradition an *Offenbarungswort*. He cites Otto Michel, but Michel does not define the term either (Otto Michel, "*oikos*," *Theological Dictionary of the New Testament*, ed. Gerhard Friedrich, trans. and ed. Geoffrey W. Bromily 5 [Grand Rapids, Mich.: Wm. B. Eerdmans Publishing Company, 1967]:132). Karl Kundsin speaks of *Offenbarungswörter*, *Offenbarungssprüche*, referring to core elements of the Johannine speeches, such as the "I am" sayings, sayings which, according to Kundsin, arose in the visionary manifestations of the risen Christ to Christian prophets. Becker is using the term with reference to a different sort of saying, one which, on his understanding, is more like Bultmann's category of "prophetic and apocalyptic sayings" (Karl Kundsin, *Charakter und Ursprung der johanneischen Reden*, *Acta Universitatis Latviensis*, 1 [Riga, 1939]:198-99; R. Bultmann, *Die Geschichte der synoptischen Tradition*, *Forschungen zur Religion und Literatur des Alten und Neuen Testaments*, N.F. 12 [6th ed.; Göttingen: Vandenhoeck & Ruprecht, 1964]:113ff.). The term *Offenbarungswort*, "word of revelation," is particularly unhelpful to use to distinguish one piece of speech material from another; Bultmann has described the speech material as a whole as consisting of "revelation discourses."

[41]See Becker, "Abschiedsreden," p. 222, n. 36: "In der Tat spricht 14:3 für sich den Gedanken der Parusieerwartung klar aus."

[42]Ibid., pp. 222-23. Schnackenburg points out that if Becker is correct, this would be the only instance in the Gospel where a saying which is to be corrected is first attributed to *Jesus* (Schnackenburg, "Das Anliegen der Abschiedsrede in Joh 14," p. 107).

[43]Ibid., p. 223.

[44]Ibid., p. 228.

[45]*Bread from Heaven: An Exegetical Study of the Concept of Manna in the Gospel of John and the Writings of Philo, Supplements to Novum Testamentum*, Vol. 10 (Leiden: E.J. Brill, 1965).

[46]See especially ch. 2 of *Bread from Heaven* and the summary of the pattern on p. 47.

[47]Wayne A. Meeks, "The Man from Heaven in Johannine Sectarianism," *Journal of Biblical Literature* 91 (1972):58, n. 50.

[48]I owe this observation to Professor Jonathon Z. Smith, who cites Jacob Neusner's studies of the laws of purities in *A History of the Mischnaic Law of Purities, Studies in Judaism in Late Antiquity*, Vol. 6 (Leiden: E.J. Brill, 1974-). See also J.A. Neusner's article, "The Meaning of Oral Torah," in *Early Rabbinic Judaism: Historical Studies in Religion, Literature and Art, Studies in Judaism in Late Antiquity*, ed. by Jacob Neusner 13 (Leiden: E.J. Brill, 1975):3-33. In "The Meaning of Oral Torah" Neusner argues that "the Misnaic Law is separate and autonomous from Scripture, though in its unfolding it is made to interrelate, where it can, to Scripture" (p. 28).

[49]David E. Aune, *The Cultic Setting of Realized Eschatology in Early Christianity, Supplements to Novum Testamentum* 28 (Leiden: E.J. Brill, 1972):68,69. Aune cites B.W. Bacon's comparison of the Johannine use of Synoptic tradition with midrash (B.W. Bacon, *The Gospel of the Hellenists*, ed. by Carl H. Kraeling [New York: Henry Holt and Company, 1933], pp. 156, 189). The quotation which Aune cites from Bacon is not, however, found on page 189 as Aune indicates. I was unable to locate the quote in Bacon's work.

[50]Aune, *Cultic Setting*, p. 69.

[51]The discourse is a polemic "gegen die Vorstellung einer heilsleeren Gegenwart" (Becker, "Abschiedsreden," p. 228, n. 49a). Jesus is "absent" according to the *Gemeindeglaube* (ibid., p. 224). The present is characterized as "einer von Jesus 'leeren' Gegenwart" (p. 224).

[52]"Die Rede entfaltet in einer polemischen Exegese gegen eine im Traditionsstück 14:2f. benannten Christologie in ihrem Hauptteil 'die praesentia Christi,' des Erhöhten, als 'die Mitte' ihrer 'Botschaft'" (ibid., p. 228). Becker is here alluding to

Ernst Käsemann's summary of the message of the Gospel in terms
of the *prasentia Christi*, in *Jesu letzter Wille nach Johannes
17* (Tübingen: J.C.B. Mohr [Paul Siebeck], 1966), p. 33.
Käsemann's study has been translated by Gerhard Krodel as
*The Testament of Jesus: A Study of the Gospel of John in the
Light of Chapter 17* (Philadelphia: Fortress Press, 1968).

[53]The discussion is extensive. For a review of the
scholarship see Aune, *Cultic Setting*, pp. 128-32. S. Schulz also
lists with brief critical remarks, the various interpretations
that have been proposed. See Schulz, *Untersuchungen zur
Menschensohn-Christologie im Johannesevangelium* (Göttingen:
Vandenhoeck & Ruprecht, 1957), pp. 164ff.

[54]*Spirit-Paraclete*, p. 2. Spitta says of 14:21-23: "Hier
handelt es sich, kurz gesagt, um die mystische Einwohnung des
Vaters und des Sohnes in dem Gläubigen" (*Johannes-Evangelium*,
p. 348).

[55]Lindars, *The Gospel of John*, pp. 482-83. Cf. Brown,
Gospel According to John, p. 646.

[56]Macgregor interprets 14:20 as referring to a "mystic
communion of Father, Son, and Believer" (p. 310). But he has
earlier made it clear that he understands this "mystic communion"
in strictly ethical terms. Commenting on 15:4 he says, "though
the Evangelist may employ the thought-forms of the semi-physical
mysticism of his day, union with Christ is for him, 'more a
matter of will and moral effort than of feeling,' . . . To be
'in Christ' (in this Gospel) is just to accustom oneself to
breathe in the atmosphere of the moral standard Jesus has set--to
develop within us a set of Christian instincts" (G.H.C. Macgregor,
The Gospel of John, *The Moffatt New Testament Commentary* [New
York: Harper and Brothers Publishers, 1928], p. 287, citing R.H.
Strachan). Macgregor does not give the exact source of the
citation.

[57]*Gospel*, p. 581. This quotation is taken from the
discussion of 16:16-24, but it is clear that Bultmann understands
14:18-24 in exactly the same way (see p. 619, especially note 5,
which refers back to p. 581). It is important to note that
Wilhelm Heitmüller in 1908 offered a very similar interpretation
of this text. Heitmüller understands the author here to be
equating Easter, Pentecost, and Parousia and to be interpreting
all of these eschatological events as "interior" events: "Die
ungemein folgenreiche und wertvolle Arbeit, die wir als ein
besonderes Kennzeichen unseres Evangeliums ansehn müssen, die
Vereinfachung und die Verdieseitigung, bez. Verinnerlichung der
altchristlichen Vorstellungswelt zeigt sich hier [i,e., 14:18-
20] in besonders glänzendem Lichte" ("Das Johannes-Evangelium,"
pp. 827-28).

[58]*Cultic Setting*, p. 129.

[59]Karl Kundsin "Die Wiederkunft Jesu in den Abschiedsreden des Johannesevangeliums," *Zeitschrift für die neutestamentliche Wissenschaft* 33 (1934):215. The Evangelist "denkt vor allem an den auch den Jüngern bevorstehenden Leidens- und Todesweg. In der Todesstunde zeigt sich Jesus dem Sterbenden, vor allem dem Märtyrer, um ihn in die ewigen Wohnungen heimzuholen."

[60]See below, Chapter IV for a more extended discussion of the literature on this issue.

[61]For Becker the Paraclete is the "Modus der Gegenwart Jesu" ("Abschiedsreden," p. 227). Cf. Raymond E. Brown's formula. The Paraclete is "another Jesus," that is, "the presence of Jesus when Jesus is absent" (*Gospel According to John*, p. 1141). According to E.F. Scott, the Paraclete "is simply Himself returning as an unseen presence" (*The Fourth Gospel: Its Purpose and Theology* [Edinburgh: T. & T. Clark, 1908], p. 343).

[62]"Abschiedsreden," p. 227.

[63]Cf. Nils Dahl's reference to the Spirit's role in 15:26 as "comme une clé de l'Evangile de Jean." Dahl's remarks are even more appropriately applied to 14:25, 26 where the "commemorative" function which Dahl has highlighted in his article is explicit (Nils A. Dahl, "Anamnesis: Memoire et Commemoration dans le christianisme primitif," *Studia Theologica* 1 [1948]:94).

[64]Becker, "Abschiedsreden," p. 228, citing Ernst Käsemann, *Jesu letzter Wille nach Johannes 17*, p. 33.

[65]*Testament*, p. 36.

[66]Ibid.

[67]Ibid., p. 7

[68]Ibid., p. 10.

[69]It is important to observe that Käsemann does, in a note, recognize the fact that, rightly understood, "the death of Jesus does have the character of a centre of gravity." Ibid., p. 19, n. 30.

[70]Ibid., pp. 20-21.

[71]Ibid., p. 20.

[72]Ibid., p. 16.

[73]*Jesu letzter Wille*, p. 35.

[74]*Testament*, p. 23.

[75]Ibid.

[76]Ibid., p. 45

[77] Cf. Günther Bornkamm's critique of Käsemann's anachronistic use of such categories in his important essay, "Zur Interpretation des Johannes-Evangeliums. Eine Auseinandersetzung mit Ernst Käsemanns Schrift 'Jesu letzter Wille nach Johannes 17,'" *Evangelische Theologie* 28 (1968):8-25. Republished in *Geschichte und Glaube*, Part I, *Beiträge zur evangelischen Theologie* 98 (München: Chr. Kaiser Verlag, 1968):104-121. I shall quote from the latter. See pp. 120-21 for the discussion of anachronisms.

[78] Theo Preiss, "Justification in Johannine Thought," in *Life in Christ, Studies in Biblical Theology*, no. 13, trans. by Harold Knight (Chicago: Alex R. Allenson, Inc., 1954), pp. 10-11.

[79] George W. MacRae, "The Fourth Gospel and *Religionsgeschichte*," *Catholic Biblical Quarterly* 32 (1970):23. Cf. idem. "The Ego-Proclamation in Gnostic Sources," in *The Trial of Jesus, Studies in Biblical Theology*, Second Series, 13 (London: S.C.M. Press, 1970):133-34.

[80] W.D. Davies, *The Gospel and the Land: Early Christianity and Jewish Territorial Doctrine* (Berkeley: University of California Press, 1974), p. 302, n. 23.

[81] F. Hahn, "Sehen und Glauben im Johannesevangelium," *Neues Testament und Geschichte: Historisches Geschehen und Deutung im Neuen Testament: Oscar Cullmann zum 70, Geburtstag*, ed. by Heinrich Baltensweiler and Bo Reicke (Zurich: Theologischer Verlag, 1972), p. 140. Hahn takes the term from H.G. Gadamer, *Wahrheit und Methode* (1960), pp. 289f., 375, so that it has, in the first instance a specific hermeneutical significance, but Hahn does not use it in this strict sense exclusively.

[82] Rudolf Bultmann, "Die Bedeutung der neuerschlossenen mandaischen und manichaischen Quellen für das Verständnis des Johannesevangeliums," *Zeitschrift für die neutestamentliche Wissenschaft* 24 (1925):102. Cf. Rudolf Bultmann, *Theology of the New Testament*, trans. by Kendrick Grobel 2 (n.p.: Charles Scribner's Sons, 1955):66-67. Cf. also Bultmann, *Gospel*, p. 390. See Meeks, "The Man from Heaven," p. 47.

[83] Hoskyns, *The Fourth Gospel*, p. 67.

[84] Meeks, "Man from Heaven," p. 68. See also p. 55, n. 41 where he cites Hoskyns.

[85] Meeks, "Man from Heaven," pp. 68-69.

[86] See Chapter V for detailed discussion.

[87] Raymond E. Brown's translation.

[88] Bornkamm, "Der Paraklet," pp. 85-86.

[89] Ibid., p. 86.

[90]J. Louis Martyn, *History and Theology in the Fourth Gospel* (New York: Harper & Row, Publishers, 1968), p. 8.

[91]Ibid., pp. 9-10.

[92]Ibid., p. 9, n. 21.

[93]Ibid., p. 54. Emphasis in the original.

[94]Ibid., p. 77.

[95]Ibid., p. 128. Note that here Martyn refers to two *stages*.

[96]Ibid.

[97]Wilhelm Thüsing, *Die Erhöhung und Verherrlichung Jesu im Johannesevangelium, Neutestamentliche Abhandlungen*, ed. by M. Meinertz 21 (Münster: Aschendorffsche Verlagsbuchhandlung, 1960): 48-49. The second revised edition of 1970 was not available to me.

[98]Ibid., p. 48, cf. p. 289.

[99]Ibid.

[100]Ibid., p. 204.

[101]Ibid., pp. 201-4.

[102]Ibid., p. 201.

[103]Ibid., p. 204.

[104]Ibid.

[105]Käsemann, *Testament*, p. 10, n. 13; pp. 17-19.

[106]*Gospel*, p. 523.

[107]See, for example, Raymond E. Brown's argument that these were the two problems defining the *Sitz im Leben* of the Johannine Paraclete promise (*Gospel According to John*, p. 1142). A forceful statement of the view that the author was addressing the problem of distance from Jesus is to be found in Paul Minear's recent article, "The Audience of the Fourth Evangelist" (*Interpretation* 31 [1977]:339-54). According to Minear, "the distance in time and space from Jesus" created difficulties for the second generation of Christian believers, who "imagined themselves at a distinct disadvantage in comparison with their predecessors" (p. 345), and Minear speaks of "the dismay of followers who no longer have access either to Jesus or to the apostles, but who must rely upon the hearsay of later witnesses" (p. 349). He refers to the "chain of being," that is, the word of Jesus, which constituted, for the author, "a bridge over every distance of time and space" (p. 354). Minear's texts are evidence that the

author and his audience were aware of the distance in time from
Jesus (or from the founding generation of the Johannine group),
but it is not so clear that the problem created by this distance
was the problem of *access to Jesus*, as Minear holds. I maintain
that the problem created by this distance was one of hierarchy
and status. Interestingly, Minear touches on the issue of rank,
but only in a tangential way, pointing out that "in the chain of
witnesses that reaches back to the beginning, no link ranks
higher than any other, for all respond to the Word and all
become mediators of the Word" (p. 349). This leveling of all
witnesses is, according to Minear, reflected in the fact that
each disciple in John is typically enlisted "not by Jesus
directly, but by another witness" (p. 349). Minear connects the
rank of the disciples with the *indirectness* of their access to
Jesus, and even recognizes this as a positive point! Yet, from
the point of view of Minear's whole discussion, this aspect is
lost from view and is not developed.

[108]Cf. Dwight Moody Smith, Jr.'s recent attempt to characterize "Johannine Christianity." Smith emphasizes the "charismatic"
element throughout ("Johannine Christianity: Some Reflections on
its Character and Delineation," *New Testament Studies* 21 [1975]:
232, 233, 243, 244). See below, Chapter VI, for full discussion
of this argument.

[109]Cf. for example, George Johnston's observation that "it
was no fantastic, inconceivable possibility that another claimant
might arise to dispute the pre-eminent place of Jesus Christ."
Johnston goes on to cite the example of the "charismatic Montanus
who appeared to have identified himself with the Paraclete and,
as such, to have fulfilled the eschatological promises made by
Jesus in John (*The Spirit-Paraclete*, p. 95). This threat was a
particularly live possibility in the form of a contrast between
the "earthly" Jesus and the resurrected Christ in which the
believer would have understood himself to be "on the side" of the
resurrected Christ, having received post-resurrection revelations
from the heavenly Christ. See James M. Robinson's highly
relevant discussion of the two Gospel forms, the canonical Gospel
and the "gnostic" Gospel, the latter consisting of post-resurrection revelations. Robinson points to the possibility, exploited
by gnosticism, "of relegating to insignificance the early earthly
life of Jesus, as just a lower and hence irrelevant prelude"
(James M. Robinson, "On the *Gattung* of Mark (and John),"
Perspective 11 [1970]:133).

CHAPTER II

1
   See for example Raymond E. Brown, *Gospel According to John*, p. 608; Gächter, "Der formale Aufbau der Abschiedsrede Jesu," p. 176; Ibuki, *Die Wahrheit*, p. 212; Schulz, *Evangelium nach Johannes*, p. 182. "14:1ff. besitzt keine direkte Verbindung zum vorherigen Abschnitt, der Verleugnung des Petrus." On the other hand, R. Schnackenburg, though not explicitly assigning 14:1-3 to the "introduction" of the discourse, does recognize that the saying in vss. 2-3 represents "eine gewissen Abschluss" to the line of thought beginning in 13:33 (Schnackenburg, "Anliegen der Abschiedsrede," p. 101).

2
Within the context Peter becomes a representative figure as do the other disciples mentioned by name. So Bultmann, *Gospel*, p. 597, n. 1: "Peter's denial (v. 38) is only a representative event."

3
Contra Brown, *Gospel According to John*, p. 608.

4
Schnackenburg traces the *Gedankenlinie* from the announcement in 13:33, to 13:36, to 14:2-3, overlooking the announcement in terms of 'glorification" in 13:31-32 ("Anliegen der Abschiedsrede," p. 101).

5
Thus elaborating on the brief hint to this effect in 13:36.

6
It is remarkable that scholars can overlook the pervasive concern of the Gospel with Jesus' *status*. Yet Fortna takes the position that a singular attention to Jesus' status distinguishes the miracle source from the redactor! (Forna, "Christology," p. 491.)

7
Heitmüller calls 13:31-32 a "Triumphlied" (Das Evangelium des Johannes," p. 823). Schulz calls it a "Menschensohn-Hymnus" (*Evangelium*, p. 178).

8
The third line is omitted in several important witnesses including P66Bא *C* and D. It is accepted by many commentators, including Brown, Schnackenburg, Bernard, Bultmann, Lagrange, Schulz, and Thüsing. Its absence can be explained by homoioteleuton.

9
On the *doxa*, *doxasthenai* motif see Thüsing, *Erhöhung und Verherrlichung*, and Käsemann's critique of Thüsing in *Testament*, ch. II.

10
This is not to be understood in the Pauline sense, as Thüsing interprets it (*Erhöhung und Verherrlichung*, pp. 222f.). See esp. p. 224 where Thüsing comments on the "entscheidende Bedeutung" of the terminology of spatial movement in John, which

he interprets in a Pauline sense. My understanding of the
legitimating significance of the return of Jesus to heaven is
consistent with Käsemann's interpretation of the death of Jesus
(*Testament*, p. 20). The return of Jesus to heaven functions as
a legitimating act in similar fashion to the function of the
descent of Jesus in 7:25-29, for example.

[11]See pp. 27, 28.

[12]From this point of view, the "new commandment" in vss.
34-35, which calls for solidarity among the disciples left
behind in and over against "the world," is not out of place.
Cf. to the contrary Becker, "Abschiedsreden," p. 220.

[13]Cf. Wayne Meeks' comment that "the evangelist has con-
structed this whole dialogue in order to provide a new setting
for the traditional logion predicting Peter's denial (vs. 38),
so that the denial is now reinterpreted in the light of the
descent/ascent motif that *separates* Jesus from all earthly men,
even the disciples" (Meeks, "Man from Heaven," p. 65. Emphasis
not in the original).

[14]So Raymond Brown, Bultmann.

[15]Bultmann, *Gospel*, p. 75; *emprosthen mou gegonen* "refers
to his status." Bultmann notes that the basis of the usage here
is probably "the Rabbinic 'to precede'=to have the greater
dignity."

[16]Cf. the term *axios* in 1:27.

[17]Cf. 3:28-30 where the issue of rank is again to the
fore in the statement of the Baptist that "He must increase,
but I must decrease." This is followed by the further contrast
between the one who comes "from above" and the one who is "of
the earth." Twice it is stated that the one who is from heaven
is "above all." This may or may not refer specifically to the
Baptist, but in any case includes him.

[18]"Der Paraklet," p. 87. Bornkamm does note the polemic
based on Jesus' pre-existence (p. 76) but does not recognize
its implications. See below, pp. 132ff. on Bornkamm.

[19]Ibid., p. 87.

[20]On the premise that the christology of John is a projection of the self-understanding of the prophetic or charismatic
Johannine community (see below, Chapter VI), the motif of the Son
being "out of place" has significance as pointing to *itinerancy*
as a feature of the prophetic "collective." Itinerancy is
emphasized as a basic feature by Kragerud (*Der Lieblingsjünger*,
pp. 87ff.). Cf. also Gerd Theissen, "Wanderradikalismus:
Literatur-soziologische Aspekte der Überlieferung von Worten
Jesu im Urchristentum" (*Zeitschrift für Theologie und Kirche*
70 [1973]:245-71); John G. Gager, *Kingdom and Community: The
Social World of Early Christianity* (Englewood Cliffs, N.Y.:
Prentice-Hall, Inc., 1975), p. 73; and Jonathon Z. Smith on the

motifs of "out of place" and "mobility" (Jonathon Z. Smith, "Native Cults in the Hellenistic Period," *History of Religions* II [1971]:236-38); and especially the essay, "The Temple and the Magician," published as chapter 8 of the collection of essays by Professor Smith entitled *Map is Not Territory: Studies in the History of Religions, Studies in Judaism in Late Antiquity*, ed. by Jacob Neusner 23 (Leiden: E.J. Brill, 1978):see particularly 185-89. Professor Smith's essay describes the broad socio-cultural context within which the christocentrism of the Fourth Gospel is to be located, namely, the "reversal" or "shift" from temple to magician as sacred center across the Mediterranean world in Late Antiquity.

[21]Meeks follows Odeberg and Bultmann in finding a polemic against "the claim of prophets or seers to have received revelations by means of 'heavenly journeys' as for example in apocalyptic or in the *merkabah* speculation, or in the traditions of the theophanies to Moses and the Patriarchs" ("Man from Heaven," p. 52).

CHAPTER III

[1]Cf. Spitta's comment on vss. 4-11: "Jedenfalls hat es
eine absolut fremde Tonart in diese Abschiedsrede hineingebracht.
. . . An Stelle des milden Trostes, den der scheidende Jesus
seinen erschutterten Jungern spendet, tritt die Forderung der
Bedingungen für den Eingang in das Himmelreich, der Glaube an
Jesus als das Ebenbild und den wahrhaftigen Sohn Gottes"
(*Johannesevangelium als Quelle*, p. 344). The contrast is not
as sharp if we include 13:31-38 with 14:1-3 as the contrasted
section, since "gentle comfort" does not characterize 13:31-38.

[2]Another contrast between 14:4-11 and 13:31-14:3 is that
14:4-11 is predominantly in the present tense, in contrast to
the many future tense verbs in 13:31-14:3.

[3]The unity of Father and Son is expressed in a number of
different forms in the Gospel, of which the reciprocal formula
of indwelling is only one example. It is found, in reverse order,
in 10:38, and again in 17:21, with reference to the indwelling.
The reciprocal pattern is found also in 10:14 with reference to
the mutual knowledge of Father and Son. In addition to the reci-
procity forms, however, there are correlative forms which indicate
that as the Father acts *to the Son*, so the Son acts to others
(10:14; 15:9; 17:8; 18:22; 20:21), which indicate that as the
Father acts *to others*, so the Son acts to others (5:17,9,21,26;
6:57; and cf. 6:44 with 12:32), and which indicate that as the
Father commands, the Son obeys (5:30; 8:28; 12:50; 14:31). There
are also forms expressing the fact that man's action towards
Christ is equivalent to action towards the Father (14:7,9, and
see below, note 7).

[4]Cf. the statement of Yu Ibuki regarding 14:6a: "Dieses
Ego-eimi-Wort ist der Höhepunkt des ganzen Abschnittes. . . ."
Ibuki provides a very thorough analysis of 14:1-11 in *Die
Wahrheit im Johannesevangelium, Bonner Biblische Beiträge* 39
(Bonn: Peter Hanstein Verlag, 1972):222. I. de la Potterie calls
vs. 6 "une veritable charniere entre les deux subdivisions
majeures (les vv. 2-6 et 6-11)" (I. de la Potterie, "'Je suis
la Voie, la Verite et la Vie' (jn 14:6)," *Nouvelle Revue
Theologique* 88 [1966]:927). On the "I am" sayings as such see
the discussion later on in this chapter.

[5]Cf. Ibuki, *Wahrheit*, p. 218; de la Potterie, "'Je suis
le Voie,'" p. 931.

[6]With vs. 6b it becomes clear that the Father is the
destination in view in connection with the "way" symbol.

[7]The correlative forms in vss. 7 and 9 express the
mediating role of the Son. The conditional form of vs. 7 (*ei
agnokeite me, kai ton patera mou an edeite*) is found in 8:19
(and in 5:46 with reference to Moses and Jesus). The participial
correlative of vs. 9 (*ho heorakos eme heoraken ton patera*) is
found in 5:23 and 15:23 (with the negative), and in 12:44,45;
and 13:20.

[8]On the background of the "way" motif see the bibliography below, note 11. On the particular question of the relationship of the three predicates, "way," "truth," and "life," I. de la Potterie provides a comprehensive historical review of opinion in "'Je suis la Voie.'" See Raymond E. Brown's summary of de la Potterie in *Gospel According to John*, pp. 620-21. In my opinion the immediate context, especially the elaboration of the "I am" statement in vss. 6b-11, makes it clear that "the way" is the controlling predicate and that the other two predicates are subordinate.

[9]To my knowledge, no one has interpreted vss. 4-11 as already addressing the issue of succession, or 13:31-14:3 as already raising the issue, despite the fact that this is the issue taken up from vs. 12 on. Discussion of the shift that occurs at vs. 4 (or, according to some, at vs. 5 or 6) has focused on the pros and cons of some sort of eschatological reinterpretation (See Schulz, *Menschensohn-Christologie*, p. 159, n. 6 for bibliography in addition to Becker and Dodd whom we have discussed above, Chapter I).

[10]This is the common rendering of the shorter reading, *kai hopou ego hupago oidate ten hodon*, which, despite its ungrammatical construction, is accepted by most scholars as the original reading because of its strong manuscript support in p[66c], Sinaiticus, B, C*, L,W,X, 33, 1071.

[11]The "I am" sayings have been the focal point of most of the literature on the discourse material in John, from Eduard Norden on. See Eduard Norden, *Agnostos Theos: Untersuchungen zur Formengeschichte religiöser Rede* (Berlin: B.G. Taubner, 1913); Karl Kundsin, *Charakter und Ursprung der johanneischen Reden, Acta Universitatis Latviensis*, Teologisjas Fakultates, Series 1, Vol. 4 (Riga: 1939); Karl Kundsin, "Zur Diskussion über die Ego-Eimi-Sprüche des Johannesevangeliums," *Charisteria IOHANNI KOPP*. Octogenario Oblata, Papers of the Estonian Theological Society in Exile 7 (Holmiae, 1954):95-107. Heinz Becker, *Die Reden des Johannesevangeliums und der Stil der gnostischen Offenbarungsrede* (1941 Marburg dissertation, published posthumously by Rudolf Bultmann, Gottingen: Vandenhoeck & Ruprecht, 1956); J. Richter, "Ani hu und Ego eimi: Die Offenbarungsformel 'Ich bin es' im Alten und Neuen Testament" (Unpublished dissertation, Erlangen, 1956); Karl Schaedel, "Das Johannesevangelium und 'die Kinder des Lichts': Untersuchungen zu den Selbstbezeichnungen Jesu im vierten Evangelium und zur Heilsterminologie der 'En Fesha-Sekte'" (Unpublished doctoral dissertation, Vienna, 1953); S. Schulz, *Komposition und Herkunft der johanneischen Reden* (Stuttgart: W. Kohlhammer Verlag, 1960); Heinrich Zimmermann, "Das absolute Ego eimi als die neutestamentliche Offenbarungsformel," *Biblische Zeitschrift*, N.F. 4 (1960):54-69; A. Feuillet, "Les Ego eimi christologiques du quatrieme Evangile, *Recherches de Science Religieuse* 54 (1966):5-22, 213-40; George MacRae, "The Ego-Proclamation in Gnostic Sources," in *The Trial of Jesus*, ed. by Ernst Bammel, *Studies in Biblical Theology*, Second Series 13 (London: S.C.M. Press, 1970):122-34; Philip B. Harner, *The "I am" of the Fourth Gospel: A Study in Johannine Usage and Thought*

(Philadelphia: Fortress Press, 1970); Rudolf Schnackenburg, "Herkunft und Sinn der Formel ego eimi," Excursus in *Das Johannesevangelium*, Part II, *Kommentar zu Kap. 5-12, Herders Theologischer Kommentar zum Neuen Testament*, ed. by A. Wiken-hauser, A. Vogtle, R. Schnackenburg 4 (Freiburg: Herder, 1971): 59-70; D. Daube, "The 'I am' of the Messianic Presence," in *The New Testament and Rabbinic Judaism* (London: Athlone, 1956), pp.325-29; Raymond E. Brown, "EGO EIMI - 'I AM,'" Appendix 4, *Gospel According to St. John*, pp. 533-38; W.L. Knox, *St. Paul and the Church of the Gentiles* (London, 1939), pp. 55-89; E. Stauffer, *Jesus and His Story*, trans. by Richard and Clara Winston (New York: Alfred A. Knopf, 1960), pp. 174-95; E. Stauffer, "Ego," *T.D.N.T.*, 2:343-62. Eduard Schweizer, *EGO EIMI: Die religionsgeschichtliche Herkunft und theologische Bedeutung der johanneischen Bildreden*, FRLANT, N.F. 38 (2d ed.: Göttingen: Vandenhoeck & Ruprecht, 1965). Jan Bergman, *Ich bin Isis: Studien zum memphitischen Hintergrund der griechischen Isisareta-logien, Acta Universitatis Upsaliensis, Historia Religionum*, Vol. 3 (Uppsala: n/p., 1968). See also the review of Bergman by Jonathon Z. Smith, "Native Cults in the Hellenistic Period," *HR* 11 (1971):236-49.

[12]*Gospel*, p. 225, n. 3.

[13]Ibid., citing *Altorientalische Texte* I, ed. by Hugo Gressmann (Second Edition, Berlin, 1926).

[14]*Gospel According to St. John*, p. 533.

[15]Schaedel, "Das Johannesevangelium und 'die Kinder des Lichts,'" p. 15.

[16]*Gospel*, p. 255, n. 3.

[17]Ibid., p. 457, n. 4. Raymond Brown has overlooked this change of opinion in his reference to Bultmann (Brown, *Gospel According to St. John*, p. 534).

[18]Ibid.

[19]According to Karl Schaedel, the recognition formula "muss polemisch-exklusiven Charakter haben. Sie fordert aus-schliessliche Geltung, muss also jedem anderen gleichlautenden Anspruch feindlich gegenuberstehen" ("Das Johannesevangelium und 'die Kinder des Lichts,'" p. 9). Schaedel proceeds to argue as if *only* the recognition formula can express a polemic. Cf. also Schulz, *Komposition und Herkunft der Johanneischen Reden*, pp. 127-28. Brown is more careful, speaking of a "contrast" expressed in the recognition formula, rather than a "polemic." But he too slights the fact that the "identification" formula can express a contrast, given the right context.

[20]While we have made use of Bultmann's classification scheme here, it should be pointed out that a more complex analysis of the "I am" form is urgently needed, one that will take account of the whole set of factors which can affect the usage of the form, not just the one factor to which Bultmann

called attention, namely, What question is being answered? Other factors which should be used in such an analysis would include the identity of the speaker, the audience, the occasion--time and place, etc. E. Schweizer, for example, supplements Bultmann's scheme with one which he describes as "mehr inhaltlich-theo-logisch," but which could be broken down in terms of the relationship between speaker and hearer (*EGO EIMI*, pp. 27-33).

[21]The importance of this point, so elementary on the face of it, cannot be exaggerated. We have cited its importance in the development of Bultmann's interpretation of the Gospel (see above, p. 2, n. 7). Before Bultmann Wellhausen had emphasized the same fact, that "bei Joh. stösst Jesus die Juden immer nur mit der Tatsache vor den Kopf, dass Er die Wehrheit sei, worin die Wahrheit bestehe, sagt er nicht" (*Evangelium Johannis*, p. 112).

[22]*Gospel*, p. 266.

[23]This is implied by what Michael Hill, for example, calls the "relational" aspect of charismatic authority, by which he means that charismatic claims and behavior depend upon the recognition of the hearer. "It is the definition that actors in a situation give to it that is of primary importance, rather than a purely external evaluation of it" (Michael Hill, *A Sociology of Religion* [New York: Basic Books, Inc., 1973], pp. 163-64).

[24]I am placing emphasis on the *directness* of access to divine power in the definition of charismatic authority, directness relative to the prevailing, officially recognized channels of authority in a given society. I am using the term "traditional" in the sense of that order which has become recognized generally as official and legitimate in a given society. See further the discussion below, Chapter VI.

[25]Cf. Wayne Meeks's reference to self-contradictions that are "manifestly deliberate" (Meeks, "Man from Heaven," p. 48). The best discussion of John 5:31 and 8:13 is Anitra Kolenkow's address to the 1974 Society of Biblical Literature Fourth Gospel Session. See below, p. 85, n. 60.

[26]Bultmann's interpretation of the Gospel assigns prime importance to this lack of external distinguishing marks, but understands this to mean that Jesus did no miracles or offer other marks of prophetic possession. According to Bultmann the Johannine Jesus appears to be no different from other "ordinary" men. But this is hardly the Johannine viewpoint. The miracles cannot be dismissed in this fashion (see below, Chapter IV). It is, however, correct to say that for the author Jesus *appears* to be no different from other "extraordinary" men, i.e., prophetic claimants.

[27]*Agnostos Theos*, pp. 188-201.

[28]Ibid., p. 197.

[29]Ibid., p. 214. Professor Jonathon Smith has called my attention to the fact that Celsus may have been describing Christian figures, possibly Montanist prophets. According to W.L. Knox, "The language of these prophets is merely Celsus' parody of perfectly good ante-Nicene Christian preaching of a rather enthusiastic type" (W.L. Knox, *Some Hellenistic Elements in Primitive Christianity* [London: Oxford University Press, 1944], p. 83, n. 2). See Thomas W. Gillespie's recent discussion of the Celsus reference in the article, "A Pattern of Prophetic Speech in First Corinthians," *Journal of Biblical Literature* 97 (1978): 74-95.

[30]Kundsin, *Charakter and Ursprung der johanneischen Reden*, pp. 268ff.

[31]Ibid., pp. 223, 229, 267-68.

[32]*Gospel According to John*, pp. 534-35.

[33]For the literature see above, p. 52, n. 11. There has been an apologetic note in the debate which has led to the posing of all sorts of false disjunctions as regards the issue of "boasting" or self-glorification. According to Karl Kundsin, for example, the so-called distinctively Christian "soteriologi-cal clause" reflects a difference at a much deeper level between Christian and pagan "I am" forms. In the Hellenistic and Oriental texts, he writes, one finds self-glorification. The predications and attributes are listed for the sake of the god. Particularly the Babylonian and Egyptian texts are as far re-moved from the Johannine discourses as possible. Here the style reflects "absolutism . . . without reference to the receiver or hearer" (*Charakter und Ursprung*, p. 267): "Der Ichstil der babylonischen und ägyptischen Texte ist der Ausdruck für die Majestät des Redenden in ihrem reinen Für-sich-sein" (ibid., p. 268). There is "nothing even in the way of an anticipation of the idea that the transcendent being of the speaker might also signify strength and help, life and salvation for others" (ibid., p. 267). Despite certain anticipations of the Johannine style in Jewish tradition (the Pentateuch, Deutero-Isaiah, the Psalms, and Wisdom literature), Kundsin concludes that it is "auf sein tieferes Wesen gesehen durchaus etwas *sui generis*, wie es scheint, sogar etwas Schöpferisches und Neues" (ibid., p. 229).

A similar distinction is drawn by Heinrich Zimmermann between what he calls the "I-form" and the "I-style." Zimmermann lists several points of difference; however, I find the points of difference cited so confusing and as to be incapable of applica-tion. One of the most curious and revealing points is that the one who uses the "I-style" makes a "very particular claim which goes beyond the measure belonging to man" (Das absolute *Ego Eimi* als die neutestamentliche Offenbarungsformel," p. 65). Zimmermann states that within the Old Testament the "eigentlichen" "I-*style*" is found only in Proverbs and Sirach. Everywhere else in the Old Testament we find the "I-*form*" (00. 65-66). Behind what is presented as a formal literary distinction is, in fact, a theological, i.e., confessional judgment. The "I-style" is characteristically found in the mouth of the ancient Oriental

and Hellenistic gods, according to Zimmermann, and differs from
the Old Testament formula of revelation (in the "I-form") "*as
the revelation of Jahweh differs from the revelation of these
gods*" (p. 66, my emphasis).

We cite Zimmermann together with Kundsin because both
attempt to correlate a formal-stylistic distinction with a confessional distinction between Christian and non-Christian (Kundsin), or Old Testament and pagan (Zimmermann). Zimmermann's
distinction between an "I-form" and an "I-style" is not to be
equated with Kundsin's distinction between an "absolute" and a
"soteriological" style of self-testimony. However, Zimmermann's
notion that the "I-style" involves a claim which goes beyond
the measure belonging to man, which implies an illegitimate self-
aggrandizement, recalls Kundsin's notion that in the Oriental
and Hellenistic texts we find self-glorification. In both cases,
in other words, the issue is boasting, or autodoxology.

Zimmermann's two categories, I have suggested, are too
confusing to be operational. Kundson's distinction is clearer.
But it can easily be shown that the distinction between "soteriological" and "self-glorifying" types of first person self-
testimony does not coincide with the distinction between the
Christian and non-Christian literature. The introduction to the
Hammurabi law code is an example of "soteriological" self-
testimony:

> Hammurabi, the shepherd, called by Enlil, am I;
> the one who makes affluence and plenty abound;
> . . . .
> the one who made Ur prosper;
> . . . the lord, who revived Uruk;
> who supplied water in abundance to its people;
> The preamble concludes:
> When Marduk commissioned me to guide the people aright,
>   to direct the land,
> I established law and justice in the language of the land,
>   thereby promoting the welfare of the people . . .

("The Code of Hammurabi," trans. Theophile J. Meek, *Ancient Near
Eastern Texts Relating to The Old Testament*, ed. James B. Pritchard [Princeton, N.J.: Princeton University Press, 1950], pp.
163ff.) Examples could be multiplied from the Isis aretalogies.
Soteriology is implied in the claim of Alexander the False
Prophet: *Eimi Glykon . . . phaos anthropoisin* (Lucian, 18). It
should be recalled that Norden described the speech type which
he postulated on the basis of the Babylonian, Egyptian, and
Hellenistic texts as "soteriological."

A further difficulty with Kundsin's analysis is that
"soteriological" accomplishments may be cited in a particular
address for purposes of self-glorification or boasting. An
example is the Sumerian hymn, "The King of the Road." Lines 28-
35 recite the king's deeds on behalf of the wayfarer. But the
hymn as a whole is recited, as the king says explicitly, "that
my name be established unto distant days that it leave not the
mouth (of men),/that my praise be spread wide in the land,/that
I be eulogized in all the lands . . ." (Pritchard, lines 37ff.).

A step toward clarification may be made by noting that
the numerous self-laudatory royal hymns in Sumerian literature

are cited by S.N. Kramer as one expression of a psychological drive which, according to Kramer, was a pervading source of motivation in Sumerian behavior and which deeply colored their way of life--"the ambitious, competitive, aggressive, and seemingly far from ethical drive for pre-eminence and prestige, for victory and success" (S.N. Kramer, *The Sumerians: Their History, Culture, and Character* [Chicago: University of Chicago Press, 1963], p. 264). Kramer calls this drive "the will to superiority, the driving ambition for victory over a rival." Typical expressions of this "drive" are the "Copper-Silver" debate in which Copper and Silver, personified, boast of their superiority over each other, and taunt each other with insults concerning their respective shameful and humiliating social roles. Kramer cites also a "bragging speech by the shepherd-god, Dumuzi, whose plea for marriage has just been rejected by the goddess Inanna in favor of the farmer-god, Enkimdu" (p. 226). He points out that the competitive drive played a large role even in Sumerian formal education. A teacher encourages the ambitious student in the following words: "Of your brothers may you be their leader, of your friends may you be their chief; may you rank the highest among the schoolboys" (p. 266). Political rivalry between the Sumerian city-states as it is expressed in at least two epic tales reveals the same exaggerated competitiveness. "To judge from the contents of these two poems," Kramer says, "it was the driving ambition of each of these rulers to break down the morale of his rival by a kind of 'war of nerves' and thus to make submissive vassals of him and his subjects. The tales are replete with taunts and threats carried back and forth by messengers and heralds as well as with challenges and contests" (p. 267). The loser in one case acknowledges the superiority of the victor in the following words: "You are the beloved of Inanna, you alone are exalted, Inanna has truly chosen you for her holy lap; From the lower (lands) to the upper (lands) you are their lord, *I am second to you*, From the (moment of) conception, I was not your equal, you are the 'big brother.' I cannot compare with you ever!" (ibid., p. 267). We may note in passing the fact that the "I am" form is used here to express the opposite of boasting, namely submission, subordination: "I am second to you!"

In the Sumerian literature, then, which includes numerous examples of self-laudatory hymns using the "I am" form, we have unambiguous boasting, bragging speech. That such speech is not uncommon elsewhere may be demonstrated by citing an example from the nineteenth-century American frontier. Henry Adams records a quarrel overheard on a Mississippi flatboat between two boatmen:

'I am a man; I am a horse; I am a team! cried one voice;
'I can whip any man in all Kentucky, by God!' 'I am an alligator!' cried the other; 'half man, half horse; I can whip any man on the Mississippi, by God!' 'I am a man!' shouted the first; 'have the best horse, best dog, best gun, and handsomest wife in all Kentucky, by God!' 'I am a Mississippi snapping turtle!' rejoined the second; 'have bear's claws, alligator's teeth, and the devil's tail; can whip any man, by God!'

(Henry Adams, *The Formative Years*, condensed and edited by Herbert Agar I [London: Collins, 1948]:28). Cf. Mark Twain's similar account in Samuel L. Clemens, *Life on the Mississippi* (New York: Dodd, Mead & Company, 1968), pp. 17-19, which starts out, "Whoo-oop! I'm the old original iron-jawed, brass-mounted, copper-bellied corpse-maker from the wilds of Arkansaw!"

I cannot attempt here a comprehensive classification of possible functions of self-testimony language. I can only suggest that the classifications proposed to date are inadequate and misleading. There are, as the Sumerian and American frontier examples show, cases where self-testimony forms function as boasts. It is absurd, however, to suggest, as one reading of Kundsin and Zimmermann implies, that all non-Christian examples of "I-am" self-testimony have the kind of self-glorifying function of the Sumerian examples. The purpose of the self-testimony of Hammurabi which precedes the law code, for example, appears to be the legitimation of the law code. Against Zimmermann's specious distinctions there are examples of self-glorifying speech within the Old Testament, particularly in Deutero-Isaiah (See H.-M. Dion, "Le Genre Litteraire Sumerien de L'Hymne a soi-meme' et quelques Passages du Deutero-Isaie," *Revue Biblique* 74 [1967]: 215-34. Dion also provides one of the most complete catalogues of Sumerian self-laudatory hymns to be found). A comprehensive analysis of the "boasting" theme should take into account also the classical rhetorical forms which Judge has called attention to in relation to Paul (E.A. Judge, "Paul's Boasting in Relation to Contemporary Professional Practice," *Australian Biblical Review* 16 [1968]:37-50).

[34]Cf. the point made by Reiling that the problem of distinguishing between the false and the true prophet in Israel was a conflict between "prophets with an identical claim to divine authority," and as such, one which could not be solved by means of "external criteria" or "distinctive semantic terms" (J. Reiling, "The Use of PSEUDOPROPHETES in the Septuagint, Philo and Josephus," *Novum Testamentum* 13 [1971]:147-56). In other words, distinctions between true and false prophets are distinctions drawn by insiders of a given group between what, to outsiders, are equivalent figures. The resemblance of the Johannine Jesus to other savior figures has been insisted upon by only a few scholars. Cf. G.P. Wetter's conclusion that "in allem Äusseren ist dieser Christus ein echt antiker 'Sohn Gottes,' . . . ja das Evangelium scheint dazu geschrieben werden zu sein, um die Menschen davon zu überzeugen" (Wetter, *Die Sohn Gottes; Eine Untersuchung uber den Charakter und die Tendenz des Johannes-Evangeliums; Zugleich ein Beitrag zur Kenntnis der Heilandsgestalten der Antike* [Göttingen: Vandenhoeck & Ruprecht, 1916], p. 156). Cf. too, the similar conclusion of Richard Reitzenstein in *Poimandres: Studien zur griechisch-ägyptischen und frühchristlichen Literatur* (Photographic reproduction of the Leipzig, 1904 edition, Darmstadt: Wissenschaftliche Buchgesellschaft, 1966), p. 223, n. 2. Reitzenstein's statement is quoted, in agreement, by E. Schweizer, *EGO EIMI*, p. 126. Cf. too the article by Wayne A. Meeks, "The Divine Agent and His Counterfeit in Philo and the Fourth Gospel," in *Aspects of Religious Propaganda in Judaism and Early Christianity*, ed. by Elisabeth S. Fiorenze (Notre Dame: University of Notre Dame Press, 1976), pp. 43-67.

[35]Similar to Brown's distinction between autodoxology and soteriology is Robert Fortna's recent attempt to formulate the contrast between source and redaction in the Gospel in terms of a movement "from christology to soteriology." See the two articles, "From Christology to Soteriology: a redaction-critical study of Salvation in the Fourth Gospel," *Interpretation* 27 (1973): 31-47; and Fortna, "Christology in the Fourth Gospel." Fortna holds that there is a polemical thrust to this movement. The redactor's explicit "soteriology" is intended to "counter" the source's "single-minded attention to Christology" ("Christology," p. 491). Fortna himself supplies material which calls this thesis into question, for, as he points out, the redactor himself equates salvation, or life, with Jesus. "Jesus does not accomplish salvation; he is salvation" ("Christology," p. 40). The redactor's soteriology is christology, in other words. "John's most characteristic word for salvation" says Fortna, "is life, and ultimately it is not a quality, a state, to which Jesus brings men, but Jesus himself" (ibid.). If in fact the redactor was concerned about the source's christocentrism, why has he himself chosen as one of his most characteristic forms of expression the "I am" saying? That Fortna has difficulty maintaining this aspect of his argument becomes apparent in his attempt to summarize the contrast between source and redaction. There is a kind of oscillation back and forth between acknowledgment of the continuity between source and redaction, and an effort to preserve the difference between them as significant. First he points out that what John had added would not have caused offense to one who was familiar with the source, "for John has both drawn out the theological potential hidden in the source and extended it in a way that makes its original meaning clearer and deeper" (ibid.). Then he checks himself and insists that John's "advance" on the source is "a major one." One expects a summary statement of the "advance" to follow. And, indeed, there follows first a description of the source: it is a gospel of signs, a demonstration of the Messiahship of Jesus, and "its soteriology is entirely subjected to Christology." As for the redactor, one finds the concession that "this christological emphasis is not diminished by John--on the contrary." Then where is the difference? Fortna proceeds: the redacted Gospel is "a Gospel not only of signs, that is, of Jesus and his identity, but much more of salvation, of life." But then he must add, "Or rather, it finally asserts that the two are one, that to know who Jesus is and to believe in him is to live (20.31). Presumably John's experience, and that of his church, showed him that christology alone is insufficient; belief in Jesus, unless perceived soteriologically, is of no account" (ibid., p. 41). I suggest that whatever John may have "countered" in his source, if anything, it was not a single-minded attention to christology. He is as guilty of this charge as is his source. He has a more *explicit* soteriology, as Fortna points out, but one which ends up even more insistently directing the reader's attention back to Jesus as in some way or other the source and the substance of salvation. In other words, both source and redaction are equally christocentric.

[36]Dieter Georgi, *Die Gegner des Paulus im 2. Korintherbrief: Studien zur religiösen Propaganda in der Spätantike*, Wissenschaftliche Monographien zum Alten und Neuen Testament 11 (Neukirchen-Vluyn: Neukirchener Verlag, 1964):210-13.

[37]Ibid., p. 232.

[38]Ibid., p. 229.

[39]Ibid., p. 213.

[40]See, for example, W. Nicol's observation that "a more or less general consensus of opinion has been reached that the Jesus of the S[igns Source] was in some way or other influenced by *theios aner*-ideas,"--in contrast to the author or redactor (W. Nicol, *The Semeia in the Fourth Gospel: Tradition and Redaction, Supplements to Novum Testamentum* 32 [Leiden: E.J. Brill, 1972]:49).

[41]I am suggesting, in other words, that the hypothesis of a Signs Source and its redaction by the author may not be used to dissociate the author from the image of Jesus as a miracle worker. Even though to the author Jesus is more, much more, than this, he knows that this is what Jesus *looked like*, outwardly.

[42]See below, pp. 150ff.

[43]Cf. Bultmann's statement that "I am the Way" is "the pure expression of the revelation idea" (*Evangelium*, p. 467, my translation. Cf. *Gospel*, p. 605).

[44]Wetter called it a "Streitschrift" (*Sohn Gottes*, p. 127). Wilhelm Wrede held that a historical understanding of the Gospel would only be achieved when it was seen "als eine aus dem Kampfe geborene und für den Kampf geschriebene Schrift" (Wrede, *Charakter und Tendenz des Johannesevangeliums* [Tübingen: J.C.B. Mohr [Paul Siebeck], 1903], p. 40).

[45]Notably Louis Martyn among recent scholars, in *History and Theology*, and "Source Criticism and Religionsgeschichte in the Fourth Gospel," *Perspective* 11 (1970):247-73.

[46]See for example Oscar Cullmann, *The Johannine Circle*, trans. by John Bowden (Philadelphia: The Westminster Press, 1976), p. 60. On this point Cullmann follows W. Baldensperger, W. Bauer, and R. Bultmann.

[47]O. Cullmann, "The Significance of the Qumran Texts for Research into the Beginnings of Christianity," *Journal of Biblical Literature* 74 (1955):225; Schaedel, Das Johannesevangelium und 'die Kinder des Lichts,' p. 231.

[48]Bultmann, *Gospel*, p. 377.

[49]E.C. Colwell, *John Defends the Gospel* (Chicago: Willett, Clark & Company, 1936), p. 13.

[50]Ibid., p. 376. Cf. Schweizer, *EGO EIMI*, p. 126, who follows Bultmann on this point.

[51]Ibid., emphasis in original

[52]Ibid.

[53]Ibid., p. 377.

[54]*Journal of Biblical Literature* 91 (1972):44-72.

[55]Ibid., p. 69.

[56]Ibid., pp. 69-70. My emphasis.

[57]Ibid., p. 71.

[58]Ibid., p. 69.

[59]Ibid., p. 70.

[60]Ibid., pp. 70-71.

[61]This point needs stressing, since some may view our reading of the farewell discourse as a polemic as arising from current fashion in New Testament scholarship. The fact is, however, that I have not introduced the idea of a polemic into the discourse, but rather suggested an alternative issue to the eschatological polemic usually found there.

[62]Cf. the "we" of 3:11, which associates the author and his group, with the one who is "from above" in 3:31ff. For the question of the *Sitz im Leben* of the Gospel this observation may be reversed. The earthly locus of those whose standpoint is heaven is some form of prophetic calling or vocation.

CHAPTER IV

[1]For the literature, see above, p. 3, n. 11.

[2]Brown, *Gospel According to St. John*, p. 645; Schnackenburg, *Johannesevangelium*, Part III, p. 90, n. 98; Dodd, *Interpretation*, p. 405; Bultmann, *Gospel*, p. 619.

[3]See Schnackenburg's summary of the problem and the alternative solutions proposed. Schnackenburg concludes that the two texts, 14:16, 17 and 18ff. refer to different theological aspects "und nicht knofrontiert werden dürfen" *Johannesevangelium*, Part III, p. 88).

[4]Berlin: Georg Reimer, 1907. The literary break within the farewell material at 14:31 served, in fact, as the starting point for Wellhausen's investigation.

[5]Julius Wellhausen, *Das Evangelium Johannis* (Berlin: George Reimer, 1908), p. 77: "Es hat sich in Kap. 14 ein innerer Zwiespalt gezeigt."

[6]Ibid.

[7]*Spirit-Paraclete*, p. 3.

[8]Ibid., p. 5.

[9]Ibid., p. 24.

[10]Ibid., p. 13.

[11]Ibid., p. 17.

[12]Ibid., p. 19.

[13]Ibid.

[14]Ibid., p. 3.

[15]Ibid., p. 2.

[16]Ibid., p. 24.

[17]Ibid., p. 10. That this is a speculation is clear from the note Windisch adds, which proposes an alternative possible understanding of the sequence (note 27).

[18]Ibid., p. 20.

[19]Bornkamm, "Der Paraklet im Johannes-Evangelium." See also the rector's address by Bornkamm, published as "Die Zeit des Geistes: Ein johanneisches Wort und seine Geschichte," in *Geschichte und Glaube*, 1:90-103.

[20]"Der Paraklet," p. 70.

[21]Ibid., p. 71.

[22]Ibid., p. 84.

[23]Ibid., p. 79. A further indication of the unsatisfactory nature of Bornkamm's understanding of the Paraclete is his ambiguity on the identification of the Paraclete with the glorified Son. Though Bornkamm claims that the Paraclete is none other than the Son of Man glorified, he subsequently states that "the evangelist does not speak of a new 'Spirit-form' of the exalted one, but rather places the Spirit in the service of the dying exalted one," and adds that "the unity with the Father which is reserved for Jesus alone is consequently not attributed to the Paraclete" (p.88).

[24]Ibid., p. 87.

[25]Ibid.

[26]Ibid., p. 88.

[27]Ibid., p. 85.

[28]Bultmann pointed out, in criticism of the original version of Bornkamm's article (published in *Festschrift für R. Bultmann* [Stuttgart: Kohlhammer, 1949], pp. 12-35), that the two changes introduced by the author in applying the forerunner-fulfiller conception leave nothing of the original pattern (Bultmann, *Gospel*, p. 567, n. 2). In his reply to Bultmann, incorporated into the revised version of the article, Bornkamm held that the eschatological relationship of the two times remained. Despite the changes introduced by the evangelist, Bornkamm asserted, the idea retained significance "because it was able to express the qualitative difference between Then and Now and at the same time the indissoluble connection of both, the time of the historically limited preparation and the time of the eschatological fulfilment" (Der Paraklet," p. 86). But this reintroduces the notion of rank.

[29]As in Acts 2:16ff., for example. See Bultmann, *Theology of the New Testament*, trans. by Kendrick Grobel 1 (New York: Charles Scribner's Sons, 1951):155. Cf. Robin Scroggs' important article, "The Exaltation of the Spirit by Some Early Christians," *Journal of Biblical Literature* 74 (1965):359-73.

[30]Brown cites Spitta, Delafosse, Windisch, Sasse, Bultmann, and Betz as holding to the position that the Paraclete was once an independent salvific figure, later confused with the Holy Spirit (Brown, "The Paraclete," p. 113, no. 4).

[31]*Der Paraklet*, p. 149ff., cf. p. 2.

[32]Ibid., p. 127.

[33]Ibid., p. 149.

[34]Ibid., p. 150.

[35]The one subsequent reference to the text (page 163) does not resolve this problem.

[36]We have not touched on interpretations of the Paraclete where the Paraclete is identified with the Beloved Disciple. In such interpretations the distinction between the Paraclete and Jesus, the Son, receives its most pointed expression. See especially H. Sasse, "Der Paraklet im Johannesevangelium," *Zeitschrift für die neutestamentliche Wissenschaft* 24 (1925): 275; Kragerud, *Der Lieblingsjunger im Johannesevangelium*, p. 82. Brown agrees "in principle" with those who see in the Beloved Disciple the "incarnation" of the Paraclete (Brown, *Gospel According to St. John*, p. 1142). Cf. also Culpepper, *The Johannine School*, pp. 267-70. Although Culpepper makes it clear that for the author the Beloved Disciple "was *not* the Paraclete" (p. 268), nevertheless, he suggests that for the Johannine community the Beloved Disciple was "their first Paraclete" (p. 269).

[37]Windisch, *Spirit-Paraclete*, p. 25.

[38]Becker, "Abschiedsrede," p. 227; Bultmann, *Gospel*, pp. 581, 619. Betz cites also Heitmuller, Corssen, Holtzmann, and Feine (Betz, *Paraklet*, p. 149, n. 5). Cf. also Brown, *Gospel According to St. John*, p. 646, and the discussion by Ernest Scott (Ernest F. Scott, *The Fourth Gospel: Its Purpose and Theology* [Edinburgh: T. & T. Clark, 1906] pp. 346-49).

[39]As noted above (p. 70, n. 3) Schnackenburg concludes that these two parts of the text should not be brought into confrontation!

[40]Windisch, *Spirit-Paraclete*, p. 3.

[41]With this cf. the promise of authority to Peter in Matt. 16:18, 19, later extended to all the disciples, Matt. 18:18. See also John 20:22, 23, discussed below in Chapter V.

[42]Becker recognizes that this formula introduces a new section or subsection, but pays little attention to the disciples as the subjects of Jesus' announcement ("Abschiedsrede," p. 224). Spitta likewise quotes B. Weiss on v. 12 as follows: "Die feierliche Versicherung zeigt, dass hier eine neue Gedankenreihe beginnt. . . ." (Spitta, *Johannes-Evangelium als Quelle*, p. 344).

[43]Fortna assumes that the uniqueness precludes a sharing in the divine power of the Son by the disciples. But such a sharing is just what is in view in vss. 12-24. See above, p. 3 n. 10.

[44]On the "magical potency" of Jesus' self-identification see Knox, *Some Hellenistic Elements*, p. 87. It is the effect of Jesus' words in the narrative which demonstrates their power.

The argument over whether or not the absolute *ego eimi* without predicate appears in the magical literature is beside the point (See Zimmermann, "Das absolute *ego eimi*," p. 56). What the parallels cited by Knox and others show is the well-known role of identification, of knowing the identity of the deity, or proclaiming the name of the deity, in magic.

[45]See under *ekballo* in William F. Arndt and F. Wilbur Gingrich, *A Greek-English Lexicon of the New Testament and Other Early Christian Literature* (Chicago: University of Chicago Press, 1957).

[46]Cf. Caird's comments in his article, "The Glory of God in the Fourth Gospel" An Exercise in Biblical Semantics," p. 266.

[47]Cf. the magical parallels for the use of *tarasso* cited by Campbell Bonner, "Traces of Thaumaturgic Technique in the Miracles," *Harvard Theological Review* 20 (1927):177. Cf. Morton Smith, *Clement of Alexandria and a Secret Gospel of Mark* (Cambridge: Harvard University Press, 1973), p. 223. According to Bonner we have in John 13:21 "a clear case of the phrenetic agitation of the prophet" (p. 178).

[48]Bultmann, *Gospel*, p. 119, n. 2 raises the question explicitly as to whether "the Evangelist" believed the miracle (in 2:1-11) to have been "an actual historical occurrence" or not, without giving an answer. But when he argues that "the divinity of the figure of Jesus in John is completely lacking in visibility" (*Theology of the New testament*, 2:42), and concludes that the miracles "are neither more nor less than words, *verba visibilia* (ibid., p. 60), he points the way to the conclusion that their actual historicity as demonstrations of divine power is a matter of indifference to the author. According to Bultmann miracles are a "a concession to the weakness of man" (*Gospel*, p. 696).

[49]The primary statement of the "hiddenness" theme is to be found in Bultmann's comments on John 1:14, *ho logos sarx egeneto* (*Gospel*, p. 63).

[50]Bultmann, *Theology of the New Testament*, 2:59-60.

[51]Jürgen Becker, "Wunder und Christologie," *New Testament Studies* 19 (1970): 130-148.

[52]Ibid., p. 146.

[53]Ibid., pp. 146-47.

[54]Fortna, "Christology in the Fourth Gospel," p. 491. Fortna here follows Paul Achtemeier, "Gospel miracle tradition and the divine man," *Interpretation* 26 (1972): 174-97.

[55]Ibid., p. 492.

[56]Ibid., p. 493.

[57]Ibid., p. 491. Cf. above, p. 61, n. 35, for a specific critique of Fortna.

[58]See above, p. 61.

[59]*Testament*, p. 22.

[60]The miracles have become events freighted with a significance which places them on a level with creation, resurrection, and judgment, but this symbolic importance which they have acquired as a result of the one who performs them does not take away from their importance as events. As events, in fact, they belong to the time of "the beginning." The symbolic importance of the miracles does not make them any the less miraculous or magical. Anitra Kolenkow's term "goetic" to describe the outright assertion of claims to divine power such as one finds in the Johannine discourse material is legitimate, and underscores the fact that the motifs found in the discourses, such as the power to give life, to judge, and even the identity and indwelling motifs (14:10, 11, for example) "may be associated with a miracle milieu." Kolenkow's study was presented as an address at the Annual Meeting of the Society of Biblical Literature in 1974, under the title "Argument Among Miracle Believers: Johannine Use of 'Goes' Motifs to Modify 'Miracle Apology' Motifs in John 5 and 8." Unfortunately it has not been published.

[61]Cf. Brown, *Gospel According to John*, p. 1037; Bultmann, *Gospel*, p. 692; Schnackenburg, *Johannesevangelium*, Part III, p. 387.

[62]See Büchsel on common use of the terms "bind" and "loose" in magic (Friedrich Büchsel, *"deo,"* *Theological Dictionary of the New Testament*, 2:60-61).

[63]Brown, *Gospel According to John*, p. 384.

[64]Karl Preisendanz, *Papyri Graecae Magicae* (2d rev. ed.; Stuttgart: Verlag B.G. Teubner 2 [1974]:45ff).

[65]Ignored completely by C.K. Barrett, C.H. Dodd, and R.E. Brown, for example, in their discussions of the background of the Gospel as well as in their detailed comments on the text. Schnackenburg in his three volume commentary does not cite Preisendanz anywhere in his bibliography, nor *PGM* in the list of abbreviations. In the study of early christian literature generally a shift in attitude to magic is occurring. Hull's book on *Hellenistic Magic and the Synoptic Tradition* is an example of a new willingness to take the magical literature seriously. David Aune's forthcoming article, "Magic in Early Christianity," in W. Haase, ed., *Aufstieg und Niedergang der römischen Welt* (Berlin: W. de Gruyter, 198?, is another important example.

[66]A.-J. Festugière, "La valeur religieuse des papyrus magiques," in *L'ideal religieux des grecs et l'évangile* (Paris: n.p., 1932), pp. 281-328. See esp. p. 285.

[67]On the concern with transmission and succession see, for example, the instruction in *PGM*, 1:193ff.: "These things deliver to no one except to your own actual son alone." Cf. also the instructions in the so-called Mithras Liturgy, *PGM*, 4:734f. The "Mithras Liturgy" has been translated by Marvin W. Meyer in the SBL Texts and Translations series: *The "Mithras Liturgy," SBL Texts and Translations*, No. 10, Graeco-Roman Religion, Series 2, ed. and trans. by Marvin W. Meyer (Missoula, Montana: Scholars Press, 1976). See A. Dieterich, *Eine Mithrasliturgie* (3d expanded ed., published by Otto Weinreich; Leipzig: B.G. Teubner, 1923), p. 52, for other examples.

[68]In the spell for a light oracle (*luchnomantias*) the deity is called on to "enter in" (*eiselthe*) seven times (*PGM*, 4:955-1034. Cf. also 4:24, 75, 91, 879).

[69]Martyn, *History and Theology*, p. 7. Cf. Windisch, *Spirit-Paraclete*, pp. 19-20.

[70]Aune, *Cultic Setting*, p. 78.

[71]Bultmann, *Gospel*, p. 610; Schnackenburg, *Johannesevangelium*, 3:80-81; Brown, *Gospel According to John*, p. 633.

[72]*Johannesevangelium*, 3:81.

[73]*Gospel*, pp. 610-11.

[74]*Perspective*, 9 (1970):110.

[75]Ibid.

[76]Ibid., p. 114.

[77]Examples of this gospel form would be the *Pistis Sophia*, *The Apocryphon of James*, *The Apocryphon of John*. See also W. Schneemelcher's discussion of types of apocryphal gospels in Edgar Hennecke, *New Testament Apocrypha*, ed. by Wilhelm Schneemelcher, English translation ed. by R. McL. Wilson, 1 (Philadelphia: The Westminster Press, 1963):p. 82ff.; also H.-Ch. Puech ibid, pp. 231ff. The contrast in the gospel forms is valid, regardless of whether or not the non-canonical gospel form is usefully described as "gnostic."

[78]Robinson, "*Gattung*," p. 107.

[79]Ibid., p. 113.

[80]This phrase is from Peter Worsley, *The Trumpet Shall Sound: A Study of 'Cargo' Cults in Melanesia* (2d, augmented ed.: New York: Schocken Books, 1968), p. 1. See below, Chapter VI for further discussion of the term "charisma."

[81]Cf. Georgi's observation that in the case of the charismatic or "pneumatic" apostle "der Triumph in der Konkurrenz" is in essence the content of their message (*Gegner*, p. 213). Goergi emphasizes the element of competition throughout

his analysis. Worsley points to the "fissiparity" of charismatic movements, but traces this phenomenon to the primacy of the message, rather than the person of the prophet. Worsley cites Talmon in support, but this is misleading since in Talmon's analysis the kind of message is only one of several factors contributing to the fissiparous tendency of millenarian movements. Talmon also points out that "millenarian movements suffer from frequent cessation and fission partly because they base their recruitment of their leaders on inspiration." (Y. Talmon, "Pursuit of the Millennium: The Relation Between Religious and Social Change," *Archives Europeennes de Sociologie* 3 [1962]: 134). Cf. also Lewis Coser's analysis of sectarian dynamics in *Greedy Institutions*, Ch. 7, "Sects and Sectarians," (London: Free Press, 1974). Coser points out, for example, that the sect often "invents" inner enemies in order to strengthen its solidarity (p. 110). Again, "The world of the sect is a stern world where the sheep and the goats are continually sorted anew . . ." (p. 14).

[82]See in particular Klaus Haacker, *Die Stiftung des Heils: Untersuchungen zur Struktur der johanneischen Theologie, Arbeiten zur Theologie*, First Series 47 (Stuttgart: Calwer Verlag, 1972: 75ff).

[83]See Chapter V below on 14:25, 26.

[84]*Gospel*, p. 611. The whole of verse 14 is omitted in two minor uncials, and some other MSS, "no doubt because it seemed redundant after v. 13," as Barrett points out. Commentators have in one way or another stumbled at the extreme christocentrism of the verse. Bernard omits the *me*, though acknowledging the strong MSS support. Wellhausen and Spitta change *poieso* into *poiesei*. But Bultmann's argument for the verse as it stands is very much to the point.

[85]The basic formal structure of the thought in vs. 20 is hierarchical; that is, it sets forth two levels in which one is subordinate to the other. *Superior level*: "I (am) in my Father." *Subordinate level*: "You (are) in me." The third element ("and I (am) in you") introduces the *reciprocal* structure of vss. 10, 11 into the subordinate relationship. The hierarchical structure is present in 10:14; 15:9,10; 17:21,22; 13:16; 15:20; 17:18, repeated in 20:21. It is insisted upon polemically in 13:16 (recalled in 15:20) though here it is the superiority of the middle party, Jesus, to the disciples, which is in view, at least by inference. With this we should compare 14:28, which indicates the superiority of the first party, the Father, to Jesus. On 17:18, the hierarchical correlation of the sending of Jesus with the sending of the disciples, see Robert M. Grant, "Chains of Being in Early Christianity," in *Myths and Symbols: Studies in Honor of Mircea Eliade*, ed. by J.M. Kitagawa and C.H. Long (Chicago: University of Chicago Press, 1969), pp. 279-89, esp. 285.

[86]On the polemic in 3:13 see Meeks, "Man from Heaven," p. 52. David Aune argues that the polemic in 3:13 "against those who claim to have ascended into the heavenly realm, should *not* be interpreted to exclude that experience on the part of the Johannine community. The prophetic revelation of the exalted

and glorified Jesus was mediated to the community through just such visionary and auditionary pneumatic experiences" (*Cultic Setting*, p. 99). My reading of the farewell discourse suggests, however, that for the author there was an important, basic, distinction between the descent and ascent of the Son which were primal, archetypical events, and the access of the believer to the Father which was, precisely, *"mediated"* (Aune's word) *by the Son*. The author denies the possibility of ascent and access *independent* of Jesus.

CHAPTER V

[1] Cf. Hugo Odeberg's observation that 5:30-47 is "a typical *coda*-section, of the same category as 3:22-36 in relation to 3:3-21 and 4:31-42 in relation to 4:7-30" (*The Fourth Gospel: Interpreted in its Relation to Contemporaneous Religious Currents in Palestine and the Hellenistic-Oriental World* [Amsterdam: B.R. Grüner, Publisher, 1968], p. 217.

[2] Miller, "Parakletenvorstellung," p. 46.

[3] This is not to say that an association of the Spirit with the task of interpreting tradition is uniquely Johannine. Far from it. See, for example, Georgi on Philo and the Jewish apologetic literature (*Gegner*, pp. 127-30). Though the general idea is not unique, the *explicitness* with which our text ascribes the office of "remembering" to the Spirit is striking, and, taken with the other references in John to the remembering motif, in 2:17, 2:22; 12:16, constitutes a fundamental clue to the redactional point of view of the Gospel. Wead and Mussner in particular have emphasized this, though I take issue with their interpretations (see David W. Wead, *The Literary Devices in John's Gospel*, University of Basel Dissertation [Basel: Friedrich Reinhardt Kommissionsverlag, 1970], ch. I; and Franz Mussner, *Die johanneische Sehweise und die Frage nach dem historischen Jesu*, Quaestiones Disputatae 28 [Freiburg: Herder, 1965]: esp. pp. 38ff., 45ff. and ch. V).

[4] For bibliography on the remembering motif see, in addition to the commentaries to the passages cited and the discussion in Wead and Mussner (see previous note), Nils A. Dahl, "ANAMNESIS"; O. Michel, "mimneskomai," *Theological Dictionary of the New Testament*, 4:675-83 (disappointingly brief on John); W. Theiler, "Erinnerung," *Reallexikon für Antike und Christentum*, Vol. 6, cols. 43-54; Muller, "Parakletenvorstellung"; Robinson, "*Gattung*"; Haacker, *Stiftung*, pp. 154-162; Nicol, *Semeia*, pp. 125-130; Betz, *Paraklet*, pp. 94ff., 184ff.

[5] Schnackenburg, *Johannesevangelium*, 1:362.

[6] Bultmann, *Gospel*, p. 128.

[7] Cf. the expository pattern of the farewell discourse itself as a formal expression of this "remembering."

[8] See above on Bornkamm, pp. 132ff.

[9] I return to the rank issue and the notion of "the beginning" referred to here in the following chapter.

[10] Cf. Haacker's discussion of the Johannine idea of tradition, especially the discussion of *terein*, where he refers specifically to the "remembering" motif (*Stiftung*, pp. 74-75, and his discussion of the conditional promises of the farewell discourse (ibid., pp. 148ff).

[11]One of the better discussions of the Johannine idea of tradition is Klaus Haacker's monograph *Die Stiftung des Heils*. I do not think Haacker has acknowledged sufficiently the extent to which the Gospel reflects a prophetic, charismatic community such as Kragerud, for example, sets forth, but neither do I think that the prophetic, charismatic character of Johannine Christianity precludes the sort of attitude to tradition which Haacker develops.

[12]See the discussion below (Chapter VI) of Bornkamm's notion of the "retrospective" point of view in the Gospel.

[13]Nils Dahl, "Der erstgeborene Satans und der Vater des Teufels (Polyk 7:1 und John 8:44)," *Apophoreta: Festschrift für Ernst Haenchen, Beihefte zur Zeitschrift für die neutestamentliche Wissenschaft* 30 (Berlin: Verlag Alfred Töpelmann, 1964):70-84.

[14]Ibid., pp. 80-81.

[15]Schnackenburg, *Johannesevangelium*, 2:293.

[16]John 8:30 suggests that the polemic is in fact against Christian "heretics" (Cf. Dahl, "Der erstgeborene Satans," p. 80).

[17]Windisch, *Spirit-Paraclete*, pp. 8-9.

[18]*Gospel*, p. 576, n. 2.

[19]"Parakletenvorstellung," p. 51. Müller cites Sasse, Mussner, Brown, and Kümmel as sharing this view (p. 51, n. 63).

[20]Citing 4 Ezra 14, Ass. Mos. 10:11; Slavic Enoch 33:5ff., 36:1; 47:1-3; 66:7 as examples, Müller concludes "dass die literarische Gattung Abschiedsrede dazu dient, dass der anonyme Autor dieser Schriften die sterbende Gestalt der Vergangenheit den Anstoss zur Abfassung von Schriften geben lasst, die auf die jeweils vorliegende Schrift jenes Autors verweisen. Die Gattung Abschiedsrede dient der Legitimation der pseudepigraphen Literaten" ("Parakletenvorstellung," p. 56).

[21]Ibid., p. 57.

[22]Müller cites Windisch to the effect that 2 Peter is in fact the "Testament of Peter" (Müller, "Parakletenvorstellung," p. 57; Hans Windisch, *Die katholischen Briefe, Handbuch zum Neuen Testament* 15 [3d. extensively revised edition by Herbert Preisker; Tübingen: J.C.B. Mohr (Paul Siebeck), 1961]:87).

CHAPTER VI

[1]Charles H.H. Scobie, "The Origin and Development of the Johannine Community," a paper delivered to the SBL Fourth Gospel Section, 31 October, 1976 (unpublished), p. 3. Cf. Käsemann, *Testament*, p. 2; I am not convinced that the state of knowledge about the social situation of the other three canonical gospels is that much further advanced.

[2]Ibid.

[3]Meeks, "Man from Heaven"; Smith, "Johannine Christianity"; James M. Robinson, "The Johannine Trajectory," in *Trajectories through Early Christianity*, by James M. Robinsin and Helmut Koester (Philadelphia: Fortress Press, 1971), pp. 232-68; Culpepper, *The Johannine School*; Käsemann, *Testament*; Cullman, *The Johannine Circle*; Martyn, *History and Theology*; Kragerud, *Lieblingsjünger*.

[4]Smith, Scobie and Cullmann.

[5]Meeks (sectarianism); Culpepper (school); Käsemann (conventicle).

[6]Smith, "Johannine Christianity," p. 222.

[7]Ibid., pp. 223-24.

[8]Ibid., p. 224. It is not even completely clear that for Smith sectarianism is incompatible with universalism. Cf. the question at the conclusion of his article: "Finally, the extent to which the widely perceived universalism of the Gospel is rooted in the intention of the evangelist seems to me also to be a question worthy of further reflection . . ." (p. 248).

[9]Herbert Leroy, *Rätsel und Missverständnis: Ein Beitrag zur Formgeschichte des Johannesevangeliums, Bonner Biblische Beiträge*, Vol. 30 (Bonn: Peter Hanstein Verlag, 1968).

[10]"Man from Heaven,' pp. 70-71.

[11]*SBL 1975 Seminar Papers*, ed. by George MacRae 2 (Missoula, Montana: University of Montana for The Society of Biblical Literature, 1975):233-64.

[12]Ibid., pp. 240, 249.

[13]*Testament*, p. 15, cf. pp. 31, 38.

[14]Ibid., p. 38.

[15]Ibid., pp. 37-38.

[16]"Johannine Christianity," p. 243.

[17]Ibid., p. 233.

[18]Ibid., p. 232, cf. p. 244. Smith's view here recalls Kundsin's earlier argument that the "I am" self-testimony form in John goes back to early Christian prophetic experience. Smith cites Kundsin in this connection (p. 233, n. 2). I accept the connection between the Johannine self-testimony and Christian prophecy, but do not accept Kundsin's corollary that this makes it a uniquely Christian form. Cf. also the use made by David Aune of Kundsin's thesis. Aune, *Cultic Setting*, pp. 66-73, esp. p. 72.

[19]"Johannine Christianity," p. 233.

[20]Ibid., p. 239.

[21]Ibid., pp. 236-37.

[22]Ibid., p. 232.

[23]Ibid., p. 244.

[24]Michael Hill, *A Sociology of Religion* (New York: Basic Books, Inc., 1973), chs. 7 & 8. Other sources used include especially Worsley, *The Trumpet Shall Sound*; Peter L. Berger, "Charisma and Religious Innovation: The Social Location of Israelite Prophecy," *American Sociological Review* 28 (1963): 940-50; *Max Weber on Charisma and Institution Building*, ed. by S.N. Eisenstadt (Chicago: University of Chicago Press, 1968); Edward Shils, "Charisma, Order, and Status," *American Sociological Review* 30 (1965):199-213; John Howard Schütz, "Charisma and Social Reality in Primitive Christianity," *Journal of Religion* 54 (1974):51-70; Kenelm Burridge, *New Heaven New Earth: A Study of Millenarian Activities* (New York: Schocken Books, 1969). Following a suggestion made by Professor Jonathon Smith I have placed my interpretation of charismatic authority within the framework of Peter Brown's contrast between "articulate" and inarticulate" power. See Peter Brown, "Socery, Demons and the Rise of Christianity: From Late Antiquity into the Middle Ages," *Religion and Society in the Age of Saint Augustine* (London: Farber and Farber, 1972), pp. 119-46.

[25]*Max Weber on Charisma*, p. 51.

[26]Ibid.

[27]Ibid., p. 52.

[28]*Sociology of Religion*, p. 179.

[29]Ibid., p. 162, citing Norman Cohn, *The Pursuit of the Millennium* (London: Paladin, 1970), p. 268.

[30]*Sociology of Religion*, p. 164.

[31]See Jonathon Z. Smith, "The Garments of Shame," *History of Religion* 5, No. 2 (Winter, 1966): esp. p. 223, n. 23.

[32]Cf. Cohn, *Pursuit of the Millennium*, p. 268.

[33]P. 124. My emphasis.

[34]Ibid.

[35]*Weber on Charisma*, p. 46.

[36]Ibid., pp. 46-47. My emphasis.

[37]*Sociology of Religion*, pp. 153-54. My emphasis.

[38]*Weber on Charisma*, p. 48.

[39]*Trumpet Shall Sound*, p. xii. My emphasis.

[40]*Sociology of Religion*, p. 171.

[41]Ibid., pp. 140-42, and 163.

[42]Worsley, *Trumpet Shall Sound*, p. xiii; Hill, *Sociology of Religion*, p. 153.

[43]Ibid., p. 163.

[44]Ibid., p. 164.

[45]*Trumpet Shall Sound*, p. xxxvi.

[46]*Sociology of Religion*, p. 174. Hill is here following Robert C. Tucker, "The Theory of Charismatic Leadership," *Daedalus* 97, No. 3 (Summer 1968):754.

[47]*Weber on Charisma*, p. 54.

[48]It is all the more imperative to stress this side of the matter in relation to the Fourth Gospel because of the extreme concentration of authority in the Son which characterizes it. On the other hand, it is just this radical concentration which constitutes the single most important clue to the kind of social situation out of which the Gospel arose. The quest for the social context of the Gospel must begin with the question of the social context of its christocentrism.

[49]*New Heaven New Earth*, p. 105.

[50]Ibid., pp. 107-8.

[51]Ibid., p. 111.

[52]Ibid., p. 112.

[53]Meeks, "Man from Heaven," p. 50.

[54]The view that Johannine christology reflects the self-understanding of the Johannine group and, therefore, may be used as evidence of the kind of group it constitutes is hardly novel. David Aune has, perhaps, made the point most explicitly in observing that "the Johannine Jesus becomes comprehensible as a projection (or retrojection) of the religious needs and experiences of the Johannine community in combination with other more traditional historical and conceptual factors" (*Cultic Setting*, p. 77, cf. p. 76). Wayne Meeks similarly suggests that the book of John may be regarded as an "etiology" of the Johannine group in which "the fate of the community [is] projected onto the story of Jesus" ("Man from Heaven," pp. 69, 71). Cf. too the way Louis Martyn uses his concept of the Christian witness as the "double" of Jesus (*History and Theology*, p. 140). Cf. too Haacker's related point that "Johannes ersetzt den Begriff der Kirche durch die Beschreibung der Christusrelation, die nach seiner Auffassung das Wesen der Kirche ausmacht" (*Stiftung*, pp. 66-67). This is the principle underlying Käsemann's argument in *Testament of Jesus*. Cf. for example the relationship between the "docetic" Christology and the "ecclesiology" (*Testament*, p. 70, for example). Aune has overlooked this in his critique of Käsemann (Aune, *Cultic Setting*, pp. 75-76).

[55]The "sectarianism" reflected in the Gospel has been emphasized especially by Wayne Meeks in the article, "The Man from Heaven in Johannine Sectarianism." We have cited above D. Moody Smith, Jr.'s assumption of a "sectarian consciousness" in the Gospel ("Johannine Christianity," pp. 223-24).

[56]Peter Berger, "The Sociological Study of Sectarianism," *Social Research* 21 (1954):467-85. See Hill's discussion of Berger's article, *Sociology of Religion*, pp. 91ff.

[57]"Sectarianism," p. 474.

[58]Ibid., p. 475.

[59]Ibid.

[60]Ibid., p. 476. My emphasis.

[61]In making this distinction I have in mind the distinction between the setting in the life of the church (Sitz im Leben der alten Kirche) and the setting in the gospel (Sitz in Evangelium), to use the terms proposed by R.J. Sneed and cited by Norman Perrin (R.J. Sneed, "The Kingdom's Coming: Luke 17:20-21, Studies in Sacred Theology," Vol. 130 [Washington D.C., 1962]). See Norman Perrin, *Rediscovering the Teaching of Jesus* (New York: Harper & Row, Publishers, 1967), p. 256 and Norman Perrin, *What is Redaction Criticism?* (Philadelphia: Fortress Press, 1969), pp. 34-35.

[62]"Zur Interpretation," p. 114.

[63]P. 136. Emphasis in the original

[64]Ibid.

[65]*Testament*, p. 33. The debate over John's use of tradition "really centres upon John's conception of history."

[66]Ibid., p. 34.

[67]I have run across two other New Testament scholars who have used the word "protology." David Aune uses the term in *Cultic Setting*, pp. 7, 8. John C. Meagher states, in the conclusion of *The Way of the Word: The Beginning and the Establishing of Christian Understanding* (New York: The Seabury Press, 1975): "Earliest Christian thought is radically protological." This means, among other things, the notion of "participation in the fulfillment of original creation" (pp. 184-85). The use of the term "protology" in NT scholarship is symptomatic of increasing attention to mythological aspects in early Christian attitudes towards the past, a much needed relaxation of its one-sided preoccupation with eschatology. Another indication of this shift is the attention to the "founder" as a category (see Haacker, *Die Stiftung des Heils* and Culpepper, *The Johannine School*).

[68]*Testament*, pp. 34ff.

[69]Ibid., p. 7.

[70]"Zur Interpretation," p. 112.

[71]Ibid., p. 113.

[72]Ibid., pp. 113-14.

[73]Note that Käsemann has very significantly qualified his statement later on: "The hour of the passion and death is in a unique sense the hour of his glorification because in it Jesus leaves the world and returns to the Father." To this statement he adds the following note: *"In this respect, the death of Jesus does have the character of a centre of gravity . . ."* (*Testament*, p. 19, n. 30)!

[74]Given the stress laid by Käsemann on this perspective as the "hermeneutical key" to the Gospel, Bornkamm's discussion of it is startlingly brief, consisting of one paragraph ("Zur Interpretation," p. 119).

[75]Ibid.

[76]Note that the first occurrence of the remembering motif, in connection with the temple destruction saying, is followed immediately by the reference to Jesus' complete knowledge, 2:23-25.

[77]One of the most striking formal features of the Fourth Gospel supports the thesis developed here. I have in mind the fact that the author has taken "revelation discourses" (that is to say, discourses by a revealer figure speaking in the first person using, characteristically, the "I am" form), and placed them in the mouth of the pre-resurrection "earthly" figure of

Jesus. This "revelation discourse" form is, everywhere else in
Christian literature, found in a post-resurrection setting.
Whatever the specific historical reasons for the author's anachronistic projection of post-resurrection "Christian" discourses back into the pre-resurrection narrative, the effect
is to insure "against the possibility--exploited by gnosticism--
of relegating to insignificance the early earthly life of Jesus,
as just a lower and hence irrelevant prelude" (Robinson, "*On
the Gattung* of Mark (and John)," p.113).

[78]My understanding of the unity of the discourse is that
it is an illogical, but nevertheless *systematic* unity. The fact
that a set of statements can be illogical and still be systematic
is beautifully illustrated by Milton Rokeach in an article on
"the nature and meaning of dogmatism" in which he quotes a saying
believed to be from Sholom Aleichem: "I did not borrow your
pot; besides it was broken when you lent it to me; besides I
have already returned it to you." As Rokeach points out,
"despite its illogical character, the statement is nevertheless
systematic. While each of the beliefs expressed is contradictory
to the others, they all reinforce each other to serve the end of
protecting the central authority (in this case, the person speaking) against threat" (Milton Rokeach, "The Nature and Meaning
of Dogmatism," *Current Perspectives in Social Psychology*, ed.
W.P. Hollander and R.H. Hunt [New York: Oxford University Press,
1967], p. 163, n. 1)

[79]It is even possible that they were understood to be
claiming to be Jesus himself. Evidence of such a phenomenon
is perhaps to be found in the warning of Jesus in the apocalyptic
discourse in Mark 13. Jesus tells the disciples, "Take heed
that no one leads you astray. Many will come in my name, saying
ego eimi, and they will lead many astray" (Mark 13:5,6). According to Werner Kelber, the *ego eimi* is a "formula of theophany"
(following Stauffer), and affirms the presence of Jesus in such
a way that those who come in the name of Jesus "assert the
identity of the very one in whose name they come. The people
the Markan Apoclypse opposes come in the name of Jesus, because
they claim to be Jesus himself" (Werner H. Kelber," Kingdom and
Parousia in the Gospel of Mark" [unpublished dissertation,
University of Chicago Divinity School, 1970], p. 155).

BIBLIOGRAPHY

Achtemeier, Paul. "Gospel Miracle Tradition and the Divine Man," *Interpretation* 26 (1972):174-97.

Adams, Henry. *The Formative Years*. Condensed and edited by Herbert Agar, Vol. 1. London: Collins, 1948.

Arndt, William F. and Gingrich, F. Wilbur. *A Greek-English Lexicon of the New Testament and Other Early Christian Literature*. Chicago: University of Chicago Press, 1957.

Aune, David Edward. *The Cultic Setting of Realized Eschatology in Early Christianity, Supplements to Novum Testamentum* Vol. 28. Leiden: E.J. Brill, 1972.

_____. "Magic in Early Christianity." Edited by W. Haase. *Aufstieg und Niedergang der römischen Welt*. Berlin: W. de Gruyter, 198?

Bacon, B. W. *The Gospel of the Hellenists*. Edited by Carl H. Kraeling. New York: Henry Holt and Company, 1933.

Barrett, C. K. *The Gospel According to St. John: An Introduction with Commentary and Notes on the Greek Text*. London: S.P.C.K., 1965.

Becker, Heinz. *Die Reden des Johannesevangeliums und der Stil der gnostischen Offenbarungsrede*. Dissertation accepted March 10, 1941 by the Theological Faculty of the University of Marburg. Published posthumously by Rudolf Bultmann. Göttingen: Vandenhoeck & Ruprecht, 1956.

Becker, Jürgen. "Wunder und Christologie." *New Testament Studies* 19 (1970):130-48.

_____. "Die Abschiedsreden Jesu im Johannesevangelium." *Zeitschrift für die neutestamentliche Wissenschaft* 59 (1970):215-46.

Behler, G. B. *Die Abschiedsworte des Herrn: Johannesevangelium Kapitel 13-17*. Salzburg: Otto Müller Verlag, 1962.

Berger, Peter L. "Charisma and Religious Innovation: The Social Location of Israelite Prophecy." *American Sociological Review* 28 (1963):940-50.

_____. "The Sociological Study of Sectarianism." *Social Research* 21 (1954):467-85.

Bergman, Jan. *Ich bin Isis: Studien zum memphitischen Hintergrund der griechischen Isisaretalogien. Acta Universitatis Upsaliensis, Historia Religionum*, Vol. 3. Uppsala: n.p., 1968.

Bernard, J. H. *A Critical and Exegetical Commentary on the Gospel According to St. John, The International Critical Commentary*. New York: Charles Scribner's Sons, 1929.

Betz, Otto. *Der Paraklet: Fürsprecher im häretischen Spätjudentum, im Johannes-Evangelium und in nue gefundenen gnostischen Schriften, Arbeiten zur Geschichte des Spätjudentums und Urchristentums*. Vol. 2. Leiden: E.J. Brill, 1963.

Bonner, Campbell. "Traces of Thaumaturgic Technique in the Miracles." *Harvard Theological Review* 20 (1927):171-81.

Borgen, Peder. *Bread from Heaven: An Exegetical Study of the Concept of Manna in the Gospel of John and the Writings of Philo, Supplements to Novum Testamentum*. Vol. 10. Leiden: E.J. Brill, 1965.

Borig, Rainer. *Der Wahre Weinstock: Untersuchungen zu Jo 15:1-10, Studien zum Alten und Neuen Testament*. Vol. 16. München: Kösel-Verlag, 1967.

Bornkamm, Günther. "Der Paraklet im Johannes-Evangelium." *Geschichte und Glaube*, Part I, *Collected Essays*, Vol. 3. München: Chr. Kaiser Verlag, 1968. Pp. 68-89.

_____. "Die Zeit des Geistes: Ein johanneisches Wort und seine Geschichte." *Geschichte und Glaube*, Part I, *Collected Essays*. Vol. 3. München: Chr. Kaiser Verlag, 1968. P. 90-103.

_____. "Zur Interpretation des Johannesevangeliums: Eine Auseinandersetzung mit Ernst Käsemann's Schrift "Jesu letzter Wille nach Johannes 17.'" *Evangelische Theologie* 28 (1968):8-25.

Brown, Peter. "Sorcery, Demons and the Rise of Christianity: From Late Antiquity into the Middle Ages." *Religion and Society in the Age of Saint Augustine*. London: Farber and Farber, 1972. P. 119-146.

Brown, Raymond E. *The Gospel According to John, The Anchor Bible*. Vols. 29 and 29a. Garden City, N.Y.: Doubleday & Company, Inc., 1966, 1970.

_____. "The Paraclete in the Fourth Gospel." *New Testament Studies* 13 (1966/67):113-32.

Buchsel, Friedrich. "*deo.*" *Theological Dictionary of the New Testament*. Edited by Gerhard Kittel, translated and edited by Geoffrey W. Bromiley. Vol. 2. Grand Rapids, Mich.: Wm. B. Eerdmans Publishing Company, 1964.

_____. *Das Evangelium nach Johannes, Das Neue Testament Deutsch*. Vol. 4. Göttingen: Vandenhoeck & Ruprecht, 1946.

Bultmann, Rudolf. "Die Bedeutung der neuerschlossenen mandäischen und manichäischen Quellen für das Verständnis des Johannesevangeliums." *Zeitschrift fur die neutestamentliche Wissenschaft* 24 (1925):100-46.

_____. *Die Geschichte der synoptischen Tradition, Forschungen zur Religion und Literatur des Alten und Neuen Testaments*. N.F., Vol. 12 6th ed. Göttingen: Vandenhoeck & Ruprecht, 1964.

_____. *The Gospel of John: A Commentary*. Translated by G.R. Beasley-Murray. Oxford: Basil Blackwell, 1971.

_____. *Theology of the New Testament*. Translated by Kendrick Grobel. Vol. 2. n.c.: Charles Scribner's Sons, 1955.

Burridge, Kenelm. *New Heaven New Earth: A Study of Millenarian Activities*. New York: Schocken Books, 1969.

Caird, G. B. "The Glory of God in the Fourth Gospel: An Exercise in Biblical Semantics." *New Testament Studies* 15 (1968-69):265-77.

Charlier, C. "La Presence dans l'absence (Jean 13:31-14:31)." *Bible et vie chretienne* 2 (May-July 1953):61-75.

Clemens, Samuel L. *Life on the Mississippi*. New York: Dodd, Mead & Company, 1968.

Colwell, Ernest Cadman. *John Defends the Gospel*. Chicago: Willett, Clark & Company, 1936.

Corssen, P. "Die Abschiedsreden Jesu in dem vierten Evangelium." *Zeitschrift für die neutestamentliche Wissenschaft* 8 (1907):125-42.

Coser, Lewis A. *Greedy Institutions: Patterns of Undivided Commitment*. London: Free Press, 1974.

Crossan, Dominic. *The Gospel of Eternal Life: Reflections on the Theology of St. John*. Milwaukee: The Bruce Publishing Company, 1967.

Cullman, Oscar. *The Johannine Circle*. Translated by John Bowden. Philadelphia: The Westminster Press, 1976.

_____. "The Significance of the Qumran Texts for Research into the Beginnings of Christianity." *Journal of Biblical Literature* 74 (1955):213-26.

Culpepper, R. Alan. *The Johannine School: An Evaluation of the Johannine-School Hypothesis Based on an Investigation of the Nature of Ancient Schools, Society of Biblical Literature Dissertation Series*. Number 26. Missoula, Montana: Scholars Press, 1975.

Dahl, Nils A. "Anamnesis: Memoire et Commemoration dans le christianisme primitif." *Studia Theologica* 1 (1948): 69-95.

_____. "Der erstgeborene Satans und der Vater des Teufels (Polyk. 7:1 und John 8:44)." *Apophoreta: Festschrift für Ernst Haenchen, Beihefte zur Zeitschrift für die neutestamentliche Wissenschaft.* Vol. 30. Berlin: Verlag Alfred Töpelmann, 1964. Pp. 70-84.

Daube, David. "The 'I am' of the Messianic Presence." *The New Testament and Rabbinic Judaism.* London: Athlone, 1956. Pp. 325-29.

Davies, W. D. *The Gospel and the Land: Early Christianity and Jewish Territorial Doctrine.* Berkeley: University of California Press, 1974.

Dieterich A. *Eine Mithrasliturgie.* 3d expanded ed., published by Otto Weinreich; Leipzig: B.G. Teubner, 1923.

Dion, H.-M. O.P. "Le Genre littéraire Sumerien de l' 'hymne a soi-même' et Quelques Passages du Deutéro-Isaie." *Revue Biblique* 74 (1967):215-34.

Dodd, C. H. *The Interpretation of the Fourth Gospel.* Cambridge: At the University Press, 1965.

Eisenstadt, S. N., ed. *Max Weber on Charisma and Institution Building: Selected Papers.* Chicago: University of Chicago Press, 1968.

Festugière, A.-J. "La valeur religieuse des papyrus magiques." *L'idéal religieux des grecs et l'évangile.* Paris: J. Gabalda et Cie, Editeurs, 1932. Pp. 281-328.

Feuillet, A. "Les *Ego eimi* christologiques du quatrieme Evangile." *Recherches de Science Religieuse* 54 (1966): 5-22.

Fortna, R. T. "Christology in the Fourth Gospel: Redaction-Critical Perspectives." *New Testament Studies* 21 (1974-75):489-504.

_____. "From Christology to Soteriology: A Redaction-Critical Study of Salvation in the Fourth Gospel." *Interpretation* 27 (1973):31-47.

Gachter, P. "Der formale Aufbau der Abschiedsrede Jesu." *Zeitschrift für katholische Theologie* 58 (1934):155-207.

Gager, John G. *Kingdom and Community: The Social World of Early Christianity.* Englewood Cliffs, N.J.: Prentice-Hall, Inc. 1975.

Gillespie, Thomas W. "A Pattern of Prophetic Speech in First Corinthians." *Journal of Biblical Literature* 97 (1978): 74-95.

Grant, Robert M. "Chains of Being in Early Christianity."
    Myths and Symbols: Studies in Honor of Mircea Eliade.
    Edited by J.M. Kitagawa and C.H. Long. Chicago: University
    of Chicago Press, 1969. Pp. 279-89.

Haacker, Klaus. *Die Stiftung des Heils: Untersuchungen zur
    Struktur der johanneischen Theologie, Arbeiten zur
    Theologie.* Series 1. Vol. 97. Stuttgart: Calwer Verlag,
    1972.

Hahn, Ferdinand. "Sehen und Glauben im Johannesevangelium."
    *Neues Testament und Geschichte: Historisches Geschehen
    und Deutung im Neuen Testament: Oscar Cullmann zum 70.
    Geburtstag.* Edited by Heinrich Baltensweiler and Bo
    Reicke. Zürich: Theologischer Verlag/Tübingen: Mohr,
    1972. Pp. 125-41.

Harnack, Adolf von. "Zur Textkritik und Christologie der
    Schriften des Johannes." *Sitzungsberichte der preussischen
    Akademie der Wissenschaften,* Phil. - his. Klasse, 1915.

Harner, Philip B. *The "I am" of the Fourth Gospel: A Study in
    Johannine Usage and Thought.* Philadelphia: Fortress Press,
    1970.

Heitmuller, Wilhelm. "Das Johannes-Evangelium" Edited by J.
    Weiss. *Die Schriften des Neuen Testaments.* Vol. 2. 2d
    improved and expanded edition; Göttingen: Vandenhoeck &
    Ruprecht, 1908.

Hennecke, Edgar. *New Testament Apocrypha.* Edited by Wilhelm
    Schneemelcher, translated by R. McL. Wilson. Vol. 1.
    Philadelphia: The Westminster Press, 1963).

Hill, Michael. *A Sociology of Religion.* New York: Basic Books,
    Inc., 1973.

Hoskyns, E. C. *The Fourth Gospel.* Edited by F.N. Davey. 2d
    ed., rev.; London: Farber and Farber Limited, 1961.

Howard, W. F. *The Fourth Gospel in Recent Criticism and
    Interpretation.* 4th ed. Revised by C.K. Barrett.
    London: Epworth Press, 1955.

Hull, John M. *Hellenistic Magic and the Synoptic Tradition,
    Studies in Biblical Theology.* Second Series, No. 28.
    London: SCM Press Ltd., 1974.

Ibuki, Yu. *Die Wahrheit im Johannesevangelium, Bonner Biblische
    Beiträge.* Vol. 39. Bonn: Peter Hanstein Verlag, 1972.

Johnston, G. *The Spirit-Paraclete in the Gospel of John.*
    Cambridge: University Press, 1970.

Judge, E. A. "Paul's Boasting in Relation to Contemporary
    Professional Practice." *Australian Biblical Review* 14
    (1968):37-50.

Käsemann, Ernst. *Jesu letzter Wille nach Johannes 17.*
Tübingen: J.C.B. Mohr (Paul Siebeck), 1966. Translated by
Gerhard Krodel, *The Testament of Jesus.* Philadelphia:
Fortress Press, 1968.

Kelber, Werner H. "Kingdom and Parousia in the Gospel of Mark."
Unpublished Ph.D. dissertation, University of Chicago,
1970.

Knox, Wilfred. *Some Hellenistic Elements in Primitive Christianity.* London: Published for the British Academy, 1944.

Kolenkow, Anitra B. "Argument Among Miracle Believers: Johan-
nine Use of 'Goes' Motifs to Modify 'Miracle Apology'
Motifs in John 5 and 8." Paper presented to the Annual
Meeting of the Society of Biblical Literature, Fourth
Gospel Section, 1974.

Kragerud, A. *Der Lieblingsjünger im Johannesevangelium. Ein
exegetischer Versuch.* Oslo: Osloer-Universitätsverlag,
1959.

Kramer, S. N. *The Sumerians: Their History, Culture, and
Character.* Chicago: University of Chicago Press, 1963.

Kundsin, Karl. "Charakter und Ursprung der johanneischen Reden."
Acta Universitatis Latviensis. Teologisjas Fakultates,
Series 1, No. 4. Riga, 1939.

_____. "Die Wiederkunft Jesu in den Abschiedsreden des
Johannesevangeliums." *Zeitschrift für die neutestamentliche Wissenschaft* 33 (1934):210-15.

_____. "Zur Diskussion über die Ego-Eimi-Sprüche des
Johannesevangeliums." *Charisteria IOHANNI KOPP.* Octo-
genario Oblata. Papers of the Estonian Theological
Society in Exile Vol. 7. Holmiae, 1954. Pp. 95-107.

Kysar, Robert. *The Fourth Evangelist and His Gospel: An
Examination of Contemporary Scholarship.* Minneapolis,
Minn.: Augusburg Publishing House, 1975.

Leroy, Herbert. *Rätsel und Missverständnis: Ein Beitrag zur
Formgeschichte des Johannesevangeliums, Bonner Biblische
Beiträge.* Vol. 30. Bonn: Peter Hanstein Verlag GMBH,
1968.

Lindars, Barnabas. *The Gospel of John, New Century Bible.*
Edited by Ronald E. Clements and Matthew Black. London:
Oliphants, 1972.

Macgregor, G.H.C. *The Gospel of John, The Moffatt New Testament
Commentary.* New York: Harper and Brothers Publishers,
1928.

MacRae, George. "The Ego-Proclamation in Gnostic Sources."
The Trial of Jesus. Edited by Ernst Bammel. *Studies in
Biblical Theology,* Second Series. Vol. 13. London: S.C.M.
Press, 1970. Pp. 122-34.

_____. "The Fourth Gospel and Religionsgeschichte." *Catholic Biblical Quarterly* 32 (1970):13-24.

Martyn, J. Louis. "Source Criticism and Religionsgeschichte in the Fourth Gospel." *Perspective: A Journal of Pittsburgh Theological Seminary* 11 (1970):247-73.

_____. *History and Theology in the Fourth Gospel.* New York and Evanston: Harper & Row, Publishers, 1968.

Meagher, John C. *The Way of the Word.* New York: The Seabury Press, 1975.

Meeks, Wayne. "The Man from Heaven in Johannine Sectarianism." *Journal of Biblical Literature* 91 (1972):44-72.

_____. "The Divine Agent and His Counterfeit in Philo and the Fourth Gospel." *Aspects of Religious Propaganda in Judaism and Early Christianity.* Edited by Elisabeth Schüssler Fiorenza. Notre Dame: University of Notre Dame Press, 1976. Pp. 43-67.

Meyer, Marvin W., ed. and trans. *The "Mithras Liturgy," Society of Biblical Literature Texts and Translations.* No. 10, Graeco-Roman Religion Series 2. Missoula, Montana: Scholars Press, 1976.

Michaels, J. Ramsey. "The Johannine Words of Jesus and Christian Prophecy." *Society of Biblical Literature 1975 Seminar Papers.* Edited by George MacRae. Vol. 2. Missoula, Montana: Univeristy of Montana for the Society of Biblical Literature, 1975. Pp. 233-64.

Michel, Otto. "*oikos.*" *Theological Dictionary of the New Testament.* Edited by Gerhard Friedrich, translated and edited by Geoffrey W. Bromiley. Vol. 5. Grand Rapids, Mich.: Wm. B. Eerdmans Publishing Company, 1967. Pp. 119-59.

Minear, Paul S. "The Audience of the Fourth Gospel." *Interpretation* 31 (1977):339-54.

Morris, Leon. *The Gospel According to John, The New International Commentary on the New Testament.* Grand Rapids, Mich.: Wm. B. Eerdmans Publishing Co., 1971.

Müller, U. B. "Die Parakletenvorstellung im Johannesevangelium." *Zeitschrift für Theologie und Kirche* 71 (1974):31-77.

Mussner, Franz. *Die Johanneische Sehweise und die Frage nach dem historischen Jesus.* Quaestiones Diputatae. Vol. 28. Freiburg: Herder, 1965.

Neusner, Jacob. *A History of the Mishnaic Law of Purities, Studies in Judaism in Late Antiquity.* Vol. 6. Leiden: E.J. Brill, 1974- .

_____. "The Meaning of Oral Torah." *Early Rabbinic Judaism: Historical Studies in Religion, Literature and Art, Studies in Judaism in Late Antiquity*. Edited by Jacob Neusner. Vol. 13. Leiden: E.J. Brill, 1975. Pp. 3-33.

Nicol, W. *The Semeia in the Fourth Gospel: Tradition and Redaction, Supplements to Novum Testamentum*. Vol. 32. Leiden: E.J. Brill, 1972.

Norden, Eduard. *Agnostos Theos: Untersuchungen zur Formen-geschichte religiöser Rede*. Berlin: B.G. Teubner, 1913.

Odeberg, Hugo. *The Fourth Gospel: Interpreted in its Relation to Contemporaneous Religious Currents in Palestine and the Hellenistic-Oriental World*. Amsterdam: B.R. Grüner, 1968.

Perrin, Norman. *Rediscovering the Teaching of Jesus*. New York: Harper & Row, 1967.

_____. *What is Redaction Criticism?* Philadelphia: Fortress Press, 1969.

Potterie, I. de la. "'Je suis la Voie, la Verite et la Vie' (Jn 14:6)." *Nouvelle Revue Theologique* 88 (1966):907-42.

Preisendanz, Karl. *Papyri Graecae Magicae*. Vol. 2. 2d rev. ed.; Stuttgart: Verlag B.G. Tuebner, 1974.

Preiss, Theo. "Justification in Johannine Thought." *Life in Christ, Studies in Biblical Theology*. No. 13. Translated by Harold Knight. Chicago: Alex R. Allenson, Inc., 1954.

Pritchard, James B. *Ancient Near Eastern Texts Relating to the Old Testament*. Princeton, New Jersey: Princeton University Press, 1950.

Purvis, James D. "Samaritan Traditions on the Death of Moses." Edited by George W.E. Nickelsburg, Jr. *Studies on the Testament of Moses: Seminar Papers*. Septuagint and Cognate Studies, No. 4. Cambridge, Mass.: Society of Biblical Literature, 1973. Pp. 93-227.

Reiling, Jr. "The Use of PSEUDOPROPHETES in the Septuagint, Philo and Josephus." *Novum Testamentum* 13 (1971):147-56.

Reitzenstein, Richard. *Poimandres: Studien zur griechisch-ägyptischen und frühchristlichen Literatur*. Photographic reproduction of the Leipzig, 1904 edition. Darmstadt: Wissenschaftliche Buchgesellschaft, 1966.

Richter, Georg. "Die Deutung des Kreuzestodes Jesu in der Leidensgeschichte des Johannesevangeliums (Jo 13-19)." *Bibel und Leben* 9 (1968):21-36.

_____. *Die Fusswaschung im Johannesevangelium: Geschichte ihrer Deutung, Biblische Untersuchungen*. Vol. 1. Regensburg: Verlag Friedrich Pustet, 1967.

Richter, Georg. "Zur Formgeschichte und literarischen Einheit von Joh 6:31-58." *Zeitschrift fur die neutestamentliche Wissenschaft* 40 (1969):21-55.

Richter, J. "Ain Hu und Ego eimi: Die Offenbarungsformel 'Ich bin es' im Alten und Neuen Testament." Unpublished dissertation, Erlangen, 1956.

Robinson, James M. "Introduction: The Dismantling and Reassembling of the Categories of New Testament Scholarship." James M. Robinson and Helmut Koester, *Trajectories Through Early Christianity*. Philadelphia: Fortress Press, 1971. Pp. 1-19.

_____. "On the *Gattung* of Mark (and John)." *Perspective* 11 (1970):99-129.

_____. "The Johannine Trajectory." James M. Robinson and Helmut Koester, *Trajectories Through Early Christianity*. Philadelphia: Fortress Press, 1971. Pp. 232-68.

Rokeach, Milton. "The Nature and Meaning of Dogmatism." *Current Perspectives in Social Psychology*. Edited by W.P. Hollander and R.H. Hunt. New York: Oxford University Press, 1967. Pp. 158-67.

Sasse, H. "Der Paraklet im Johannesevangelium." *Zeitschrift für die neutestamentliche Wissenschaft* 24 (1925):260-77.

Schaedel, Karl. "Das Johannesevangelium und 'die Kinder des Lichts': Untersuchungen zu den Selbstbezeichnungen Jesu im vierten Evangelium und zur Heilsterminologie der 'En Fesha-Sekta.'" Unpublished Dissertation, Vienna, 1953.

Schnackenburg, Rudolf. "Das Anliegen der Abschiedsrede in Joh 14." Edited by H. Feld and J. Nolte. *Wort Gottes in der Zeit: Festschrift Karl Hermann Schelkle zum 65. Geburtstag dargebracht von Kollegen, Freunden, Schülern*. Dusseldorf: Patmos-Verlag, 1973. Pp. 95-110.

_____. "Herkunft und Sinn der Formel ego eimi." *Das Johannesevangelium*, Part II, *Kommentar zu Kap. 5-12, Herders Theologischer Kommentar zum Neuen Testament*. Edited by A. Wikenhauser, A. Vögtle and R. Schnackenburg. Vol. 4. Frieburg: Herder, 1971. Pp. 59-70.

_____. *Das Johanesevangelium*, Part III, *Herders Theologischer Kommentar zum Neuen Testament*. Vol. 4. Frieburg; Herder, 1975.

Schneider, Johannes. "Die Abschiedsreden Jesu: Ein Beitrag zur Frage der Komposition von Johannes 13:31-17:26." *Gott und die Götter: Festgabe für Erich Fascher zum 60. Geburtstag*. Berlin: Evangelische Verlagsanstalt, 1958. Pp. 103-12.

Schulz, Siegfried. *Komposition und Herkunft der johanneischen Reden*. Stuttgart: W. Kohlhammer Verlag, 1960.

_____. *Das Evangelium nach Johannes, Das Neue Testament Deutsch*, II. 12th ed.; Göttingen: Vandenhoeck & Ruprecht, 1972.

_____. *Untersuchungen zur Menschensohn-Christologie im Johannesevangelium*. Gottingen: Vandenhoeck & Ruprecht, 1957.

Schütz, John Howard. "Charisma and Social Reality in Primitive Christianity." *Journal of Religion* 54 (1974):51-70.

Schweizer, Eduard. *EGO EIMI . . . Die religionsgeschichtliche Herkunft und theologische Bedeutung der johanneischen Bildreden, zugleich ein Beitrag zur Quellenfrage des vierten Evangeliums*. 2d ed. *Forschungen zur Religion und Literatur des Alten und Neuen Testaments*. New Series, Vol. 38. Göttingen: Vandenhoeck & Ruprecht, 1965.

Scobie, Charles H. H. "The Origin and Development of the Johannine Community." Unpublished paper presented to the Society of Biblical Literature Fourth Gospel Section, 31 October, 1976.

Scott, Ernest F. *The Fourth Gospel: Its Purpose and Theology*. Edinburgh: T. & T. Clark, 1906.

Scroggs, Robin. "The Exaltation of the Spirit by Some Early Christians." *Journal of Biblical Literature* 84 (1965): 359-73.

Shils, Edward. "Charisma, Order and Status." *American Sociological Review* 30 (1965):199-213.

Smith, D. Moody, Jr. *The Composition and Order of the Fourth Gospel: Bultmann's Literary Theory*. New Haven: Yale University Press, 1965.

_____. "Johannine Christianity: Some Reflections on its Character and Delineation." *New Testament Studies* 21 (1974-75);222-48.

Smith, Jonathon Z. "The Garments of Shame." *History of Religion* 5 (1966):217-38.

_____. *Map is Not Territory: Studies in the History of Religions, Studies in Judaism in Late Antiquity*. Edited by Jacob Neusner. Vol. 23. Leiden: E.J. Brill, 1978.

Smith, Jonathon Z. "Native Cults in the Hellenistic Period." *History of Religions* 11 (1971):236-49.

_____. "The Social Description of Early Christianity." *Religious Studies Review* 1 (1975):19-25.

Smith, Morton. *Clement of Alexandria and a Secret Gospel of Mark*. Cambridge: Harvard University Press, 1973.

Sneed, R. J. "The Kingdom's Coming: Luke 17:20-21, Studies in Sacred Theology." Vol. 130. Unpublished Dissertation, Catholic University of America, Washington, D.C., 1962.

Spengler, Oswald. *Der Untergang des Abendlandes*. Vol. 2. Münich: C.H. Becksche Verlagsbuchhandlung, 1924.

Spitta, Friedrich. *Das Johannes-Evangelium Als Quelle der Geschichte Jesu*. Göttingen: Vandenhoeck & Ruprecht, 1910.

Stauffer, Ethelbert. *"Ego." Theological Dictionary of the New Testament*. Edited by Gerhard Kittel, translated and edited by Geoffrey W. Bromiley. Vol. 2. Grand Rapids, Mich.: Wm. B. Eerdmans Publishing Company, 1964.

_____. *Jesus and His Story*. Translated by Richard and Clara Winston. New York: Alfred A. Knopf, 1960.

Talmon, Yonina. "Pursuit of the Milennium: The Relation Between Religious and Social Change." *Archives Europeennes de Sociologie* 3 (1962):125-48.

Theiler, W. "Erinnerung." *Reallexikon für Antike und Christentum*. Vol. 6, Cols. 43-54. Stuttgart: Anton Hiersmann, 1966.

Theissen, Gerd. "Wanderradikalismus: Literatursoziologische Aspekte der Überlieferung von Worten Jesu im Urchristentum." *Zeitschrift für Theologie und Kirche* 70 (1973): 245-71.

Thüsing, Wilhelm. *Die Erhöhung und Verherrlichung Jesu im Johannesevangelium, Neutestamentliche Abhandlungen*. Edited by M. Meinertz. Vol. 21. Münster: Aschendorffsche Verlagsbuchhandlung, 1960.

Tucker, Robert C. "The Theory of Charismatic Leadership." *Daedalus* 97, No. 3 (Summer, 1968):731-56.

Wead, David W. *The Literary Devices in John's Gospel*. University of Basel Dissertation. Basel: Friedrich Reinhardt Kommissionsverlag, 1970.

Wellhausen, Julius. *Erweiterungen und Änderungen im vierten Evangelium*. Berlin: Reimer, 1907.

_____. *Das Evangelium Johannis*. Berlin: Reimer, 1908.

Westcott, B. F. *The Gospel According to St. John*. Photolithograph reprint of the 1908 edition. Two volumes in one. Grand Rapids, Mich.: Eerdmans Publishing Company, 1954.

Wetter, Gillis Petersson. *"Der Sohn Gottes"; Eine Untersuchung über den Charakter und die Tendenz des Johannes-Evangeliums: Zugleich ein Beitrag zur Kenntnis der Heilandsgestalten der Antike. Forschungen zur Religion und Literatur des Alten und Neuen Testaments*, N.F. 9. Göttingen: Vandenhoeck & Ruprecht, 1916.

Wikenhauser, Alfred. *Das Evangelium nach Johannes, Das Neue Testament übersetzt und kurz erklärt*. Edited by A. Wikenhauser and Otto Kuss. Vol. 4. Regensburg: Verlag Friedrich Pustet, 1948.

Windisch, Hans. *Die katholischen Briefe, Handbuch zum Neuen Testament*. Vol. 15. 3d extensively revised edition by Herbert Preisker; Tübingen: J.C.B. Mohr (Paul Siebeck), 1951.

_____. *The Spirit-Paraclete in the Fourth Gospel*. Translated by James W. Cox. Philadelphia: Fortress Press, 1968.

Worsley, Peter. *The Trumpet Shall Sound: A Study of 'Cargo' Cults in Melanesia*. 2d augmented ed.; New York: Schocken Books, 1968.

Zimmermann, Heinrich. "Das absolute Ego eimi als die neutestamentliche Offenbarungsformel." *Biblische Zeitschrift*, N.F. 4 (1960):54-69.

_____. "Struktur und Aussageabsicht der johanneischen Abschiedsreden (Jo 13-17)." *Bibel und Leben* 8 (1967): 279-90.